The Citizen in European Private Law: Norm-setting, Enforcement and Choice

Editors:
C. Cauffman
J. Smits

The Citizen in European Private Law: Norm-Setting, Enforcement and Choice

intersentia

METRO

Ius Commune Europaeum

Intersentia Ltd
Sheraton House | Castle Park
Cambridge | CB3 0AX | United Kingdom
Tel.: +44 1223 370 170 | Fax: +44 1223 370 169
Email: mail@intersentia.co.uk
www.intersentia.com | www.intersentia.co.uk

Distribution for the UK and Ireland:
NBN International
Airport Business Centre, 10 Thornbury Road
Plymouth, PL6 7PP
United Kingdom
Tel.: +44 1752 202 301 | Fax: +44 1752 202 331
Email: orders@nbninternational.com

Distribution for Europe and all other countries:
Intersentia Publishing nv
Groenstraat 31
2640 Mortsel
Belgium
Tel.: +32 3 680 15 50 | Fax: +32 3 658 71 21
Email: mail@intersentia.be

Distribution for the USA and Canada:
International Specialized Book Services
920 NE 58th Ave. Suite 300
Portland, OR 97213
USA
Tel.: +1 800 944 6190 (toll free) | Fax: +1 503 280 8832
Email: info@isbs.com

The Citizen in European Private Law: Norm-setting, Enforcement and Choice

ISBN 978-1-78068-373-7
D/2016/7849/2
NUR 822

British Library Cataloguing in Publication Data. A catalogue record for this book is available from the British Library.

CONTENTS

PART II: NORM-SETTING AND ENFORCEMENT

LIST OF AUTHORS

Anna Beckers, Assistant Professor of Private Law and Legal Methodology, Maastricht University and Max Weber Fellow, European University Institute

Caroline Cauffman, Associate Professor of Contract, Consumer and Competition Law, Maastricht University

Naomi Creutzfeldt, ESRC Research Fellow, University of Oxford

Nicole Kornet, Senior Lecturer in Commercial Law, Maastricht University

Vanessa Mak, D.Phil, M.Jur (Oxon); Professor of Private Law, Tilburg University

Stephan Rammeloo, Associate Professor EU Company Law, Private International Law and Comparative Law, Maastricht University

Wolf-Georg Ringe, Professor of International Commercial Law, Copenhagen Business School, and University of Oxford

Susan Rutten, Associate Professor of Family Law, Maastricht University

Jan Smits, Professor of European Private Law, Maastricht University and Academic Director of the Maastricht European Private Law Institute (MEPLI).

Veerle Van Den Eeckhout, Professor of Comparative and European Private International Law, University of Antwerp, fellow at Radboud University Nijmegen

Frans van der Velden, Visiting Professor of Islamic Law at the University of Maastricht and Leuven

Patrick Wautelet, Professor of Private International Law, University of Liège

LIST OF ABBREVIATIONS

AbgÄG	Abgabenänderungsgesetz
ADR	Alternative Dispute Resolution
AG	Advocate-General
ApS	Anpartselskab
ARN	Allmänna reklamationsnämnden
ASIC	Australia Securities and Investments Commission
BGH	Bundesgerichtshof
BGmbH	Basis-GmbH
BV	Besloten Vennootschap
CA	Court of Appeal
CA 2006	Companies Act 2006
CDR	Consumer Dispute Resolution
CESL	Common European Sales Law
CJEU	Court of Justice of the European Union
COMI	Centre of Main Interests
CSR	Corporate Social Responsibility
DGS	De Geschillencommissie
EC	European Commission
ECFR	European Company and Financial Law Review
ECHR	European Court of Human Rights
ECJ	European Court of Justice
EEC	European Economic Community
EU	European Union
EUR	Euro
FAME	Financial Analysis Made Easy
GesRÄG	Gesellschatsrechts-Änderungsgesetz
GmbH	Gesellschaft mit beschränkter Haftung
GmbHG	GmbH-Gesetz
ICGI	Maastricht Institute for Corporate Law, Governance and Innovation Policies
ILO	International Labour Organization
KiFiD	Klachteninstituut Financiële Dienstverlening
KmbH	Kammanditgesellschaft mit beschränkter Haftung

LLP	Limited Liability Partnership
Ltd.	Limited Liability Company
MEPLI	Maastricht European Private Institute
MindestkapG	Gesetz zur Neuregelung des Mindestkapitals der GmbH
MoMiG	Modernisierung des GmbH-Rechts und zur Bekämpfung von Missbräuchen
NCP	National Contact Point
ODR	Online Dispute Resolution
OECD	Organisation for Economic Co-operation and Development
OJ	Official Journal
OLG	Oberlandesgericht
PIL	Private International Law
PmbH	Personengesellschaft mit beschränkter Haftung (partnership with limited liability)
SA	Société Anonyme
SARL	Société à Responsabilité Limitée
SAS	Société par Actions Simplifiée
SLNE	Sociedad Limitada Nueva Empresa
SL/SRL	Sociedad de Responsabilidad Limitada
TFEU	Treaty on the Functioning of the European Union
UG	Unternehmersgesellschaft
UK	United Kingdom
UN	United Nations
US	United States

PREFACE

It is not a particularly surprising revelation that the citizens of the European Union are often not aware of the rights that they have, nor of the possibilities to enforce these rights. This was a reason for the European Commission to declare 2013 the 'European Year of Citizens.' The explicit aim of both the Commission and the European Parliament was - twenty years after the establishment of European Union citizenship under the Maastricht Treaty - to boost the idea of EU citizenship and to develop strategies to better inform European citizens about their rights. It was in this context that the Faculty of Law of Maastricht University decided to initiate a number of events around this 'Year of Citizens.' One of these events was devoted to the role of private actors (meaning: citizens, consumers and companies) in norm-setting, enforcement and choice of law. It took the form of a conference entitled 'The Citizen in European Private Law', organised on 18 October 2013 in cooperation between the Maastricht European Private Law Institute (MEPLI) and the Maastricht Institute for Corporate Law, Governance and Innovation Policies (ICGI). Caroline Cauffman, Mieke Olaerts and Jan Smits were able to take care of the practical organisation thanks to the highly proficient help of Marina Jodogne and Marjo Mullers. Damla Cavusoglu and Lotte Meurkens wrote an elaborate report on the conference that was published in the European Review of Private Law 22 (2014), p. 469-480.

This volume contains most of the contributions that were presented at the conference, together with some new articles. Its structure reflects the wish of the editors to look at citizen empowerment from a thematic perspective and not from the viewpoint of separate fields of law. Thus, part I looks at choice and regulatory competition in both company law and family law, while part II considers norm setting and enforcement in consumer law, commercial law and family law. The introduction to this volume explains the set-up in more detail.

We would like to thank Marina Jodogne, Eve Meurgey, Alina Anapyanova and Christopher Mondschein for essential help in preparing this volume. We also acknowledge the financial support received from the University Fund Limburg/SWOL and from the Faculty of Law of Maastricht University to organise the conference.

The editors, 31 August 2015

C. Cauffman
J. Smits

INTRODUCTION

1. Introduction

Private law traditionally allows citizens a large role in shaping their legal relationships. Although this private autonomy always needs to be balanced against other instrumental goals that the law aims to achieve, it seems that during the last decades the importance of autonomy has increased.[1] Private actors (not only citizens, but also companies) increasingly set their own rules (by way of codes of conduct and other types of private regulation, but also by allowing religious and cultural minorities to set their own norms), revert to private enforcement of these rules (such as Alternative Dispute Resolution and Online Dispute Resolution), and choose their applicable law (according to some authors leading to a true 'law market'[2]). This tendency is visible in a wide range of subfields, including contract law, company law, consumer law and family law. Unfortunately, however, this phenomenon of increasing autonomy in choosing, setting and enforcing norms was until now seldom studied from a horizontal perspective. What is missing so far is how increasing autonomy (and its limits) is perceived in the various sub-fields of private law, and in what these perceptions differ. It is true that in company law there is much attention for private codes, while in consumer law dispute resolution is a hot topic and in family law religious norms are scrutinised. But there is very little attention for looking at these phenomena together and to try to draw conclusions from this that go beyond one specific field. This is a clear lack in the study of this important phenomenon.

The aim of this book is to fill this gap. Of course, this is not a full horizontal survey of how autonomy works out in all subfields of private law. This volume must rather be seen as a collection of essays highlighting various aspects of party autonomy. The contributing authors, coming from various fields of private law, where invited to reflect on three central questions: (1) is the increased reliance on

1 See on the (mostly American) debate on private law as reflecting autonomy and the limits thereto: Dagan 2008, p. 809-833 and Herstein 2015, p. 99-132, as well as Kessedjian 2013.

2 O'Hara & Ribstein 2009.

private actors supported by empirical evidence?; (2) what are the perceived benefits of this increased reliance, if any?; and (3) what should be the limits of party autonomy in your field? The original papers were presented at the conference of 18 October 2013 and subsequently adapted to fit this book. The original set-up of the conference is reflected in the different types of contributions that one finds here: next to the main papers, more succinct comments that served as a stimulus for discussion are reproduced.

This introduction briefly presents the papers and comments thereto. They are organised in two different parts. The first part (section 2 below and Part I of the book) is devoted to choice and regulatory competition, the second part (section 3 below and Part II of the book) to norm-setting and enforcement.

2. Choice and Regulatory Competition

The rise of the global economy and the subsequent surge of information about other jurisdictions is leading private actors to make increasingly use of choice of law and forum. In fields such as contract and commercial law, parties can often opt-out of their own national legal system and choose for another jurisdiction. It seems that such 'legal tourism' is on the rise, not only in a commercial context but also in consumer and family law.[3] This is not only because of the growing desire of parties to regulate their legal relationship as much as possible themselves, but also because of the policy of some national organisations of lawyers and even countries to deliberately promote a choice for one jurisdiction or the other.[4] A related trend in the last decade is the attempt of the European Commission to create optional regimes as '29th jurisdictions.' However, in view of the now withdrawn proposals for the CESL and a European Foundation,[5] it remains to be seen whether these efforts will continue in the years to come.

Part I starts off with a contribution by Veerle Van den Eeckhout. She looks at private international law (PIL) as the main tool for parties to exercise their autonomy in addressing one court rather than another (choice of forum) and in choosing the law that the court is to apply (choice of the applicable law). She rightly indicates that at the moment such choices are often hidden for both private individuals and companies. And although PIL offers a myriad of possibilities for strategic planning by private actors, it is usually only the well-informed parties that are able to do this in fact. A complicating factor in this respect is the fact that

3 Recent empirical surveys of choice of law by commercial parties are offered by Cuniberti 2014, p. 455-517 and by Vogenauer 2013, p. 13-78. Vogenauer has reservations about the rise of regulatory competition.

4 *Cf.* the well-known brochures published by the Law Society of England and Wales (*England and Wales: The Jurisdiction of Choice*, London, 2007) and the German Ministry of Justice (*Law – Made in Germany*, Berlin, 2008).

5 Proposal for a Regulation on a Common European Sales Law, COM(2011) 635 final and Proposal for a Council Regulation on the Statute for a European Foundation, COM(2012) 035 final, both withdrawn in Commission Work Programme 2015: A New Start, COM(2014) 910 final (16 December 2014), Annex II 12.

European rules often come about in a 'stormy and capricious way', triggered by what is the problem of the day and not by a well-considered policy of balancing choice against protection of weaker parties and limiting the risks of regulatory competition. This is an oft-heard refrain in assessing European harmonisation and one to which PIL is not immune.

Patrick Wautelet subsequently explains how party autonomy is now indeed one of the leading principles in European private international law, including the fields of cross-border family relationships, successions, divorces and maintenance matters. It is such family relations for which Wautelet develops a research agenda. Such an agenda should first of all entail the mapping out of the concept of party autonomy in PIL, including the empirical question of how frequent for example marriage tourism actually is. In addition the consequences of exercising party autonomy must be addressed, not only from the angle of coherence to avoid the risk of contradictory rules being applicable through choice of law, but also from the angle of regulatory competition. Wautelet doubts that any real competition will emerge in the field of family law because of a lack of visibility of choices being made: how should member states know that their citizens make 'exit choices' and what interest do they have in responding to this? Although Wautelet is surely right that the incentive for a legislator to change the existing law is more likely to exist in company law because it may have financial consequences, it is not unlikely that there are other reasons for a state to act under competitive pressure. Increasing a country's prestige could be one such reason. A further aspect Wautelet rightly points at concerns the protection of parties: the balance of power may be different in family law than in contract law or company law.

Unlike it is the case in international family law, there is no lack of empirical data on choice of law in the field of European company law. Wolf-Georg Ringe provides insightful empirical data on such corporate mobility in Europe. His main finding is that, although German start-up companies were at first very much inclined to choose for the English limited company when this became possible with the ECJ's *Centros* case of 1999, there was a sharp decline after 2006. Ringe gives five possible reasons for this development, of which the simple reason that both Germans and English law closed down the loopholes that made the Limited attractive for German business is the most compelling one (which does not rule out that the other reasons also played a role).

In his reaction to Ringe's analysis of possible reasons for choosing some national corporate form, Stephan Rammeloo emphasises that choices by entrepreneurs are not always rational and may also be influenced by other factors than those mentioned by Ringe. For example, the mere fact that English law is better accessible because of language reasons may partly explain the success of the Limited company. This underscores the importance of looking at all possible factors in understanding increasing or decreasing choice of law.

3. Norm-setting and Enforcement

The increased role of private actors in shaping their legal relationships not only comes out in choice of law or forum. It is also visible in the seemingly more frequent use of private regulation and in the increased possibilities for private enforcement. Part II of this volume focuses on these phenomena.

Private regulation as such is nothing new and has always filled a vacuum left by the official rule makers. One could think of the international law merchant (*lex mercatoria*), as posited in modern time in the form of global or European principles[6] or of transnational sports law (*lex sportiva*).[7] The use of standardised general conditions in business-to-business or business-to-consumer transactions and Corporate Social Responsibility codes[8] provides additional examples. These private regimes offer what a national legal system is not able to provide, namely a set of rules that is not territorially limited and that can therefore be effectively used across borders.[9]

In her contribution Vanessa Mak considers the possible advantages and disadvantages of using private regulation in setting norms. After having identified different types of self-regulation, she emphasises that private regulation is difficult to reconcile with traditional views of law making. This calls for a method to accommodate private regulation in a broader framework. This is a concern with defining the scope for law making by private actors in relation to other law making actors in today's multi-level legal order. Here lies indeed a major challenge, both when it comes to how to deal with a plurality of different sources and with which legal actor should be entrusted with law making competences in the first place.[10]

Possibly the most controversial cases of private norm-setting can be found in the area of family law. Both the contributions of Susan Rutten and Frans van der Velden deal with questions of marriage and divorce in situations where people have a strong affiliation with religious values. This raises the much-discussed question of the extent to which the law must accommodate these religious values. Rutten discusses the reasons why people wish to enter into a religious marriage and the limits to people's autonomy in doing so as well as in getting divorced in the current law. This leads her to ask three questions about what limits the law should pose in upholding religious norms. Van der Velden builds upon this by discussing the phenomenon of forced marriages. He claims that a sharp dichotomy between secular and religious marriage could obstruct the autonomy of the divorced.

Next to norm-setting attention is paid to enforcement. The rise of alternative dispute mechanisms in commercial and consumer transactions can be seen as another instance of giving more opportunities to citizens in 'enforcing' rights. Clearly stimulated by the wish to improve access to justice and encourage consumer confidence in the internal market, the European legislator has introduced new rules that facilitate alternative dispute resolution for consumers as well as online dispute resolution. Naomi Creutzfeld provides an overview of this legislation, but also shows how at the moment different jurisdictions have quite different approaches to

6 Such as the *Unidroit Principles of International Commercial Contracts* (Unidroit, 3rd edn., Rome, 2010).

7 *Cf.* Michaels & Jansen 2006, p. 843.

8 See for a quest to reconstruct CSR-codes as contractual obligations Beckers 2015.

9 See e.g. Gessner 2008, p. 3.

10 See on this question most recently Akkermans *et al.* 2015.

consumer ADR that are partly inspired by different national cultures of disputing. This provokes the question of how likely it is that European harmonisation in this field will be successful.

Caroline Cauffman builds upon Creutzfeld's analysis by discussing the weaknesses of the current ADR Directive. The directive surely has a worthy aim in trying to provide consumers with a low-cost and fast access means of dispute resolution, but it does not always guarantee that consumers can enforce the rights that they have, nor does it meet the standard for a proper administration of justice. It would be better to amend the existing national court procedures in dealing with low value consumer claims.

Not only consumer disputes could do with a better framework for dispute resolution. This is also true for disputes between commercial parties. Nicole Kornet emphasizes that a commercial party usually has a choice between litigation, arbitration and mediation. She explores the different normative frameworks in commercial transactions and asks what influence these frameworks should have on adjudication and mediation. Her main point is that each of these dispute settlement mechanisms requires a different way of dealing with the normative framework. Reliance on legal norms instead of on social, business or economic norms would jeopardise effective mediation, while traditional adjudication should be based on legal norms. Put differently: each form of dispute resolution requires application of different norms. This as such does not necessarily imply that party choice determines which normative framework should take precedence when dealing with a dispute, but it is the conclusion that Kornet reaches.

Anna Beckers places Kornet's contribution in the broader frameworks of 'contracting worlds' and contract governance. She criticises two main elements of Kornet's argument. First, Beckers is critical about the view that it is a matter of party choice which of the normative frameworks applies. Second, she questions the value of a strict separation between mediation and adjudication, that are in reality very much interwoven.

4. Conclusions

All contributions to this book take up the issue of party autonomy, be it in choosing the applicable law or forum, in setting the relevant norms or in their enforcement. It is no surprise that the respective role that is attached to party autonomy differs from one field to another. The importance of the principle seems to reflect the nature of the subfield: the more a field aims to achieve public goals (as in consumer law) or is about issues that are regarded as sensitive by the public at large (as in family law), the less important the role of autonomy is. This also explains the relatively large role of autonomy in contract law and commercial law, that are generally seen as less influenced by overriding interests of the State. But this conclusion should not conceal the fact that autonomy is on the rise in all subfields of private law. Perhaps the more important conclusion to draw is that this forces us to think through once more where the limits of autonomy lie.

Bibliography

Akkermans *et al.* 2015
Akkermans, B. *et al.* (eds.), *Who Does What? On the Allocation of Regulatory Competences in European Private Law*, Cambridge/Antwerp: Intersentia, 2015.

Beckers 2015
Beckers, A., *Taking Corporate Codes Seriously: Towards Private Law Enforcement of Voluntary Corporate Social Responsibility Codes*, Oxford: Hart Publishing, 2015.

Cuniberti 2014
Cuniberti, G., 'The International Market for Contracts: The Most Attractive Contract Laws', *Northwestern Journal of International Law & Business*, 2014, Vol. 34, p. 455-517.

Dagan 2008
Dagan, H., 'The Limited Autonomy of Private Law', *American Journal of Comparative Law*, 2008, Vol. 56, p. 809-833.

Gessner 2008
Gessner, V., 'Towards a Theoretical Framework for Contractual Certainty in Global Trade', in: Gessner, V. (ed.), *Contractual Certainty in International Trade*, Oxford: Hart Publishing, 2008, p. 3-27.

Herstein 2015
Herstein, O.J., 'How Tort Law Empowers', *University of Toronto Law Journal*, 2015, Vol. 65, p. 99-132.

Kessedjian 2013
Kessedjian, C. (ed.), *Autonomie en droit Européen: stratégie des citoyens, des entreprises et des États*, Paris: Éditions Panthéon-Assas, 2013.

Michaels & Jansen 2006
Michaels, R. & Jansen, N., 'Private Law beyond the State? Europeanization, Globalization, Privatization', *American Journal of Comparative Law*, 2006, Vol. 54, p. 843-890.

O'Hara & Ribstein 2009
O'Hara, E. & Ribstein, L.E., *The Law Market*, Oxford: Oxford University Press, 2009.

Vogenauer 2013
Vogenauer, S., 'Regulatory Competition through Choice of Contract Law and Choice of Forum in Europe: Theory and Evidence', *European Review of Private Law*, 2013, Vol. 21, p. 13-78.

PART I

CHOICE AND REGULATORY COMPETITION

V. Van Den
Eeckhout

CHOICE AND REGULATORY COMPETITION. RULES ON CHOICE OF LAW AND FORUM

1. Introduction: The Abstract and Peculiar Character of PIL

The field of private international law (hereinafter 'PIL') is known as an abstract and peculiar discipline. PIL could be considered peculiar because through the application of PIL a new dimension is added to the law: PIL is a field that determines whether, in private disputes with cross-border elements, a judge can hear a case according to rules of international jurisdiction and subsequently, according to the rules of applicable law, which law will be applied by this court. This entails that it may very well be the case that, considering the added value given by PIL rules, this will possibly make the solution of the case more difficult and complicated. However, the very fact that a new dimension is added to the law through the application of PIL may grant to private actors - both individuals and companies - additional legal options in which new additional strategies can be followed.

When we talk about options and strategies for individuals and companies - both types of private actors will be involved in this contribution - this contribution will essentially deal with the options or strategies concerning the right to address a certain *judge* (choice of forum) rather than another and the *law* that the judge should apply (the applicable law). Most attention will be given to the issue of the applicable law.

In this contribution I will explore in a non-exhaustive way some ongoing dynamics and focus on a number of issues relating to the possibilities to choose (the judge or law applicable) c.q. to 'shop' for private individuals and companies. I will briefly mention in this context a number of 'hot issues' in current politically sensitive topics, namely on labour law and Corporate Social Responsibility.

I shall focus on the rather *indirect*, sometimes almost hidden ways for actors - both private individuals and companies - to seek the application of a desired law.

2. The Two Basic Lessons of PIL, Placed in the Current Situation of Europeanisation of PIL

The highlighting of options concerning jurisdiction and applicable law leads to the essence of PIL: by highlighting the question of international jurisdiction and the question of applicable law, two of the three main issues of PIL are raised. The first basic lesson of PIL is, indeed, to distinguish the three main questions in PIL: issues of jurisdiction, issues of applicable law, and issues of recognition and enforcement. Here it is important to keep in mind that when answering the first question - the question for international jurisdiction - the question of applicable law has not yet been answered.

Also the second basic lesson of PIL should be recalled here. This lesson consists of always keeping in mind that PIL basically is national law.

Given that PIL is in essence national law, one can speak of Dutch PIL, Belgian PIL, etc. In national PIL there often appear to exist certain options for individuals and companies, such as possibilities for *forum* shopping (*e.g.* by allowing for the option of choice of forum i.e. an option concerning international jurisdiction) and/or for choice of *law* (an option concerning the applicable law). It can be, however, that such options are prohibited or only allowed under limited conditions; one could say that national PIL has certain 'defence mechanisms' built in that allow the authorities to control unlimited situations of *forum shopping* or *law shopping* between legal systems - *e.g.* by allowing the invocation of an exception of international public order or by allowing the application of rules that are qualified as internationally mandatory rules in the forum, or by refusing to recognize the judgment obtained abroad.

In a situation where PIL rules are not unified, it is imaginable that, for example, a Dutch judge, according to Dutch PIL rules, applies Belgian substantive law, while a Belgian judge, according to Belgian PIL rules, applies French substantive law, whilst a German judge, according to German PIL rules, applies German substantive law. This is a situation that can create options for actors, by for example strategically addressing the Belgian judge - when this judge accepts international jurisdiction over the case - when aiming to have substantive French law as the applicable law. This leads to a situation in which it is imaginable that one can 'shop' a judge to select the applicable law, thereby taking into account the possibility of recognition and enforcement of the ruling of that judge in the states where the recognition and enforcement is of importance.

PIL is, as already mentioned, in essence national law: however sometimes PIL also contains supranational sources, such as those from EU origin. Before 1997 there were barely any European PIL sources. Since then, however, a process of Europeanisation of PIL started, during which a large number of PIL regulations were produced. The European ambition for the unification of the PIL of the EU Member States is clearly visible in the rules governing the *recognition and enforcement* of foreign judgments (where the impact of the principle of mutual recognition is clearly visible), as for the rules concerning *international jurisdiction* (where the impact of the principle of access to justice is visible, usually resulting in a situation where more than one national judge has jurisdiction), and the rules concerning the *applicable law* (where no matter the Member State, the judges would come to the same result). According to the Commission *'one day the courts in all the Member States of the European Union will apply the law of the same country to a given international situation'*.[1] In such a situation there would be no difference whether the parties seize the Dutch, Belgian or German court; all judges would apply the same law (for example German substantive law) based on a uniform European rule on choice of law.

The traditionally national character of PIL does not impede the existence of the various supranational PIL sources. In the domestic PIL of EU Member States, these supranational sources are more and more of EU origin. Through the process of the Europeanisation of PIL, which started several years ago with the objective of increasing legal certainty and predictability, a growing number of PIL rules are created on the supranational level by the *EU legislator*, often replacing national PIL rules. The EU interference in Member States' PIL rules also causes attention for the *Court of Justice* of the European Union (hereinafter the 'Court of Justice'), in a double way. On the one hand, this European judicial institution explains and interprets the European PIL rules, as its *Hadadi* judgment[2] - a way in which it contributes to the development of European PIL-rules. On the other hand, it also interferes in the PIL rules of the EU Member States by reviewing them, on request, with conformity with European law. Such has already been the case in the matter of the international laws on names and international company law. The manner in which the Court of Justice interferes will, in addition to the manner of interference by the EU legislator, appear to be of influence on the possibility to 'controlling' citizens and businesses.

Hereafter the possibility and/or impossibility of *forum shopping* will be placed in the context of the process of the Europeanisation of PIL. One of the ambitions, if not the main ambition, of Europe in this process of the Europeanisation of PIL is exactly that of creating legal certainty and preventing *forum shopping*. A point of attention here is, however, that the European PIL rules are being established in fits and starts and that the Court of Justice judges on a case-by-case basis. The process of Europeanisation of PIL is stormy but capricious; in addition, it goes hand in hand with many questions of interpretation. For now, one cannot (yet) speak about a complete unification of PIL rules, as in some areas only certain aspects of PIL are harmonized, for example when only two of the three basic questions have been regulated on a European level in a particular field of PIL.

1 See also e.g. <http://ec.europa.eu/civiljustice/applicable_law/applicable_law_ec_en.htm>.
2 Case C-168/08, *Hadadi*, ECR 2009, I-06871.

3. Shopping in a Situation of a Continuing but not Completely Realized Europeanisation of PIL

3.1. Requests for the Court of Justice of the European Union to Explain European PIL

The abovementioned case of *Hadadi* is illustrative for situations that can occur in the context of a partial Europeanisation of PIL, where the Court of Justice has been asked to interpret European PIL rules. The judgment of the Court of Justice concerning the explanation of Article 3 Brussels II*bis* Regulation[3] is relevant in the context of possibilities of *forum shopping* for EU citizens concerning divorce. *Hadadi* is an example for the manner in which competing norms allow citizens to explore and challenge the Court of Justice to take stand.

At the time of the *Hadadi* case, there was a situation of partial European unification of PIL rules concerning divorce: following the Brussels II*bis* Regulation, procedural rules of PIL - including rules concerning jurisdiction and rules concerning recognition within Europe of a divorce pronounced in a EU State - were already unified, the rules on applicable law were not, just as there was no unification of the substantive law on divorce.

In *Hadadi,* the Court of Justice had to deal with a couple who both were dual citizens in two EU Member States: the husband and wife both were of French and Hungarian nationality; they were originally Hungarian, but had been living in France for many years. A divorce procedure in Hungary could lead to a completely different application of law than a divorce procedure in France. The husband realized this and saw benefit in bringing the procedures in Hungary, where a divorce would be pronounced under conditions much more beneficial to him than if it were pronounced by a French judge.

It is clear that under certain circumstances Brussels II*bis* allows for several EU judges to exercise jurisdiction in a divorce procedure. In *Hadadi,* the Court of Justice had ultimately to judge on the jurisdiction of the Hungarian judge concerning the specific situation of the *Hadadi* couple. Through a broad interpretation of the rules of jurisdiction contained in Brussels II*bis,* the Court of Justice allowed the husband of the French-Hungarian couple to bring divorce procedures in Hungary, against the will of the wife who wanted to start procedures in France, and while being aware that the judgment of the Hungarian judge would allow the husband to ask for recognition and enforcement of that judgment in other EU countries. Essentially the husband thus seems to be allowed "to get law elsewhere". It also seems that the Court of Justice thus gives a green light for forum shopping and the rush to the courts, even if that is at the expense of the defendant - in this case the wife - and

3 Regulation (EC) No 2201/2003.

even if one is allowed to escape the applicability of the French rule of applicable law/the substantive law that is made applicable through the French PIL rule.[4]

In the current situation, the European unification of PIL concerning divorce has further developed: meanwhile, a Regulation has been promulgated that concerns the applicable law, namely the Rome III Regulation.[5] One could ask in how far the rush to the courts has thus been made impossible or useless. In any case, if a unification of the rules on applicable law concerning divorce has taken place, there should be no difference in the law applied by any EU judge, contrary to the case of *Hadadi* where the applicable law depended on the seized court. However, even if rules on applicable law have been unified, one should keep in mind that differences concerning rules of applicable law that deal with certain *consequences* of divorce would still be imaginable as far as these rules are not unified.

It is remarkable that the Rome III Regulation is a form of European unification of PIL in which not all EU Member States participate. The Rome III Regulation has been created through the process of 'enhanced co-operation', which has as a consequence that, currently, only a part of the EU Member States are party to the Rome III Regulation. Indeed, several EU States demonstrated reluctance and aversion during the preparations of the Rome III Regulation against the manner of unification of the rules concerning divorce. Amongst other things, there was a difference of opinion regarding the acceptance of permitting a choice of law concerning the extent in which the applicable law concerning divorce could lead to a liberal or restrictive divorce settlement - differences in insight that are partially connected to differences of opinion on the question of how substantive divorce-law is best arranged. It may also be noted that there is a fear that the position taken in the context of PIL could lead to a domino effect that would influence the internal context, being the domestic law of a particular EU Member State. Here, situations of 'reversed discrimination' could emerge and the need to permit 'U-turns' could be feared by EU Member States.[6]

In any case, the result was that only a limited number of Member States agreed to become party to the proposed Rome III Regulation, with the consequence that also now, anno 2015, forum shopping and the rush to the court by one or both partners is still possible, although in a lesser degree than at the time of the *Hadadi* case.

4 See on this issue e.g. also the Report from the Commission to the European Parliament, the Council and the European Economic and Social Committee on Brussels II*bis*, 15 April 2014 COM(2014) 225 final.

5 Regulation (EU) No 1259/2010.

6 See on some of these aspects (including issues such as 'fraud on the law') in international family law e.g. also Yetano 2010, p. 155-193. See also on some of these issues in a more general way/in other areas of law e.g., in 2006, Sorenson 2006, p. 423-459 and more recently, Deacon 2013, to be consulted on <www.euroblawg.com/eu-law-2/the-eu-law-doctrine-of-abuse-of-rights-should-it-be-a-general-principle-of-eu-law-and-is-it/>. See also the case law of the CJEU on the 'Belgium route' particularly in migration law (cases C-456/12 and 457/12).

3.2. *Requests for the Court of Justice to Review National PIL*

The Court of Justice of the European Union is not only asked to explain or interpret European PIL rules, as in the *Hadadi* case, but the Court can also be asked to review domestic PIL rules for compatibility with EU law. The Court has been asked to intervene in this manner in both matters of the international law on names and in the matter of international company law.

The rulings in the cases *Garcia Avello*[7] and *Grunkin Paul*[8] concerning the (international) law on names could be interpreted as the Court of Justice, partly under the influence of push factors such as the free movement of persons and non-discrimination, breaking through the opposition of Member States. It seems that the national obstacles against the ways in which citizens try to get the law they please, are being broken by the Court of Justice.

In rulings concerning international company law, such as *Centros*[9] and *Inspire Art*,[10] the Court allows companies a certain degree of leeway under the impulse of freedom of establishment.

Although the Court formulates considerations here and there concerning the 'required connection' and pretends it does not want to give leeway to completely artificial situation, a question that arises is: when does the Court consider that it deals with either a case of fraud or a case of forum shopping?

Besides this, it is remarkable that the Court of Justice doesn't break *all* national opposition under the impulse of push factors, such as the EU fundamental freedoms and the principle of non-discrimination. In a more recent case such as *Sayn-Wittgenstein*,[11] it can be imagined as if the Court of Justice allows for the, in this case, Austrian 'obstacles' to remain.

Finally, it is remarkable that EU Member States sometimes, after conviction of their domestic PIL provisions by the Court of Justice, proceed to a different arrangement between intra-Community situations, where the Court of Justice can make a final and binding ruling, and non-intra-Community cases, in which the Member States consider themselves sovereign. Illustrative is the Dutch PIL arrangement concerning company law, where clearly two separate policies are applied: after the ruling in *Inspire Art*, Dutch PIL rules combating situations sentenced as 'fraud' are still, as such, applicable on situations that are not in a purely intra-Community. The Dutch authorities had to obey to the ruling in *Inspire Art*, an intra-Community case, in which Dutch PIL rules were convicted by the Court: 'forum shopping' was allowed, according to the Court of Justice, and thus it was ruled that some Dutch PIL rules combating 'fraud' could not apply. But in cases that are not in a purely intra-Community setting and where the context is almost equal to that of the *Inspire Art* case, the same acts are currently still sentenced as fraud by Dutch PIL rules.

7 Case C-148/02, *Garcia Avello*, ECR 2003, I-11613.
8 Case C-353/06, *Grunkin*, ECR 2008, I-07639.
9 Case C-212/97, *Centros*, ECR 1999, I-01459.
10 Case C-167/01, *Inspire Art*, ECR 2003, I-101555.
11 Case C-208/09, *Sayn-Wittgenstein*, ECR 2010, I-13693.

4. Forum Shopping in a Situation of (Completed) European Unification of Rules on Applicable Law

What if the rules on applicable law are unified in Europe? In the discussion on the international law on names and international company law rulings of the Court of Justice, the rules of applicable law were not (yet) unified on the European level. Here I will discuss the situation where the EU legislator has already intervened, in particular by promulgating uniform rules on applicable law. In such a situation the starting point is that both Member State A, Member State B, Member State C, etc. apply law X. I would like to bring to attention again the quote cited above stating that '*one day the courts in all the Member States of the European Union will apply the law of the same country to a given international situation*'. Such a situation usually takes place in a context in which judges of various Member States have international jurisdiction (which often also provides for a possible choice of forum) and where, in addition, the starting point is that recognition of the judgment is in principle secured, but where there also still exist differences concerning substantive law between Member States.

In such situations, in which differences between Member States concerning substantive law still exist, the question arises which law will be deemed the applicable law. Quid in this context of competing substantive norms? Which possibilities are offered by connecting factors and the (European) PIL mechanisms? Does unification of the rules on applicable law provide here for exclusion of forum shopping possibilities, or is the contrary the case and do forum shopping possibilities continue to exist?

4.1. *Direct Possibilities for Choice of Law*

In the case of the European unification of rules on applicable law, sometimes possibilities for choice of law are provided.[12] One can indicate, for example, Article 3 Rome Convention[13] and Article 3 Rome I Regulation[14] on applicable law concerning agreements in which broad possibilities for choice of law are provided (with the difficult issue of the possibility or impossibility in this context for a European sales law), Article 14 Rome II Regulation[15] concerning the applicable law on torts, and Article 5 Rome III Regulation concerning the applicable law on divorce. Under certain circumstances such a choice of law is subjected to restrictions. For example, according to Article 6 Rome Convention and Article 8 Rome I Regulation an employee, as the weaker party, cannot deprive himself of certain rights through a choice of law. The following other limitations also come to mind: the limitation contained in Article 3(3) Rome I Regulation concerning choice of law in an internal situation; the one contained in Article 3(4) Rome I Regulation

12 See on some of these possibilities and issues e.g. Rutgers & Zilinsky 2013.
13 Convention on the Law Applicable to Contractual Obligations 1980.
14 Regulation (EC) No 593/2008.
15 Regulation (EC) No 864/2007.

concerning the choice of law of a state that is not party to the Rome I Regulation; the limitation contained in Article 14(1) Rome II Regulation on limitations concerning the moment on which a choice of law is made; and lastly, Article 5 Rome III Regulation in which the choice between legal systems is limited.

If a choice of law possibility is explicitly foreseen and is actually used by the parties, there is a direct possibility to choose the applicable law; all Member States will apply this applicable law, and if PIL rules concerning recognition allow for it, the recognition and enforcement of the judgment in which this law has been applied is also secured.

4.2. *Indirect Possibilities for Choice of Law*

If there is no case of choice of law (because it is not allowed or used by the parties) the question arises on how far the law can be chosen indirectly.

Points of attention are the question whether the connecting factors that are being used in the absence of a choice of law honours strategic practice from one party (the strong party) and whether that connecting factor lends itself for strategic use by one party (the strong party). In other words: which possibilities are given to the strong party? The foregoing could be explored in two domains: first of all in the area of Corporate Social Responsibility, with the possible focus on rules on the law applicable to torts as contained in the Rome II Regulations, and in the domain of international labour law, with a possible focus on rules applicable to employment agreements as contained in the Rome Convention and the Rome I Regulation. To what extent do risks of unregulated competition arise?

These two 'hot topics' – the topic of Corporate Social Responsibility and the topic of international labour law – could serve as case-studies[16] if one were to analyse PIL from the perspective of regulatory function. The first example could be situated mainly in situations that are not purely intracommunatarian but should be placed in the 'global context', namely situations dealing with damage created outside of Europe by European multinationals. The second example could focus on the pure EU context, where it touches on labour migration from Eastern European

16 For a first exploration of these questions on both domains I refer to the abovementioned PowerPoint Presentation as well as to several publications on each of both domains which contain further references to legislation, jurisprudence and legal doctrine, to be consulted on <http://papers.ssrn.com/sol3/cf_dev/AbsByAuth.cfm?per_id=919707>; see also the paper 'The (Boundaries of) the Instrumentalisation of European Private International Law' (<http://papers.ssrn.com/sol3/papers.cfm?abstract_id=2485759>) on which section 4.2 of this chapter has been based. The paper 'The (Boundaries of) the Instrumentalisation of European Private International Law' was presented on a conference in Louvain-La-Neuve in June 2014 and has been published in an extensive version in the congress book of that conference (Bergé, Francq & Gardenes Santiago 2015). As for the topic of international labour law, on the Directive on the enforcement of the Posting Directive of 15 May 2014 (Directive 2014/67/EU), see recently: Van Overbeeke 2014. See also, for cases about (international) labour law, recently, Case C-91/13, *Essent Energie Productie BV*, not yet reported; Case C-549/13, *Bundesdruckerei GmbH*, not yet reported and Case C-396/13, *Sähköalojen ammattiliitto ry*, not yet reported.

countries to Western European countries. Both themes are at least partly covered by rules of European PIL. And rules of European PIL can make a difference in these fields: eventually, it is, in first instance, PIL rules in respect of jurisdiction and applicable law that determine to what extent and on what basis a European parent company and its non-European subsidiary can be sued in an EU country under civil law and, thus, to what extent multinationals must actually take notice of certain rules. Similarly, PIL rules also determine which employment conditions must be respected in case of international posting and hence to what extent competition on employment conditions is possible.

De facto, already the manner in which PIL is regulated - and the level at which this happens - has in any case effect on, inter alia, the possibilities for victims of environmental pollution to have recourse against European multinationals. The issue then could be examined in terms of how European PIL currently serves the protection of planetary commons or whether it works in the opposite way, namely by creating or allowing phenomena such as the race to the bottom at the expense of environmental protection, the protection of human rights and ultimately at the expense of weak parties.

In both areas - in international labour law and in Corporate Social Responsibility -, some PIL rules have already been indicated by Muir-Watt[17] as 'tools of governance' - namely the Posting Directive[18] as well as Article 7 of the Rome II Regulation. However, the question also has already been raised in how far these rules are indeed to be seen as tools of governance, facilitating *e.g.* access to justice or, conversely, as another tool of power in the hands of the powerful party and another legal hurdle for victims or weak parties. The answer to this depends in the area of labour law, inter alia, on the interpretation of the Posting Directive as a tool of minimum or maximum protection of posted workers and the interaction of this Directive with other PIL rules as well as, in the area of Corporate Social Responsibility, on the interpretation of Article 7 Rome II Regulation, allowing or not allowing the victim to choose for the law of the country where the mother company has taken decisions in the area of environment protection.

In both abovementioned debates, *several* legal arguments and principles are at stake, including or touching EU fundamental freedoms - such as the freedom of establishment, the freedom of services, possibly also the freedom of movement of workers within Europe as well as human rights. These issues also revolve around questions of flexibility versus predictability, around protection of weak parties, around allowing or prohibiting choice of law, and around creating or avoiding dynamics of races to the bottom. What position should PIL assume towards the issues and dynamics that are currently at play in these areas?

17 See the Guest Editorial of Muir-Watt, published on <http://conflictoflaws.net/2008/guest-editorial-muir-watt-on-reshaping-private-international-law-in-a-changing-world/>.

18 Directive 96/71/EC of 16 December 1996.

5. The EU as a Protector of Weak Parties and Human Rights? Risks and Opportunities

Currently, PIL finds itself at the crossroads of several force fields, *both* in the European and the global context. This implies discussions revolving around the fundaments of PIL and around various principles influencing PIL. The necessity to discuss the abovementioned is underlined when studying the PIL aspects of tort, in particular environmental pollution, and in studying PIL aspects of contract law, in particular employment contracts.

The overall question arises whether 'Europe' (the EU legislator and the Court of Justice) is or has the potential to be a central regulator that stands up for weak parties and for the protection of human rights.

Sometimes the interference by the EU seems indeed to offer some capabilities to protect and to enforce the rights of vulnerable parties and to limit the risks of competition. Think for example of the Posting Directive which (as far as the Directive is indeed considered to provide a minimum threshold of protection) lays down a minimum protection to mobile workers. Alternatively, the possible effects of the freedom of movement of persons in PIL is a fitting illustration for a beneficial outcome to EU intervention, in the sense that it would regulate the use of a minimum of the local law to mobile workers. Also, Article 7 Rome II Regulation is able to have beneficial effects - at least if Article 7 Rome II Regulation is given a broad interpretation.

But, looking at the issue from up close, it turns out that also risks can be found in relation to the role of the EU: it sometimes seems that the interference of European institutions in PIL has lead in some cases to a race to the bottom and to situations that sometimes are viewed as excesses, potentially culminating in unregulated competition. This might include, for example, the effects of the freedom of establishment in international corporate law - with judgments such as *Centros* and *Inspire Art* as fitting illustrations. And in some cases, the effect could be a reduction in the level of protection of weaker parties - thus creating 'adverse effects'. Noteworthy in this context is the impact of Article 6 Rome Convention in international labour law: as far as, through Article 6 Rome Convention, the foundation is laid or green light is given to situations of social dumping, adverse effects emerge. Further, the possible effects of the freedom of establishment and freedom to provide services in international labour law are indicative of such a development: as far as companies are allowed here to seek (or try to seek) the application of a law that is prejudicial to the employee, adverse effects on the protection of weak parties emerge also here. Such adverse effect could also be evidenced (at least in some cases) by Article 4 Rome II regulation.

The above is only treated in an exploratory and selective manner but still consequently, the question arises to the regulatory function of PIL.[19]

[19] See on this issue for example the abovementioned Guest Editorial of Muir-Watt, published on <http://conflictoflaws.net/2008/guest-editorial-muir-watt-on-reshaping-private- →

6. Conclusion: PIL and Social Justice?

Whatever may become of a possible regulatory function of PIL in the future, there is without a doubt a need for awareness about the role of PIL. As Robert Wai[20] recently stated regarding international economic law, the question is not so much whether PIL has to play a role, but it is more about which role it needs to play.

Awareness is needed of PIL's impact on the protection of weak parties and on the protection of human rights and protection of the environment, both inside and outside of Europe.

The doctrine[21] has already framed issues in terms of 'social *environmental* justice and the role of PIL'. The role of PIL on social justice could be broader; it is then necessary to analyse how PIL could in general terms play a role in ensuring or achieving social justice.

In this chapter, I have treated some ongoing developments selectively, which may give the reader a somewhat incomplete or distorted picture. Nevertheless, my contribution hopefully was successful in bringing some pressing issues surrounding the use of PIL to the attention of the readers. The above should be read as a warning in order to be alert to the role of European or national PIL in ensuring or achieving social justice. All in all, it appears that mindfulness and awareness of the very real effects of the abstract, peculiar discipline of PIL is required.

international-law-in-a-changing-world/>) as well as her call for studying PIL as 'Global Governance', published *inter alia* in her paper (Muir Watt 2011). *Cf.* also earlier literature (referred to also by Muir-Watt) such as several publications of R. Wai (see for several publications of R. Wai <http://papers.ssrn.com/sol3/cf_dev/AbsByAuth.cfm?-per_id=114304>) and R. Michaels (see for several publications of R. Michaels <http://papers.ssrn.com/sol3/cf_dev/AbsByAuth.cfm?per_id=105373>); see also e.g. Romano 2011; Joerges, Kjaer & Ralli 2011, and Bomhoff & Meuwese 2011.

20 See e.g. the paper of Wai presented at the Conference 'What is Private International Law' (Wai 2012).

21 For the use of the term 'Social *environmental* justice', see e.g. recently Bright-Staath & Wray 2012.

Bibliography

Bergé, Francq & Gardenes Santiago 2015
Bergé, J.S., Francq, S. & Gardenes Santiago, M. (eds.), *The Boundaries of European Private International Law*, Bruxelles: Bruylant, 2015.

Bomhoff & Meuwese 2011
Bomhoff, J. & Meuwese, A., 'The Meta-Regulation of Transnational Private Regulation', *Journal of Law and Society*, 2011, p. 138-162.

Bright-Staath & Wray 2012
Bright-Staath, C. & Wray, B., 'Corporations and Social Environmental Justice: the Role of Private International Law', in: Duval, A. & Moreau, M.-A. (eds.), *Towards Environmental Justice*, EU Working Paper Law 2012/02, EUI (European University Institute, Florence).

Deacon 2013
Deacon, N., *The EU Law Doctrine of Abuse of Rights: Should it Be a General Principle of EU Law; and is it?'*, to be consulted on: <http://www.euroblawg.com/eu-law-2/the-eu-law-doctrine-of-abuse-of-rights-should-it-be-a-general-principle-of-eu-law-and-is-it/>.

Joerges, Kjaer & Ralli 2011
Joerges, Chr., Kjaer, P. & Ralli, T., 'A New Type of Conflicts Law as Constitutional Form in the Postnational Constellation', *Transnational Legal Theory*, 2011, p. 153-165.

Muir Watt 2008
Muir Watt, H., 'Reshaping Private International Law in a Changing World', available at: <http://conflictoflaws.net/2008/guest-editorial-muir-watt-on-reshaping-private-international-law-in-a-changing-world/>.

Muir Watt 2011
Muir Watt, H., 'Private International Law Beyond the Schism', *Transnational Legal Theory*, 2011, Vol. 2(3), p. 347-427.

Romano 2011
Romano, J.P., 'Le droit international privé à l'épreuve de la théorie kantienne de la justice', in: Lorandi, F. & Stachelin, D. (eds.), *Festschrift für Ivo Schwander*, Zürich/St Gallen: Dike Verlag, 2011, p. 613-642.

Rutgers & Zilinsky 2013
Rutgers, J.W. & Zilinsky, M. (eds.), *Begrensde vrijheid in het IPR*, Apeldoorn: Maklu, 2013.

Sorenson 2006
Sorenson, K.E., 'Abuse of Rights in Community Law: A Principle of Substance or Merely Rhetoric?', *Common Market Law Review*, 2006, p. 423-459.

Van Den Eeckhout 2014
Van Den Eeckhout, V., 'The (Boundaries of) the Instrumentalisation of European Private International Law', available at: <http://papers.ssrn.com/sol3/-papers.cfm?abstract_id=2485759>.

Van Overbeeke 2014
Van Overbeeke, F., 'Het toepasselijk recht op gedetacheerde werknemers na de Handhavingsrichtlijn inzake de Detacheringsrichtlijn', *Arbeidsrecht,* 2014, Vol. 44, p. 1-8.

Wai 2012
Wai, R., 'Already Transnational Private Law', paper presented at the Conference 'What is Private International Law' of the Duke Law School, November 2012.

Yetano 2010
Yetano, T.M., 'The Constitutionalisation of Party Autonomy in European Family Law', *Journal of Private International Law,* 2010, p. 155-193.

P. Wautelet

PARTY AUTONOMY IN INTERNATIONAL FAMILY RELATIONSHIPS: A RESEARCH AGENDA

In recent years, there has been quite a lively debate by citizens on the choice of legal regime.[1] The debate has focused on concepts such as empowerment, enhancing participation of citizens in the European integration process and other items.[2] For once, private international law may play a part in this discussion. The idea of choice by citizen indeed nicely fits in with one of the cornerstones of modern private international law, i.e. the concept of party autonomy.[3] This mechanism is well known in the field of cross-border contracts. Parties to such contracts may select which law governs their contract, as has recently been confirmed by the Rome I Regulation, whose Preamble indicates that the parties' freedom to choose the applicable law 'should be one of the cornerstones of the system of conflict-of-law rules in matters of contractual obligations'.[4] [5] The nature, effects and consequences of such choice have been studied, against a background of intense debate on the legitimacy of allowing parties to choose the law applicable to their contract.[6]

More recently, party autonomy has conquered new grounds in cross-border private relationships.[7] Building on first attempts in national codifications,[8] party

1 See e.g. the papers published in Kessedjian 2013.

2 See e.g. Smits 2010, p. 68-74.

3 The link between choice in general and party autonomy in private international law is made by Smits 2010, p. 70.

4 Regulation (EC) No 593/2008 of the European Parliament and of the Council of 17 June 2008 on the law applicable to contractual obligations (Rome I), *OJ* 2008, L177/6.

5 Recital 11. The Court of Justice has confirmed the central role of party autonomy in its *Unamar* ruling: Case C-184/12, *United Antwerp Maritime Agencies (Unamar) NV v Navigation Maritime Bulgare,* not yet reported, para. 49.

6 See Jacquet 2011, p. 1-15; Kohler 2013, p. 155-262. For a recent attempt to question the foundations of party autonomy see Muir Watt 2010a, p. 1-34.

7 Another area where party autonomy has also been considered is that of property law. Even though scholars have convincingly pleaded for the introduction of party autonomy in this field (see e.g. Westrik & Van der Weide 2011. See already Flessner 2010, p. 125-146 and Van →

autonomy has become one of the leading principles used in various EU regulations dealing with cross-border family relationships. It can now be found in successions,[9] in divorce[10] and in maintenance matters.[11] It is widely expected that the future Regulation dealing with matrimonial property regimes[12] will also allow parties to choose the applicable law.[13] This new trend sometimes has been greeted with enthusiasm, sometimes with scepticism.[14]

While these Regulations constrain the choice that parties can make, it cannot be denied that the principle of freedom of choice has been openly embraced by the European legislator. This principle evolved, at least within the EU, from what was until recently a marginal phenomenon to a well-respected solution for cross-border family relationships. This (r-)evolution occurred quite fast and has attracted much attention. However, much of the research in this area has adopted a limited perspective, focusing exclusively on the possibilities and limits of choice in one specific instrument[15] or adopting a comprehensive outlook but with a strong positive flavour.[16] While it is true that a number of contributions provide excellent food for thought,[17] the overall impression is that more time and more research is needed to start apprehending the fundamental questions raised by this evolution.[18] In part, this may be due to the relative novelty of the concept of party autonomy in

der Weide 2006), not much progress has been made so far. More recently, a plea has been made to allow party autonomy in intellectual property issues, see Matulionyte 2013, p. 77-99.

8 Most notably the Dutch act adopted in 1981 dealing with cross-border divorces allowed the spouses to make a choice for the application of Dutch law, see Art. 1 para. 4 of the *'Wet houdende regeling van het conflictenrecht inzake ontbinding van het huwelijk en scheiding van tafel en bed...'* adopted on 25 March 1981.

9 Art. 22 of Regulation 650/2012.

10 Art. 5 of Regulation 1259/2010.

11 Art. 15 of Regulation 4/2009, which refers to the 2007 Hague Maintenance Protocol.

12 A Proposal was published by the Commission in 2011: Proposal for a Council Regulation on jurisdiction, applicable law and the recognition and enforcement of decisions in matters of matrimonial property regimes COM(2011) 126 final.

13 And may also one day be accepted in matters of name, see the proposal made by Dutta *et al.* 2014, p. 33-44. Art. 37 of the Swiss Federal Act on Private International Law (1987) already makes it possible for a person to prefer the application of the national law over the law of one's domicile.

14 E.g. Bourdelois 2014, p. 137-154.

15 Such as the role of party autonomy in the area of cross-border maintenance claims (see e.g. Lipp 2012, p. 847-866), of cross-border divorce (see e.g. Röthel 2013, p. 3-15), of succession matters (see e.g. Cach & Weber 2013, p. 263-269 (studying choice of law in succession matters) or cross-border matrimonial property regimes (see e.g. Sotiropoulou 2013, p. 21-38).

16 See e.g. Heinrich 2012, p. 701-713.

17 See e.g. the various contributions published in *NIPR* 2012/4 (Hook 2012, p. 587-596; Torga 2012, p. 547-554; Viarengo 2012, p. 555-561; Peari 2012, p. 597-604 and Nagy 2012, p. 576-586). *Adde* Terradas 2013, p. 119-131 and Carruthers 2012, p. 881-913.

18 It is notable that in two recent fundamental papers on party autonomy leading scholars have almost exclusively focused on the use of party autonomy in contracts, leaving other fields untouched - see e.g. Lehmann 2008a, p. 381-434 and Basedow 2011, p. 32-59. See, however, the various contributions published in Spickhoff 2013. The same applies to older publications, such as e.g. Jessurun d'Oliveira 1974.

international family relationships.[19] It may also be due to the unavoidable tendency to look for inspiration to the field of cross-border contracts, where party autonomy can claim a much longer history. There is indeed a clear genealogy of rules which can be traced to the Rome I Regulation and previous instruments dealing with cross-border contracts. This 'copy-paste' attitude, which can be found both in legislative acts and in scholarship, does not do justice to the peculiarities of the concept of party autonomy in cross-border family relationships.

At this stage, it may be too early to offer a comprehensive study of all questions raised concerning the growing importance of the concept of party autonomy in private international law. New developments may in fact modify the picture soon and add to the fields conquered already by party autonomy, such as divorce and succession. At the same time, the relative novelty of the changes brought to the field of private international law by the rise of the concept of party autonomy makes it difficult to take full stock of all issues raised by the development of party autonomy. This is why scholars should first attempt to define a research agenda. This paper offers a first glimpse into such a research agenda by exploring a number of questions which should figure prominently in such agenda. It is by no means meant to be exhaustive. Rather, an attempt will be made to shed some light on the main questions raised by recent evolutions in the hope of being an invitation for further research.

1. Mapping out the Concept of Party Autonomy in Private International Law

A first item on the research agenda should be to map out the extent and limits of party autonomy under the current private international law regulations.

It will be fairly easy to describe all opportunities for choice existing under the various regulations adopted by the EU. In fact, such work has already been undertaken. A comprehensive mapping should, however, also include a comparison of the differences existing between the European instruments. To give but one example: under the Succession Regulation,[20] one may choose to subject its succession to the law of its nationality.[21] In the absence of an express provision to that effect, Article 22(2) of the Succession Regulation makes it possible to infer a choice of law from the 'terms' of a disposition of property upon death. Hence, it may be possible to find out that a person has chosen a law even though such choice

19 The issue is not entirely novel. In the past, some scholars have already devoted quite some attention to the issue of party autonomy in family law. See most notably Carlier 1992 and Gannagé 1992, p. 424-454. While very inspiring, these two contributions could not look back at actual use of party autonomy by rules dealing with cross-border family relationships.

20 Regulation (EU) No 650/2012 of the European Parliament and of the Council of 4 July 2012 on jurisdiction, applicable law, recognition and enforcement of decisions and acceptable and enforcement of authentic instruments in matters of succession and on the creation of a European certificate of succession, *OJ* 2012, L201/107.

21 A person holding two or more nationalities may choose whichever nationality suits him best.

has not been expressly stated.[22] By contrast, it is unclear whether such an implicit choice of law may be accepted under the Rome III Regulation.[23] While some commentators have argued that the terms of the Regulation may accommodate an implicit choice of law,[24] it has also been suggested that Rome III Regulation leaves no room for such choice.[25] Other differences may exist between the European private international law Regulations, which should be thoroughly analysed.

Going beyond choice possibilities offered by regulations and other EU instruments, research should also extend to *less visible* forms of party autonomy. Indirect choice possibilities have always existed. To refer to one traditional example: in a not-so-distant past, some couples travelled to Scotland to get married or to Nevada to obtain a divorce, both of which would have been very difficult to obtain in their home jurisdiction.[26] In some regions of the world, such marriage tourism is still alive and kicking, with couples willing to get married sometimes travelling to neighbouring countries to avoid having to comply to what is perceived as cumbersome requirements.[27] More recently, the advent of registered partnerships and same-sex marriages in some jurisdictions may have encouraged some form of legal tourism. This may have been especially noticeable in jurisdictions which did not impose strict jurisdictional requirements to access such legal status.[28] It may also have been encouraged by the special treatment afforded under private international law to same sex marriages.[29] These forms of legal tourism come very close to strategies of legal engineering. They do not arise out of direct recognition of party autonomy. At the end of the day, this phenomenon comes, however, very close to a choice by the parties concerned regarding their legal status. These mechanisms

22 See the explanations of Bonomi & Wautelet 2013, p. 321-325.

23 Council Regulation (EU) No 1259/2012 of 20 December 2010 implementing enhanced cooperation in the area of the law applicable to divorce and legal separation, *OJ* 2010, L343/10.

24 See e.g. Devers & Farge 2012.

25 Azzi 2013, p. 165.

26 See the account by Van Poppel 1968, p. 427-457. On marriages celebrated in Gretna Green, see e.g. CA Brussels, 17 January 1962, *Pasicrisie*, 1963, II, 30.

27 Some Danish islands attract many couples living in Germany who are wishing to get married, see 'Marriage migration makes Denmark "Europe's Las Vegas" - Lenient laws for marrying bi-national couples makes Denmark a haven for Germans and their foreign fiancees', *The Copenhagen Post*, 12 October 2012 (http://cphpost.dk/news/marriage-migration-makes-denmark-europes-las-vegas.3031.html).

28 For the situation in Germany, see Martiny 2012, p. 190.

29 For various reasons, Member States allowing same sex marriages have indeed made it easier for couples to marry by introducing nuances to the application of the national law of the future spouses. In Belgium, Art. 46 of the Code of Private International Law makes to possible to disregard the fact that under the national law of one of the spouses, a marriage would not be possible because of the fact that the two spouses share the same sex. According to Verhellen, this caveat to the application of the national law of the spouses has been frequently applied (Verhellen 2013, p. 561, No. 74). In France, a similar provision has been adopted - see Art. 202 of the French Civil Code, as modified by the Act N) 2013-404 of 17 May 2013 'ouvrant le mariage aux couples de personnes de même sexe'.

should therefore also be taken into account when discussing the role and limits of party autonomy.

Many of the instruments adopted by the EU to deal with cross-border situations also afford the parties a measure of choice, even if only indirectly. This is especially the case when rules of jurisdiction make it possible for a plaintiff to select between jurisdictions. The EU has adopted uniform rules determining the relevant jurisdiction in private law matters. These apply among other fields in contract, liability in tort but also in divorce and maintenance matters. What is striking with these rules is that they often offer the possibility to choose between two (or more) courts. If a car accident occurs, say, in Maastricht between a Dutch national riding a bike and a car with a Belgian license plate, the injured biker may bring proceedings either in Netherlands[30] or in Belgium.[31] He has in other words a choice between two courts. This choice has in turn been facilitated by the fact that regardless where he chooses to bring proceedings, the plaintiff may be certain that the judgment will be recognised in other Member States.[32] The same may be said when one spouse wants to file for divorce: under Article 3 of the Brussels *IIbis* Regulation,[33] there will often be a choice between several jurisdictions.

These two examples concern the possibility to choose the court, and not the law which the chosen court will apply to a given case. The possibility to choose the court in those circumstances may be less apparent than an outright possibility to choose the law enshrined in an explicit provision to that effect. It does not have the same, radical effect as a choice for the law of one Member State.[34] However, by choosing the court, a plaintiff exercises a great impact on the conduct of litigation and on the law which will eventually be applied to the matter at hand. Such choice possibility, which is a key part of the private international law system, should therefore not be underestimated.

In recent years, important evolutions in case law, in particular in the case law of the Court of Justice (ECJ), have also expanded the possibility for parties to exercise an 'indirect' choice in certain contexts. This is particularly the case for the treatment of persons with dual or multiple nationalities in the EU. Dual nationals have always been a challenge for private international law. Special rules have been

30 Art. 7(2) Brussels *Ibis* Regulation (recast).

31 Art. 4 Brussels *Ibis* Regulation (recast).

32 According to Art. 39 of the Brussels *Ibis* Regulation (recast), 'A judgment given in a Member State which is enforceable in that Member State shall be enforceable in the other Member States without any declaration of enforceability being required'.

33 Council Regulation (EC) No 2201/2003 of 27 November 2003 concerning jurisdiction and the recognition and enforcement of judgments in matrimonial matters and the matters of parental responsibility, repealing Regulation (EC) No 1347/2000, *OJ* 2003, L338/1.

34 This is in particular the case since account should be taken of the fact that the EU has also adopted uniform rules of conflict of laws, which in many fields reduce the importance of the choice between several jurisdictions. This is the case in matters of tortious liability (Rome II Regulation) and divorce proceedings (Rome III Regulation).

developed to allow the application of conflict rules in case the person concerned possesses more than one nationality.[35]

One striking feature in the recent developments of EU law is that the ECJ has issued strict guidelines on how Member States should handle cases of multiple nationalities: in brief, Member States no longer have the freedom to consider that a person who possesses two nationalities among which their nationality, may be treated as only one of their nationals for the purpose of conflict of laws rules based on the law of the nationality. The Court has established a set of rules constraining how Member States should handle multiple nationalities.[36] The ECJ has even broadened the scope of these rules by considering cases involving persons with multiple nationalities, one of which was the nationality of a third state. In this respect, the Court clarified that Member States should also forgo their traditional rules in order to let the persons concerned enjoy the benefits of the nationality of their choice.[37]

A consequence of these guidelines is that dual or multiple nationals may end up with a possibility to choose the nationality on which they rely. This was manifestly the case in *Garcia Avello*:[38] the parents of the two children born in Belgium first relied on their two children being Belgian citizens (which opened the possibility to request a change from Belgian authorities under local law). Subsequently, they challenged the refusal by Belgian authorities to allow the change of name relying on the fact that their daughters were not only Belgian nationals, but also Spanish nationals.

The sequels to *Garcia Avello* in Belgium perfectly illustrate the fact that this case gives some forms of choice for the parties involved: for dual national children born in Belgium, with both Belgian nationality and that of another Member State, there is now an (informal) choice granted to the parents to choose which nationality prevails.[39] On a more general level, one may wonder whether the Court's ruling in *Garcia Avello* introduces the possibility for dual nationals to select the law of one of

35 Another question arises in relation to the exercise of party autonomy by dual nationals, i.e. whether the general rules dealing with cases of multiple nationalities (see in general Verwilghen 1999, p. 9-484) must be applied when party autonomy is recognised in instruments of private international law. See on this issue, Kruger & Verhellen 2011, p. 618-619.

36 This follows from a series of cases, among which Case C-369/90, *Micheletti and others v Delegacion del Gobierno en Cantabria*, ECR 1992, I-4239; Case C-168/08, *Laszlo Hadadi v Csilla Marta Mesko*, ECR 2009, I-6871 and Case C-148/02, *Carlos Garcia Avello v Belgian State*, ECR 2003, I-11613.

37 See e.g Cases C-7/10 and C-9/10, *Staatssecretaris van Justitie v Tayfun Kahveci and Osman Inan*, not yet reported. The Court held that a particular provision of a decision adopted in the framework of the Association Agreement concluded between Turkey and the EU should be interpreted as meaning that 'the members of the family of a Turkish worker duly registered as belonging to the labour force of a Member State can still invoke that provision once that worker has acquired the nationality of the host Member State while retaining his Turkish nationality' (para. 41).

38 Case C-148/02, *Carlos Garcia Avello v Belgian State*, ECR 2003, I-11613.

39 For more details, see Verhellen 2012, p. 385-388.

their nationalities to govern matters of name or rather to choose among various names they would bear under the different legislations potentially applicable.[40]

As in the previous case, the room which opens up for parties to choose is a consequence, a *by-product* of another development, i.e. the principle of non-discrimination. One could almost say that it is 'collateral damage', in the same line as the freedom granted to businesses, under *Centroos*[41] and its progeny, to incorporate in any Member State while developing activities in other Member States is a by-product of the freedom to provide services. True, the case law of the Court does not require Member States to abandon all ambition of regulating cross-border family relationships and to grant parties an unlimited autonomy to select the applicable law.[42] It remains that these developments pave the way for a greater flexibility which allows parties to manage their legal status as they see fit.[43]

It is one thing to describe with minutiae the extent to which the existing regulations allow parties to choose the law in the context of a given legal relationship. State of the art research should, however, go beyond this and also attempt to capture the extent to which choice possibilities are *effectively used*. This is particularly relevant since party autonomy is a fairly new concept in international family relationships. It may take some time for practitioners to understand and master the various choices offered today by European law. These possibilities will also need to be studied in their interactions with other rules.

This task requires going beyond traditional desk research. In order to have a good overview of how practitioners work and adapt to new possibilities offered by the law, it is not enough to draw from one's experience, however broad it may be. Rather, one should attempt to engage in a wider exercise, based on facts. One possibility is to research case law. Court rulings will indeed provide an indication of how often parties make use of the possibility to choose the law. This could work for some regulations. When parties choose the law applicable to their divorce in accordance with Article 5 of the Rome III Regulation, this may end up in court.[44] For other regulations, it will be much more difficult to rely on case law. It is well known

40 Compare Lehmann 2008b, p 158-159 (who refers to 'optional recognition') and d'Avout 2009, p. 212 (who refers to the possibility for individuals to indirectly arbitrage between two nationalities).

41 Case C-212/97, *Centros Ltd v Erhvervs- og Selskabsstyrelsen*, ECR 1999, I-1459.

42 As explained by Meeusen 2012, p. 127. According to Meeusen, the recent evolution of the case law does not lead to *'la généralisation obligatoire, sur la base du principe de non-discrimination, de l'autonomie de la volonté en matière familiale pour les citoyens de l'Union résidant sur le territoire d'un autre Etat membre'* (translation: 'the mandatory generalization, on the basis of the principle of non-discrimination, of party autonomy in family matters for citizens of the EU residing on the territory of another Member State').

43 Outside the realm of European private international law, other developments also make it possible to take into account the parties' wishes and expectations. See e.g. in relation to marriage and name the explanations of Verhellen 2013, p. 567-571.

44 This assumes that the relevant case law is duly reported and made available. This is not always the case. See for Belgium, Verschelden 2011, p. 234-236 and Verschelden 2012, p. 403-423.

that succession cases are not often brought to courts. At least in continental Europe, succession matters rarely end up being dealt with in court. Hence, drawing from court cases will not allow for obtaining a firm grasp of how much use is made of Article 22 of the Successions Regulation. A first step may be to explore the various newsletters and brochures published by specialised law firms, in order to discern whether and in which circumstances practitioners advise their clients to make a choice of law.[45] This will, however, not prove sufficient to gain insight on how choice of law is actually used.

Other tools, however, will need to be deployed if one is to find out if and to which extent parties make use of the choice possibilities. This applies in particular when one looks at the various covert forms of party autonomy. Finding out how and when an individual relies on one of his nationalities in order to avoid the application of a given national law requires sophisticated investigation methods. Social science could help. One could think of setting up interviews with seasoned practitioners and judges. This could compensate for the lack of a central database recording all instances where, for example, a will includes an express choice of law.[46] Empirical research has only recently started in the field of international contracts.[47] Family law scholars should jump on the same train and brush up their empirical research skills if they want to discover whether and how the choice possibilities they analyse are currently used in practice.

2. Reflecting on the Consequences of Party Autonomy

Once a well-developed overview of instances of choice has been developed, one should also attempt to reflect on the *consequences* of the freedom granted to individuals. Even if one lacks precise empirical data on the use, or lack thereof, of party autonomy in cross-border family relationships, this does not prevent from reflecting upon the possible consequences of such use.

Research questions are plentiful. One possible direction for further research is to look at the consequences of the multiplicity of choice possibilities in particular from the angle of coherence. As conceived under the current legal regime, a choice is expressed for a particular legal relationship and not for the whole series of questions which may arise in the course of an individual's life.[48] A citizen may

45 See e.g. the following brochure entitled 'At last... Napoleonic Succession Law Now Avoidable for Foreigners Living in France', published at: <www.blevinsfranks.com/News/-BlevinsFranks/BlevinsFranksNews?ArticleID=684>.

46 Such comprehensive research has been undertaken in the Netherlands in relation to marriage contracts. See recently, Schols & Hoens 2014, p. 43.

47 See Vogenauer 2013, p. 13-78; Vogenauer & Weatherill 2005, p. 821-837 and Cuniberti 2014, p. 455-517.

48 Compare with the system suggested by Carlier in 1990's – according to Carlier, parties could exercise an option and select the law applicable to their family relationships. In the draft Convention he put forward, Carlier contemplated a choice for the national law or the law of the habitual residence, which would apply to all questions belonging to the 'personal status' of the persons concerned (Carlier 1992, p. 391). In another part of his book, Carlier seemed, →

choose a law to govern his/her succession. If he/she is married, the spouses may have chosen the law under which they may seek to divorce and possibly to claim maintenance. It may be that all these choices are devised globally, acting upon the advice of specialised counsel, taking into account the relationships between the various fields concerned.[49] In that case, the different choices expressed by the party/parties concerned will not run the risk of bringing about contradictory consequences. However, it is far from excluded that such choice could happen in a haphazard way, without much coordination.[50]

One intriguing question is whether such uncoordinated choice could lead to difficulties for the person(s) concerned. One could think of possible contradictions between the national systems, if one and the same person has expressed a choice for different national law in different contexts.[51] Going further, one should also inquire whether such unfettered freedom leading to choice for multiple laws does not raise the risk of unravelling a person's personal status and family relationships. Rules regulating these questions may be assumed to have been conceived within each Member State with a view to guarantee intrinsic coherence. Research should therefore attempt to find out whether, as has been claimed,[52] multiple choices may imperil the balance achieved within one national family law.

Looking further, one should also inquire if the recognition of party autonomy in cross-border family relationships will have any impact on other mechanisms of conflict of laws. Conflict of laws rules indeed are peculiar in that their application comes with a series of technical devices intended to correct, qualify and/or extend their working. When applying a conflict of laws rule, one should for example inquire whether the law deemed to be applicable should be understood as covering only the substantive provisions, or also includes the conflict of laws rules of the law designated, under the well-known mechanism of renvoi.[53] Until recently, these devices have worked with conflict of laws rules leaving no or only limited room for party choice in family relationships.

Two questions come to the mind when contemplating the consequences of allowing parties to choose the law governing family relationships. First, one should examine how a greater possibility for choice will affect the role of authorities called upon to apply the law. Although the status of conflict of laws rules may vary,[54]

however, to accept the possibility that parties could select different laws for the various questions raised by their family relationships (Carlier 1992, p. 270).

49 See for an attempt to coordinate the various choice possibilities offered by European private international law instruments, e.g. Butruille-Cardew & Preney 2012, p. 385-389.

50 Any coordination should also include the tax consequences of certain choices.

51 This bears some resemblance with the difficulties raised by 'dépeçage' in cross-border contracts.

52 See e.g. Farge 2003, p. 627-628; Meziou 2009, p. 304-312. See also the observations of Meeusen 2012, p. 128.

53 The technique of 'renvoi' has lost some of its relevance due to the unification of conflict of laws rules in various European instruments. It retains some value, as shown by Art. 34 of the Succession Regulation.

54 As illustrated among others by De Boer 1996, p. 223-427.

traditional conflict of laws thinking may require the court to apply these rules *ex officio*. In some jurisdictions, a distinction is made depending on the nature of the matters covered by conflict of laws rules. The greater recognition given to the choice of law commands that the role of courts and other authorities need to be investigated. Giving parties more say on the applicable law may indeed require to scale down the role of courts and authorities when looking at cross-border relationships. This question should not be limited to the application of conflict of laws rules by the judge. It should also encompass the effects of a greater freedom to choose on the role of courts called upon to apply foreign law.

Another classic device, whose operation must be questioned in light of the wide recognition of party autonomy, is the public policy exception. If parties may choose the law, it must be questioned whether this will have an impact on the possibility for a state to refuse to apply the law chosen.[55] This question has already been debated in relation to polygamous marriages.[56] It needs to be reconsidered in view of the expansion of the realm of party autonomy.

Another area where further research is called for relates to the consequences of party autonomy on the legal systems of Member States. Allowing parties to choose the law empowers them not only to express their preference for the law of their choice, but also to avoid the application of a legal system which does not meet their expectations. A German citizen residing in Spain could opt for the application of German law for his succession not only because of the various possibilities offered by German law - and in particular the possibility of agreeing with his heirs on how his succession will be divided through the mechanism of '*Erbverträge*' - but also in order to avoid the application of Spanish law. This dual role of party choice becomes even clearer when a British citizen residing in France decides to subject his succession to English law: this choice may be motivated by the desire to avoid the application of forced heirship rules which are very strong under French law. Party choice resembles in that respect the 'voting with your feet' metaphor widely used by political scientists and economists to describe people's reaction to organizations they are dissatisfied with.[57]

Viewing choice of law as an 'easy exit option from inefficient law',[58] it has been argued that in areas where parties are indeed given the possibility to select the applicable law, the freedom of choice may result in a competition between legal systems, provided that other features of a given legal system allow for it. The paradigm of *regulatory competition* implies that lawmakers will be forced to revise their laws in order to ensure that they offer an attractive product.[59]

55 According to Carlier, the public policy exception keeps its role when a relationship is governed by the law chosen by parties, but its intervention is more limited (Carlier 1992, p. 377).

56 See e.g. the criticism voiced by Lagarde against Carlier's proposal to allow foreigners to choose the law of their country of origin: Lagarde 1993, p. 276.

57 See e.g. Hirschman 1970.

58 Schäfer & Lantermann 2006, p. 95.

59 On the requirements for such competition to exist, see Kieninger 2012, p. 301-304.

This line of argument should be considered with due care in the various fields of family law in which freedom of choice has been allowed. If persons living in one Member State are given the possibility to opt out of this Member State's law, one should investigate whether the exercise of party autonomy will exert pressure on the Member States concerned to reassess their legislative policy.[60] If all British citizens living in France decide to opt out of French law, and choose English law to govern their succession, it may be wondered what effect this will have on French policy, in particular in relation to forced heirship rules.[61] At this stage, one can only guess whether allowing party choice will open Pandora's box. Experience in other contexts has shown that to some extent Member States react to the pressure exerted by businesses shopping around for the best legal regime: following the *Centros* decision and its rich progeny which greatly opened the way for incorporation shopping, one witnessed a substantial migration of businesses to England, which in turn could explain the sudden urge of a number of Member States in continental Europe to simplify their corporate laws.[62] The fear that a similar phenomenon could also occur in family law has been voiced.[63]

It may not be easy to apply the model of competition between legal orders to the realm of family law. In contrast with choice of law in the context of incorporation made by businesses or in cross-border contracts, the impact of choices made by private individuals in matters of maintenance or divorce will not enjoy much visibility. How could the public at large know that their neighbours have been able to escape local law thanks to a choice of law? State agencies may not either have any information on such choices. Without such publicity, it may be

60 According to Muir Watt, 'in family law matters, the European version of the federal "right to travel" introduces mobility - the market factor - into conflict of law. Free choice of a more liberal personal or family regime ... is accessible to individuals who are able to cross borders, as long as no particular link to the local community is required to create a relationship prohibited by the home law of the parties... [F]ree movement, whether between laws or courts, creates a market by empowering parties to arbitrage. It is up to the conflict of laws to regulate this market by introducing limits on the mobility of private actors in order to achieve a measure of "juridical touchdown" when competition becomes distorted' (Muir Watt 2010b, p. 56).

61 Bourdelois has argued that since reserved heirship is a fundamental policy in France, application of the public policy exception may be made, which is found in Art. 35 of the Succession Regulation, in order to avoid the application of law chosen by the deceased if that law does not recognise any forced heirship. It is very interesting to note that she builds her argument on the notion of discrimination (Bourdelois 2014, p. 143).

62 The claim has been researched with great nuance by - see among others Ringe 2013, p. 230-367. On the reforms undertaken in many EU countries, see de Cordt & Navez 2014.

63 Commenting on the possibility to choose the law offered by Article 22 of the Succession Regulation, Bourdelois writes 'Introduire un choix de loi n'est donc pas qu'une modalité de désignation de la loi applicable: cela creuse les lézardes que les réformes récentes ont créées dans les fondements. A quand la ruine de l'édifice?' (Bourdelois 2014, p. 143 - translation: 'Allowing party autonomy is therefore not limited to a mere feature of the choice of law process: it further widens cracks which have been brought by recent reforms. When will the house break down?').

wondered how Member States could react to 'exit' choices made by individuals. Even if some court cases reveal the existence of 'exit' choices and lawmakers are alerted, for example through parliamentary questions, attention should be paid to the incentive structure: what interest will lawmakers have in responding to the pressure and 'improving' their 'products'? When a Member State offers an attractive legal regime for incorporation of companies, this may lead to both direct and indirect benefits, such as additional tax revenue or even job creation. The question must be addressed whether a similar incentive exists in family law. Experience in other contexts has revealed that the hypothesis of regulatory competition should be approached with caution.[64] A similar line of research is needed which would test the assumptions of regulatory competition in the new fields conquered by party autonomy.[65]

Undoubtedly, if one finds out that there is indeed a direct or indirect effect on Member States' policies, this may 'raise the ghost' of disappearing national autonomy and its impact on the democratic processes within Member States.[66] It will also raise the question of the disappearance of national legal traditions. It is submitted, however, that the fear of feeding Euroscepticism should not lead to turning away from this question. On the contrary, shedding light on the real impact of party autonomy and the existence - or absence - of a 'race to the bottom' will help feed the democratic debate. Thorough research leading to reasoned results is in any case better than mere phantasms feeding on unexplained assumptions.

Linked to the debate on regulatory competition, attention should also be paid to the effects of greater freedom on mandatory rules. Again, the experience garnered in the field of cross-border contracts puts the finger on an interesting question. Freedom of choice and mandatory rules indeed go hand in hand in cross-border contracts. Although such mandatory rules are certainly not confined to international contract law,[67] the gradual acceptance of party autonomy in cross-border contracts has led courts to discover in their substantive laws certain rules which deserve to be applied no matter what law governs the relationship at hand. Opening the possibility for citizens to select the law applicable to some of their family relationships may lead to a similar development. The question is therefore whether the recognition of party autonomy could or should foster the development of internationally mandatory rules in family law. In that respect, it is striking that while the Rome I and Rome II Regulations expressly allow courts to apply their

64 See most notable Vogenauer 2013, p. 13-78.

65 For a first, modest attempt, see Wautelet 2014, p. 131-145.

66 The existence of very liberal rules of jurisdiction and a strong imperative to recognise foreign divorces under the Brussels II*bis* Regulation has already led to a form of 'hidden' liberalisation. As Meeusen wrote, '[t]here is [...] a great paradox: the absence of substantive consensus results in a very liberal system which essentially obliges the host State to import family law concepts through the recognition of foreign judgments, while neither its national parliament nor the European Parliament never have had to approve such private international law rule, let alone such substantive concepts of family law' (Meeusen 2007, p. 304).

67 And may indeed be found in all fields of private law.

mandatory rules,[68] an equivalent provision cannot be found in the Succession Regulation, the Rome III Regulation nor in the Maintenance Regulation. This certainly calls for a thorough investigation.

3. Reflecting upon the Limits of Party Autonomy

Party autonomy has a long and sometimes troubled history. Its recognition as one of the cardinal principles of the legal regime of cross-border contracts did not come without challenges.[69] If the opposition did not succeed in challenging the very principle of party autonomy, it did manage to limit its scope. Hence, the possibility for parties to choose the law is never recognised without some limitation. Party autonomy is sometimes excluded or reduced *ex ante* - this is most notable the case for consumers contracts.[70] When parties have the possibility to choose the applicable law, Member States have kept a back door open to impose what they deem to be important regulatory concerns. This is usually done through so-called internationally mandatory rules, which limit party autonomy *ex post*. Another much discussed limitation which characterises the current European regime arise out of a Westphalian concern to preserve Member States' monopoly on regulation: under the Rome I Regulation, the freedom of parties does not allow them to opt out of the law of Member States.[71]

68 See Art. 9 Rome I Regulation and Art. 16 Rome II Regulation.

69 See most notably the crusade undertaken by Niboyet in the early decades of the 20th century to defeat the principle of party autonomy - e.g. Niboyet 1927, p. 1-116 and Niboyet 1948, p. 4-36. More recently, see the renewed efforts by Heuzé 1990.

70 Recent research has shown that consumers are protected against choice of law clauses in a very similar fashion in the EU and under US law, see Rühl 2007, p. 167-171.

71 During the process which led to the revision of the Rome Convention, it was suggested to allow a choice for another system than the law of a State. The original proposal for the Rome I Regulation made it possible for parties to choose 'the principles and rules of the substantive law of contract recognised internationally or in the Community', Art. 3(2) original Proposal for a Regulation, COM(2005) 650 final 6. This led to a rich discussion (e.g. Roth 2004; Kondring 2007, p. 241-245). It was not entirely clear whether the language suggested by the Commission would have allowed a direct reference by the parties to the rules of international law. The question has been settled with the adoption of the Rome I Regulation, which clearly confirms that a choice can only be made for municipal law. Recital 13 of the Preamble, however, allows parties to incorporate 'by reference into their contract a non-State body of law or an international convention'. On this compromise reached between the Council and the European Parliament, see Plender & Wilderspin 2009, p. 137-138, para. 6-012. Therefore, if parties, e.g., made a choice for international law, this reference to international law would probably only lead to the 'incorporation' of the rules of international law in the contract, see, e.g., Ferrari 2007, para. 19. In other words, such a choice would not prevent the application of the mandatory provisions of the national law which would be applicable to the contract in absence of a choice of law by the parties. Outside the realm of the Rome I Regulation, there is less difficulty to express a choice for something else than municipal law. This is the case for the Inter-American Convention signed in Mexico in 1994, whose provisions appear to make it possible to choose another law than that of a State - This results from a combined reading of Arts. 1, 7 and 9; see in general Juenger 1994, p. 392. Juenger wrote that 'the parties are free to →

These limitations have managed to achieve a balance between freedom and regulation. Since party autonomy in family law is to a large extent inspired by and even modelled after the regime for cross-border contracts, the question must be raised which limitations should be adopted for party choice in family law. The question is not only *whether* limitations are required, but also *how* they should be implemented.

This inquiry may be started with an assessment of how EU regulations allowing parties to select the applicable law already limit such choice. The most interesting limitation arises out of the fact that the possibility to choose the law is not an open one. Contrary to what is accepted for cross-border contracts[72] and cross-border torts,[73] the choice of law in family matters is only possible for a selected number of legal systems. The Preamble of the Rome III Regulation makes it clear that the possibility to choose the law has only been accepted provided a choice is made for a law 'with which [the spouses] have a close connection'.[74] The Preamble of the Succession Regulation likewise refers to the fact that the possibility to choose the law 'should be limited to the law of a State of their nationality in order to ensure a connection between the deceased and the law chosen...'.[75]

These limitations act as important constraints on the freedom enjoyed by parties.[76] From a conceptual point of view, they could even justify using another terminology to refer to the choice: instead of talking about party autonomy, one should maybe talk about 'party option' – or *optio iuris* – to designate the possibility to choose the law. Going further, these limitations may even be taken to mean that when parties select the applicable law, this is not a real choice of law, on equal footing with the determination by the judge on the basis of a conflict of laws rule.[77]

stipulate to the general principles of international commercial law'. See in general Michaels 2005.

72 Under Art. 3 of the Rome I Regulation, it is accepted that parties may select the law of a country which bears otherwise no connection with their contract. See e.g. Strikwerda 2010, p. 116, para. 197.

73 Art. 14 Rome II. As with the Rome I Regulation, it is accepted that the choice expressed under Art. 14 of the Rome II Regulation need not bear any connection to the relationship at hand, see e.g. Loquin 2008, p. 52-53.

74 Recital 14 Preamble Rome III Regulation.

75 Recital 38 Preamble Succession Regulation.

76 One may add that in matters of divorce, Art. 10 of the Rome III Regulation prohibits the application of the law chosen by the spouses if it does not make any provision for divorce or does not grant one of the spouses 'equal access to divorce or legal separation on grounds of their sex'. This limitation translates a substantive policy objective, i.e. guarantee the equality between spouses.

77 Leading authors have indeed argued that the choice recognised in various contexts, does not amount to party autonomy. Rather, the choice possibility is explained as a method used by the legislator to overcome the traditional opposition between the application of the law of the nationality and the law of the domicile or habitual residence: in many cases, these two connecting factors may prove equally relevant to determine the applicable law. Instead of making an abstract choice between the two, the law leaves it to the persons concerned to choose. See e.g. Audit & d'Avout 2013, p. 199, No. 211: 'Il ne s'agit nullement d'étendre en →

These limitations already call for some investigation. One could for example inquire why party autonomy is not recognised alongside identical lines in all fields of family law. It is intriguing that the choice under the Succession Regulation is limited to the law of the nationality of the person concerned, while a choice may be expressed in favour of another under other Regulations, such as the Rome III Regulation dealing with divorce. Likewise, one could ask why spouses are not afforded the possibility to choose the court in divorce matters, while a choice of court is possible, to a limited extent, in maintenance disputes. It must be asked whether there is room for several distinct brands of party autonomy depending on the subject matter concerned. It may be indeed that party autonomy needs not to be recognised alongside identical lines in all fields of family law. This should at least be investigated as a first step in defining the outer limits within which parties may exercise their freedom. At the same time, attention should be paid to the interactions between the choice of law and the regime dealing with multiple nationalities.

When looking at possible limitations of party autonomy in international family law, attention should also be paid to the consequences of party autonomy on the protection of parties. The paradigm of choice in international private relationships can be traced back to the field of international contracts. It is in relation to cross-border contracts that the idea of choice by parties arose. In contractual relationships, it may be taken for granted that parties have similar bargaining power. This explains why for a long time it was not thought useful to introduce limitations aimed at protecting certain categories of parties. It is only fairly recently that new rules have been developed to limit the exercise of party autonomy in relation to certain contracts.[78] If one leaves these developments aside, the principle remains that parties should be left to cope with the consequences of their freely assumed choice.

This assumption may not hold entirely in family relationships.[79] The balance of power between spouses or between parents and children may be very different

matière personnelle l'autonomie de la volonté telle qu'elle est comprise en matière contractuelle, où elle se fonde sur les nécessités du commerce international [...]; mais seulement de permettre aux intéressés de résoudre eux-mêmes un conflit auquel ils se trouvent spontanément soumis et dans lequel aucune loi ne jouit *a priori* d'un titre à s'appliquer supérieur à l'autre'. (translation: 'The ambition is not to apply to family law matters party autonomy as it is conceived for cross-border contracts, where it is based on the needs of international trade [...]; but only to allow the persons concerned to solve by themselves a conflict in which they are involved and in which no law enjoys a priori a stronger claim to apply than another') Carlier on the other hand sees party autonomy in family matters as a true conflict-of-laws rule (Carlier 1992, p. 255-257, paras. 237-238).

78 See e.g. Arts. 6 and 8 of the Rome I Regulation (in relation consumer and employment contracts).

79 As noted Boele-Woelki noted in 2007, 'Terwijl de zwakkere positie van de consument en werknemer in het IPR is verdisconteerd nemen de familierechtelijke Verordeningsvoorstellen de gelijkheid van partijen tot uitgangspunt. Maar is dat wel gerechtvaardigd? Is er in een familierechtelijke verhouding vaak niet ook een zwakkere partij? Kunnen verschillende economische omstandigheden niet tot ongelijkheid leiden? Zijn onderhoudsgerechtigden niet →

from that existing between parties to a contract. In family relationships, there may be a lack of equality among partners, information asymmetry or, worse, a situation where one party imposes a choice on another. Emotional considerations could also play an important role. It may not be assumed that discussions will proceed at arm's length. On the contrary, one could even start from the assumption that parties need to be protected. Recognition of party autonomy hence calls for the adoption of safeguards in order to guarantee that the choice is based on a true consent.[80]

The Rome III Regulation has attempted to tackle this issue. Article 6 of Rome III Regulation makes it possible for a spouse to draw from another law than the one chosen by the parties in order to demonstrate that he/she did not actually consent to an agreement on choice of law. Article 7 of Rome III Regulation provides additional rules dictating that the agreement between spouses meets certain formal requirements. These rules are supplemented by indications to be found in the Preamble of Rome III Regulation, which insists on the necessary information to be provided to spouses before they agree on the law applicable to their divorce.[81] It is, however, widely accepted that these safeguards, which are directly inspired by equivalent provisions found in Rome I Regulation, are insufficient to guarantee that spouses are in all cases aware of the importance and the consequences of a choice of law agreement. In family relationships, one cannot start from the premise that parties are equal and have equal access to relevant information. Further work is therefore needed to define standards ensuring that choice of law by parties is based on true, informed consent. This could be done by comparing existing standards found in substantive family law, in particular that of Member States. The goal should be to design a legal provision that ensures fairness when parties choose a law.

Research is also needed to better define the limits of party autonomy. Until now, we have witnessed a steady progression of party choice: starting with divorce proceedings, party autonomy has conquered other fields of family relationships. The principle of party choice has not raised too many difficulties in matters of

zelden vrouwen die vanwege de zorg voor kinderen financieel afhankelijk zijn van hun gewezen partner?' (Boele Woelki 2007, p. 297 – translation: 'While the weaker position of consumer and employee is taken into account in private international law, the various proposals for Regulations in family law matters start from the assumption that parties are on equal footing. But is this well justified? Is there not often in family relationships a party weaker than the other? Do various economic circumstances not lead to inequality? Are maintenance creditors not often women who happen to be dependent on their former partner because they care for the children?').

80 See already Art. 9 of the draft Convention on the law applicable to personal status matters, suggested by Carlier (Carlier 1992, p. 392).

81 According to Recital 17, spouses should have 'access to up-to-date information concerning the essential aspects of national and Union law and of the procedures governing divorce and legal separation'. Recital 18 indicates that the 'informed choice of both spouses is a basic principle of this Regulation'. The same Recital notes that '[e]ach spouse should know exactly what [...] the legal and social implications of the choice of applicable law [are]' and that '[t]he possibility of choosing the applicable law by common agreement should be without prejudice to the rights of, and equal opportunities for, the two spouses'.

succession and matrimonial assets. In domestic matters, these areas already make it possible for individuals to exercise some form of control over their relationships. Things are different for divorce: here, the resistance has been fiercer and may help explain why the Rome III Regulation could only become reality through enhanced cooperation.

Although immediate plans within the EU to venture in other areas of family law do not exist, the question must be addressed: if the Member States ever were to agree that common conflict of laws rules are needed in order to deal with cross-border marriages or the establishment of parent-children relationships, will there be any room for party choice? Looking at the current regimes in various Member States, it does not seem that party autonomy stands any chance of being accepted.[82] No Member State leaves any room for party choice in these matters. Further, the creation of a marital link or of a parent-child relationship seem to be much less amenable to party choice even in domestic matters. This is the realm of imperative regulation. At the very least, however, the question should be addressed why these areas should be treated differently from matrimonial property or divorce. If indeed party autonomy is deemed not to be welcome in these areas, this may say much about the nature of party autonomy in areas where it is welcomed.

4. Conclusion

The recent and rapid rise of party autonomy as a new paradigm for cross-border family relationships offers new possibilities to smoothen the regulations of these relationships, which are often torn between Member States' conflicting (substantive and private international law) policies. The advent of party autonomy in international family law also opens up exciting times for researchers in international family law. The recognition of party choice brings new ground for research. Questions indeed abound, which may keep researchers busy for some time.

Taken at its extreme, the possibility for citizens to opt out of a legal system and to choose another one must be appraised in the light of the relationship between a state and its citizens. What does it mean to be a citizen of a state and to reside somewhere, if one may freely opt for the legislation of another state? Does this lead to the 'commodification' of the relationship between a state and its citizen?

In the long run, research in these directions should hopefully help draw the lines of a general theory and legal framework for party autonomy in cross-border family relationships. One should hope that research of this kind will help develop party autonomy in something proper for family relationships, far from the simplistic copy-paste attitude which has prevailed until now. It may well be that the end result will not bear much resemblance to party autonomy as it exists in cross-border contracts and other commercial relationships. As such, this would only signal that private international law may no longer be able to offer a single comprehensive theory of party autonomy.

82 In this sense, Bourdelois 2014, p. 143.

Further research will hopefully also be able to answer the question whether there is a specific EU dimension to party autonomy. In view of the fact that party autonomy has also gained increased recognition outside the EU (witness recent Conventions adopted by the Hague Conference on private international law[83] or national statutes[84]), it must be asked whether there is a special EU dimension to party autonomy in family relationships. This could be the case if the very extensive mobility afforded to individuals within the EU requires that party autonomy be recognised in a distinctive way.

83 E.g. Art. 8 of the Protocol of 23 November 2007 on the Law Applicable to Maintenance Obligations.

84 See e.g. Art. 49(4) of the Czech Statute 1/2012 on private international law of 25 January 2012.

Bibliography

Anoveros Terradas 2013
Anoveros Terradas, B., 'La autonomia de la voluntad como principio rector de las normas de Derecho internacional privado comunitario de la familia', in: Forner Delaygua, J. *et al.* (eds.), *Entre Bruselas y La Haye: estudios sobre la unificacion internacional y regional del Derecho internacional privado. Liber Amicorum Alegría Borrás,* Madrid: Marcial Pons, 2013, p. 119-131.

Audit & d'Avout 2013
Audit, B. & d'Avout, L., *Droit international privé,* 7th edn., Paris: Economica, 2013.

Azzi 2013
Azzi, T., 'La volonté tacite en droit international privé', in: Comité Français de Droit International Privé, *Travaux du Comité français de droit international privé. Années 2010-2012,* Paris: Pedone, 2013, p. 147-177.

Basedow 2011
Basedow, J., 'Theorie der Rechtswahl oder Parteiautonomie als Grundlage des internationalen Privatrechts', *RabelsZ.*, 2011, p. 32-59.

Boele-Woelki 2007
Boele Woelki, K., 'Forum- en rechtskeuze in de nieuwe familierechtelijke verordeningen', *FJR,* 2007, p. 297.

Bonomi & Wautelet 2013
Bonomi, A. & Wautelet, P. (eds.), *Le droit européen des successions. Commentaire du Règlement n° 650/2012 du 4 juillet 2012,* Brussels: Bruylant, 2013.

Bourdelois 2014
Bourdelois, B.,'Relations familiales et professio iuris', in: d'Avout, L. *et al.* (eds.), *Mélanges en l'honneur du Professeur Bernard Audit. Les relations privées internationales,* Paris: LGDJ/Lextenso, 2014, p. 137-154.

Butruille-Cardew & Preney 2012
Butruille-Cardew, C. & Preney, C., 'Articulation du Règlement Rome III avec les autres instruments: clauses de juridiction et loi applicable', *AJ Famille,* 2012, p. 385-389.

Cach & Weber 2013
Cach, C. & Weber, A., 'Privatautonomie im Internationalen Erbrecht: Überlegungen zu Art 22 der Europäischen Erbrechtsverordnung', *ZfRV,* 2013, p. 263-269.

Carlier 1992
Carlier, J.-Y., *Autonomie de la volonté et statut personnel. Etude prospective de droit international privé,* Brussels: Bruylant, 1992.

Carruthers 2012
Carruthers, J.M., 'Party Autonomy in the Legal Regulation of Adult Relationships: What Place for Party Choice in Private International Law', *ICLQ*, 2012, p. 881-913.

Cuniberti 2014
Cuniberti, G., 'The International Market for Contracts: The Most Attractive Contract Laws', *Northwestern J Intl Law & Bus.*, 2014, Vol. 34(3), p. 455-517.

D'Avout 2009
D'Avout, L., 'Case note', *J.D.I.*, 2009, p. 212.

De Boer 1996
De Boer, T., 'Facultative Choice of Law: The Procedural Status of Choice-of-law Rules and Foreign Law', *Collected Courses of the Hague Academy of International Law*, 1996, Vol. 257, p. 223-427.

De Cordt & Navez 2014
De Cordt, Y. & Navez, J.-E. (eds.), *La simplification du droit des sociétés privées dans les États membres de l'UE – Étude comparée des réformes entreprises dans le paysage sociétaire européen*, Brussels: Bruylant/L.G.D.J., 2014.

Devers & Farge 2012
Devers, A. & Farge, M., 'Le nouveau droit international privé du divorce – À propos du règlement Rome III sur la loi applicable au divorce', *Dr. fam.*, 2012, étude 13, nr. 17.

Dutta *et al.* 2014
Dutta, A., Frank, R., Freitag, R., Helms, T., Krömer, K. & Pintens, W., 'Ein Name in ganz Europa. Entwurf eine Europäischen Verordenung über internationale Namensrecht', *StAZ*, 2014, p. 33-44.

Farge 2003
Farge, M., *Le statut familial des étrangers en France: de la loi nationale à la loi de la résidence habituelle*, Paris: L'Harmattan, 2003.

Ferrari 2007
Ferrari, F., 'Comment Art. 27 EGBGB', in: Ferrari, F., Kieninger, E.-M., Mankowski, P., Otte, K., Saenger, I. & Staudinger, A. (eds.), *Internationales Vertragsrecht*, München: Beck, 2007, p. 1-25.

Flessner 2010
Flessner, A., 'Rechtswahl im internationalen Sachenrecht – neue Anstösse aus Europa', in: Apathy, P. *et al.* (eds.), *Festschrift für Helmut Koziol zum 70. Geburtstag*, Vienna: Jan Sramek, 2010, p. 125-146.

Gannagé 1992
Gannagé, P., 'La pénétration de l'autonomie de la volonté dans le droit international privé de la famille', *Rev. crit. dr. int.priv.*, 1992, p. 424-454.

Heinrich 2012
Heinrich, D., 'Zur Parteiautonomie im europäisierten internationalen Familienrecht', in: Verbeke, A.-L. *et al.* (eds.), *Confronting the Frontiers of Family and Succession Law: Liber Amicorum Walter Pintens*, Antwerp: Intersentia, 2012, Vol. 1, p. 701-713.

Heuzé 1990
Heuzé, V., *La règlementation française des contrats internationaux: étude critique des méthodes*, Paris: GLN, 1990.

Hirschman 1970
Hirschman, A.O., *Exit, Voice and Loyalty. Responses to Decline in Firms, Organizations and States*, Cambridge: Harvard University Press, 1970.

Hook 2012
Hook, M., 'Party Autonomy - Yes or No? The "Commodification" of the Law Applicable to Matrimonial Property Relationships', *NIPR*, 2012, p. 587-596.

Jacquet 2011
Jacquet, J.-M., 'La théorie de l'autonomie de la volonté', in: Corneloup, S. & Joubert, N. (eds.), *Le Règlement communautaire 'Rome I' et le choix de loi dans les contrats internationaux*, Paris: Litec, 2011, p. 1-15.

Jessurun d'Oliveira 1974
Jessurun d'Oliveira, H. (ed.), *Partij-invloed in het internationaal privaatrecht*, Deventer: Kluwer, 1974.

Juenger 1994
Juenger, F.K., 'The Inter-American Convention on the Law Applicable to International Contracts: Some Highlights and Comparisons', *AJCL*, 1994, Vol 42, p. 381-393.

Kessedjian 2013
Kessedjian, C. (ed.), *Autonomie en droit européen? Stratégie des citoyens, des entreprises et des Etats*, Paris: Ed. Panthéon-Assas, 2013.

Kieninger 2012
Kieninger, M.-E., 'Competition between Legal Systems', in: Basedow, J. *et al.* (eds.), *Max Planck Encyclopedia of European Private Law*, Oxford: Oxford University Press, 2012, p. 301-304.

Kohler 2010
Kohler, Ch., *L'autonomie de la volonté en droit international privé: un principe universel entre libéralisme et étatisme*, The Hague: ADI-poche, 2013.

Kondring 2007
Kondring, J., 'Nichtstaatliches Recht als Vertragsstatut vor staatlichen Gerichten - oder: Privatkodifikationen in der Abseitsfalle?', *IPRax*, 2007, Vol. 27, p. 241-245.

Kruger & Verhellen 2011
Kruger, T. & Verhellen, J., 'Dual Nationality = Dual Trouble?', *J. Priv. Intl. L.*, 2011, Vol. 7(3), p. 601-626.

Lagarde 1993
Lagarde, P., 'La théorie de l'ordre public international face à la polygamie et à la répudiation. L'expérience française', in: Fallon, M. (ed.), *Nouveaux itinéraires en droit. Hommage à François Rigaux*, Bruxelles: Bruylant, 1993, p. 263-282.

Lehmann 2008a
Lehmann, M., 'Liberating the Individual from Battles between States: Justifying Party Autonomy in Conflict of Laws', *Vanderbilt J. Transnatl. L.*, 2008, p. 381-434.

Lehmann 2008b
Lehmann, M., 'What's in a Name? Grunkin-Paul and Beyond', *Yearb. Private Intl. L.*, 2008, p. 135-164.

Lipp 2012
Lipp, V., 'Parteiautonomie im internationalen Unterhaltsrecht', in: Verbeke, A.-L. (ed.), *Confronting the Frontiers of Family and Succession Law: Liber Amicorum Walter Pintens*, Antwerp: Intersentia, 2012, Vol. 1, p. 847-866.

Loquin 2008
Loquin, E., 'La règle de conflit générale en matière de délit dans le règlement du 11 juillet 2007 (Rome II)', in: Corneloup, S. & Joubert, N. (eds.), *Le Règlement communautaire 'Rome II' sur la loi applicable aux obligations non contractuelles*, Paris: Litec, 2008, p. 35-53.

Martiny 2012
Martiny, D., 'Private International Law Aspects of Same-sex Couples under German Law', in: Boele-Woelki, K. & Fuchs, A. (eds.), *Legal Recognition of Same-Sex Relationships in Europe. National, Cross-border and European Perspectives*, Antwerp: Intersentia, 2012, p. 189-223.

Matulionyte 2013
Matulionyte, R., 'Calling for Party Autonomy in Intellectual Property Infringement Cases', *J. Priv. Intl. L.*, 2013, p. 77-99.

Meeusen 2007
Meeusen, J., 'Instrumentalisation of Private International Law in the European Union: Towards a European Conflicts Revolution?', *Eur. J. Migration L.*, 2007, p. 287-305.

Meeusen 2012
Meeusen, J., 'Le droit international privé et le principe de non-discrimination', *Collected Courses of the Hague Academy of International Law*, 2012, Vol. 353, p. 9-184.

Meziou 2009
Meziou, K., 'Migrations et Relations Familiales', *Collected Courses of the Hague Academy of International Law*, 2009, Vol. 345, p. 304-312.

Michaels 2005
Michaels, R., 'The Re-Statement of Non-State Law: The State, Choice of Law and the Challenge from Global Legal Pluralism', *Wayne L. Rev.*, 2005, Vol. 51, p. 1209-1259.

Muir Watt 2010a
Muir Watt, H., '"Party Autonomy" in International Contracts: From the Makings of a Myth to the Requirements of Global Governance', *European Review of Contract Law*, 2010, p. 1-34.

Muir Watt 2010b
Muir Watt, H., 'The Role of the Conflict of Laws in European Private Law', in: Twigg-Flesner, Ch. (ed.), *The Cambridge Companion to European Private Law*, Cambridge: Cambridge University Press, 2010, p. 44-57.

Nagy 2012
Nagy, C.I., 'What Functions May Party Autonomy Have in International Family and Succession Law? An EU Perspective', *NIPR*, 2012, p. 576-586.

Niboyet 1927
Niboyet, J.-P., 'La théorie de l'autonomie de la volonté', *Collected courses Hague Academy*, 1927, I, Vol. 16, p. 1-116.

Niboyet 1948
Niboyet, J.-P., *Traité de droit international privé français*, Paris: Sirey, 1948, Vol. 5.

Peari 2012
Peari, S., 'Choice-of-Law in Family Law: Kant, Savigny and the Parties' Autonomy Principle', *NIPR*, 2012, p. 597-604.

Plender & Wilderspin 2009
Plender, R. & Wilderspin, M., *The European Private International Law of Obligations*, London: Sweet & Maxwell, 2009.

Ringe 2013
Ringe, W.-G., 'Corporate Mobility in the European Union - A Flash in the Pan? An Empirical Study on the Success of Lawmaking and Regulatory Competition', *Eur. Comp. & Fin. L. Rev.*, 2013, p. 230-367.

Roth 2004
Roth, W.-H., ‚Zur Wählbarkeit nichtstaatlichen Rechts', in: Mansel, H.-P., Hausmann, R., Kohler, C., Kronke, H. & Pfeiffer, T. (eds.), *Festschrift für Erik Jayme*, München: Sellier, 2004, p. 757-772.

Röthel 2013
Röthel, A., ‚Rom III-VO: Impulse für eine Materialisierung der Parteiautonomie', in: Röthel, A. (ed.), *Europäische Einflüsse auf den deutsch-italienischen Rechtsverkehr*, Heidelberg: Müller, 2013, p. 3-15.

Rühl 2007
Rühl, G., 'Party Autonomy in the Private International Law of Contracts. Transatlantic Convergence and Economic Efficiency', in: Gottschalk, E., Michaels, R., Rühl, G. & von Hein, J. (eds.), *Conflict of Laws in a Globalized World*, New York: Cambridge University Press, 2007, p. 153-183.

Schäfer & Lantermann 2006
Schäfer, H.-B. & Lantermann, K., 'Choice of Law from an Economic Perspective', in: Basedow, J. *et al.* (eds.), *An Economic Analysis of Private International Law*, Tübingen: Mohr, 2006, p. 87-119.

Schols & Hoens 2014
Schols, F.W.J.M. & Hoens, F., 'CNR-Huwelijksvoorwaardenonderzoek - deel II: verrekenbedingen en bijzondere facetten', *WPNR*, 2014, Vol. 7002, p. 33-44.

Smits 2010
Smits, J., 'Beyond Euroscepticism: On the Choice of Legal Regimes as Empowerment of Citizens', *Utrecht Law Review*, 2010, Vol. 6(3), p. 68-74.

Sotiropoulou 2013
Sotiropoulou, M.Ch., 'The Option Given to Spouses to Choose the Applicable Law Defined in the Proposal for a Council Regulation on Jurisdiction, Applicable Law and the Recognition and Enforcement of Decisions in Matters of Matrimonial Property Regimes: Progress or not?', *Revue hellénique de droit international*, 2013, Vol. 66, p. 21-38.

Spickhoff 2013
Spickhoff, A. (ed.), *Symposium Parteiautonomie in Europäischen Internationalen Privatrecht*, Bonn: DeutschNotarVerlag, 2013.

Strikwerda 2010
Strikwerda, L., *De overeenkomst in het ipr*, Antwerpen: Maklu, 2010.

The Copenhagen Post 2012
'Marriage Migration Makes Denmark "Europe's Las Vegas" - Lenient Laws for Marrying Ni-national Couples Makes Denmark a Haven for Germans and their Foreign Fiancees', *The Copenhagen Post*, 12 October 2012 (http://cphpost.dk/news/-marriage-migration-makes-denmark-europes-las-vegas.3031.html).

Torga 2012
Torga, M., 'Party Autonomy of the Spouses under the Rome III Regulation in Estonia: Can Private International Law Change Substantive Law?', *NIPR*, 2012, p. 547-554.

Van der Weide 2006
Van der Weide, J.A., *Mobiliteit van goederen in het IPR. Tussen situsregel en partijautonomie*, Deventer: Kluwer, 2006.

Van Poppel 1968
Van Poppel, V., 'Wetsontduiking bij clandestiene huwelijken', *Tijdschrift voor Privaatrecht*, 1968, p. 427-457.

Verhellen 2012
Verhellen, J., *Het Belgisch IPR-Wetboek in familiezaken. Wetgevende doelstellingen getoetst aan de praktijk*, Brugge: Die Keure, 2012.

Verhellen 2013
Verhellen, J., 'Lost in Nationality: Private International Law and Cultural Diversity', in: Foblets, M.-Cl. & Yassari, N. (eds.), *Approches juridiques de la diversité culturelle*, Leiden: Martinus Nijhoff, 2013, p. 521-572.

Verschelden 2011
Verschelden, G., 'Empirisch familierechtelijk onderzoek in België: yes we can', *Tijdschrift voor Familierecht*, 2011, p. 234-236.

Verschelden 2012
Verschelden, G., 'Pleidooi voor meer empirie in de familierechtswetenschap', in: de Mot, J. (ed.), *Liber amicorum Boudewijn Bouckaert: vrank en vrij*, Brugge: Die Keure, 2012, p. 403-423.

Verwilghen 1999
Verwilghen, M., 'Conflits de nationalités: plurinationalité et apatridie', *Collected Courses of the Hague Academy of International Law*, 1999, Vol. 277, p. 9-484.

Viarengo 2012
Viarengo, I., 'The Role of Party Autonomy in Cross-Border Divorces', *NIPR*, 2012, p. 555-561.

Vogenauer 2013
Vogenauer, S., 'Regulatory Competition through Choice of Contract Law and Choice of Forum in Europe: Theory and Evidence', *Eur. Rev. Priv. L.*, 2013, Vol. 21, p. 13-78.

Vogenauer & Weatherill 2005
Vogenauer, S. & Weatherill, S., 'The European Community's Competence for a Comprehensive Harmonisation of Contract Law: an Empirical Analysis', *Eur. Rev. Priv. L.*, 2005, Vol. 30, p. 821-837.

Wautelet 2014
Wautelet, P., 'Autonomie de la volonté et concurrence régulatoire - le cas des relations familiales internationales', in: Fulchiron, H. & Bidau-Garon, Ch. (eds.), *Vers un statut européen de la famille?*, Paris: Dalloz, 2014, p. 131-145.

Westrik & Van der Weide 2011
Westrik, R. & Van der Weide, J., *Party Autonomy in International Property Law*, München: Sellier, 2011.

W.-G. Ringe

CORPORATE MOBILITY IN THE EUROPEAN UNION – A FLASH IN THE PAN? AN EMPIRICAL STUDY ON THE SUCCESS OF LAWMAKING AND REGULATORY COMPETITION*

1. Introduction

Corporate mobility has reached a certain level of maturity in Europe. The EU legal framework is established and well understood, and it rests largely on case-law from the European Court of Justice. Beginning with the seminal *Centros* decision, the Court has effectively opened the borders between EU Member States little by little, and entrepreneurs now *de facto* have the right to select the foreign corporate law that governs the legal form of their company, at least at the company formation stage. Moreover, researchers have begun to empirically study how the case-law has impacted the market and how the market has reacted. While much effort has been spent evaluating the early market reactions, following the partial market opening made possible by *Centros*, relatively little attention has been devoted to subsequent developments. This is surprising because the various lawmakers' responses to the wave of entrepreneurial migration offer a rare glimpse at the effects of regulatory competition and subsequent business' reaction, as well as providing insights into the relevance and effects of lawmaking and regulatory responses to market pressure.

This paper explores the responses by European businesses to the (limited) occurrences of regulatory competition flowing out of *Centros* and subsequent case-law. It uses new empirical data on Germany, the most prominent example of a country that was under pressure from regulatory competition. The paper confirms

* I am grateful to John Armour, Sonja Bydlinski, Manfred Grünanger, Heribert Hirte, Peter Hubalek, Colin Mayer, Andrea Polo, Jonathan Rickford, Edmund Schuster, Beate Sjåfjell, Oren Sussman, Christoph Teichmann, Thomas Traar, as well as the participants at the Law & Finance Law Faculty seminar at the University of Oxford, a workshop at the Chamber of Commerce in Vienna, an empirical law studies workshop at the University of Oslo, and the 7th ECFR symposium in Luxembourg. This chapter has been published earlier (Ringe 2013), reprint with kind permission by the publisher.

earlier findings that entrepreneurs in continental Europe, at first, increasingly used English letterbox companies to govern their affairs, without doing any business in the UK. The present analysis goes further, however, and shows that incorporation numbers have dropped considerably since 2006, falling to remarkably low numbers today. I then go on to evaluate the role that regulatory reform may have played in this development. Many lawmakers in continental European jurisdictions claim 'success' in the sense that the legal reforms of domestic company laws have caused foreign (English) corporations to fall out of vogue with their respective entrepreneurs as these entrepreneurs have begun to increasingly use domestic company types. The data evaluated in this study seem to weaken this claim: first, I show that the number of foreign incorporations in Germany has dropped even before the law reform came into force. Secondly, I go on to compare the German data with the situation in Austria, a natural comparison to make as these two systems share many similarities - with the exception that Austria did not reform its legal system as a consequence of EU regulatory competition. Surprisingly, however, the drop in the number of foreign incorporations in Austria coincided with the development of the reform in Germany; in other words, the rate began to drop at about the same time as in Germany. This may lead to the conclusion that reasons other than legal reform must have played a role in shaping businesses' preferences. This paper is the first part of a larger research initiative to explore the merits of corporate mobility and regulatory competition in Europe.

The paper is organised as follows. Section 2 provides the legal and empirical background on developments that have led to the current (limited) scope of regulatory competition for incorporations within the EU. Section 3 evaluates these developments and offers an assessment of the academic work done so far. Sections 4 and 5 introduce new empirical data for Germany and Austria, shedding light on the implications of the German 2008 law reform and questioning traditional assumptions of its effects on foreign incorporations. Section 6 seeks to find explanations for the results and advances a number of possible conjectures. Section 7 concludes.

2. Legal and Empirical Background

Free mobility for companies across borders has been a long-standing dream for European businesses. One would imagine that the creation of the European Union - or its predecessors, the European Economic and the European Communities - with its concept of an 'Internal Market' and the instrument of 'freedom of establishment' for corporations would help this dream come true. Yet it took over forty years from the inception of the EEC for the European Court of Justice, in its famous *Centros* judgment, to allow for a certain - and limited - freedom in this field. The *Centros* saga has been discussed in sufficient detail elsewhere.[1] In summary, *Centros* effectively allows for choice of incorporation: entrepreneurs are free to form a

1 Ringe 2011, p. 107-125; Armour & Ringe 2011.

company registered in Member State A while doing business exclusively in Member State B (the latter usually being their entrepreneur's home state).[2] This means that for instance German entrepreneurs are no longer exclusively reliant on German company forms. They can form a company in any of the other EU (or EEA) Member States as a 'letterbox' company, which keeps nothing more than a registered office in that Member State, and does its business exclusively in Germany. To the extent that company laws diverge between Member States, there may accordingly be an incentive to choose any foreign company law for domestic purposes. The *Centros* case created a sudden awareness of the possibilities offered by the Internal Market, provoking a storm of academic literature[3] and corresponding business behaviour that quickly adapted to the situation.

The concept first articulated in *Centros* was later expanded and clarified. Subsequent case-law - cases like *Überseering*[4] (2002) and *Inspire Art*[5] (2003) - supported and reinforced the liberal interpretation of the European treaty framework, whereas cases like *Cadbury Schweppes*[6] (2006) and *Cartesio*[7] (2008) limited the scope of the concept. Nevertheless, it is safe to say that by the end of 2003, when the judgment in *Inspire Art* was handed down, market participants had a clear framework of permissible cross-border mobility at hand.[8]

2.1. *Legal Framework*

We can summarise the legal situation as follows:

As described, entrepreneurs can form a company in a Member State of their choice ('home Member State') and subsequently carry out business with this company in another jurisdiction ('host Member State'). The host Member State has to recognise the legal capacity and the legal characteristics of this company as such - this means that the rules of company law pertaining to internal organisation, legal status, liability of directors, etc., are all governed by the law of the home Member State. From a legal perspective, the company has to set up a branch in the host Member State, which has to be registered in the register of the host Member State in

2 Case C-212/97, *Centros Ltd v Erhvervs- og Selskabsstyrelsen*, ECR 1999, I-1459.

3 See for example Roth 2003; Rickford 2004; Armour 2005; Ringe 2005; Schön 2006; Siems 2007; Wymeersch 2000, p. 629; Munari & Terrile 2002, p. 529; Werlauff 1999; Roth 2000; Xanthaki 2001.

4 Case C-208/00, *Überseering BV v Nordic Construction Company Baumanagement GmbH*, ECR 2002, I-9919.

5 Case C-167/01, *Kamer van Koophandel en Fabrieken voor Amsterdam v Inspire Art Ltd*, ECR 2003, I-10155.

6 Case C-196/04, *Cadbury Schweppes plc, Cadbury Schweppes Overseas Ltd v Commissioners of Inland Revenue*, ECR 2006, I-7995.

7 Case C-210/06, *Cartesio Oktató és Szolgáltató bt*, ECR 2008, I-9614.

8 See, in much more detail, Paschalidis 2012.

accordance with the rules laid down in the eleventh Company Law Directive.[9] Although technically a branch, this may *de facto* be the 'head office' or even the sole place of operation for the entire company. In this case, the company keeps nothing more than a registered office in the home Member State ('letterbox company').

The case-law sets limits, however, for existing companies wishing to emigrate into another Member State.[10] For this reason, cross-border mobility so far has been confined only to the stage of company *formation*. There has not been any serious 'midstream' migration of existing companies. The possibility of a relocation of an existing business is still to some degree uncertain, due to lacunae in the Court's case law.[11] This aspect of mobility has, rather, been the realm of legislation. After the Commission officially dropped the plans for a proposed directive,[12] the European Parliament has repeatedly tried to revive the project,[13] and the Commission has now initiated a public consultation on the case for such a directive.[14] However, within the existing body of law, the Cross-Border Mergers Directive[15] and Article 8 of the European Company Statute (SE)[16] currently provide for the only means of moving an existing business across the border without being dissolved or having to register as a new company. The recent *Vale* case illustrates that the case-law developed by the ECJ may help in some situations.[17]

9 Eleventh Council Directive 89/666/EEC of 21 December 1989 concerning disclosure requirements in respect of branches opened in a Member State by certain types of company governed by the law of another State, *OJ* 1989, L395/36.

10 'Migration' can take two forms: companies may wish to move either their registered office or their head office ('real seat') across the border. Both ways have recently become easier, due to fresh case-law from Luxembourg (*Cartesio, supra* n. 7) and Case C-378/10, *Vale Építési kft,* not yet reported). Comment on the recent case-law includes Gerner-Beuerle & Schillig 2010; Szabó & Engsig Sørensen 2013.

11 Critically on this Ringe 2005.

12 Fourteenth Directive of the transfer of the seat from one Member State to another (proposal from 1997: Doc No XV/D2/6002/97-EN REV.2). Commissioner McCreevy announced in October 2007 that he would not proceed with the Directive (Speech at the European Parliament's Legal Affairs Committee, 3 October 2007, Speech/07/592), largely due to the availability of cross-border mergers under Directive 2005/56/EC (n 15).

13 See European Parliament, Committee on Legal Affairs, 'Draft Report with recommendations to the Commission on cross-border transfers of company seats' 2008/2196 (INI) of 17 October 2008. More recently, European Parliament resolution of 2 February 2012 with recommendations to the Commission on a 14th company law directive on the cross-border transfer of company seats (2011/2046(INI)), and report of 9 January 2012.

14 Consultation on the cross-border transfers of registered offices of companies (January-April 2013), see <http://ec.europa.eu/internal_market/consultations/2013/seat-transfer/-index_en.htm>. *Cf.* Communication from the Commission to the European Parliament, the Council, the European Economic and Social Committee and the Committee of the Regions – Action Plan: European company law and corporate governance – a modern legal framework for more engaged shareholders and sustainable companies (December 2012), at 4.1.

15 Directive 2005/56/EC of the European Parliament and of the Council of 26 October 2005 on cross-border mergers of limited liability companies, *OJ* 2005, L310/1.

16 Council Regulation (EC) No 2157/2001 of 8 October 2001 on the Statute for a European Company (SE), *OJ* 2001, L294/1.

17 Case C-378/10, *Vale Építési kft,* not yet reported.

Even at formation stage, where *Centros* and other cases have facilitated foreign incorporations, things did not develop as smoothly in the beginning, as there was much legal uncertainty as to the exact borderlines between permissible and abusive behaviour. This was largely due to the question as to whether the so-called 'real seat' theory was in any way impinged upon by this judgment. The real seat theory is a conflict-of-laws rule, determining the law applicable to companies (the *lex societatis*) according to the company's head office or 'real seat', which was subscribed to by a number of EU Member States.[18] Without going into the detail here,[19] this theory was applied in a way detrimental to corporate mobility which made it *de facto* impossible for foreign companies to register in a Member State, but do business exclusively in another Member State which followed the real seat theory.

The *Centros* case law has had a significant impact on company activity in Europe. With every free movement judgment handed down from Luxembourg, enterprises became increasingly assured that the freedom of establishment indeed allowed them to register in Member State A, while conducting their business exclusively in Member State B. In this manner, the Court of Justice has created a market for corporate forms within the European Union, granting entrepreneurs *de facto* a choice between the legal forms of Member States.

2.2. *Empirical Evaluations*

It is generally accepted that in this battle, English company law has proved to be the most competitive company law jurisdiction in the EU.[20] The English private company limited by shares can be set up in a comparatively fast and easy way and does not require any minimum capital or the involvement of a public notary. Because of these advantages, many companies have been set up in the years following *Centros, Überseering* and *Inspire Art* by entrepreneurs from outside the UK who conduct business exclusively in their home Member States. Special agencies sprang up like mushrooms in continental Europe, helping entrepreneurs to set up an English company seeking to further promote this legal form and to profit from its popularity.[21] These marketing agencies hailed the advantages of English company law and convinced inexperienced businessmen on the continent of the degree of ease with which an English company can be established. One of these agencies claimed to have set up over 40,000 English companies alone in Germany.[22]

18 Drury 1999, p. 356; Lowry 2004, p. 332.

19 See on this Ringe 2005, p. 626.

20 Cheffins 1997, p. 441.

21 Some examples are: <www.insolution-ltd.co.uk>, <www.easyentrepreneur.com>, <www.go-limited.de>, <www.Limited4you.de>, <www.limited24.de>, <www.france-offshore.fr> and <www.adcomp.de>.

22 See Go Ahead press release of 24 April 2012, <www.go-ahead.de/Presse/19>.

Against the total number of about 1 million private companies registered in Germany, this seems like a sizable number.[23]

This estimate may well be tainted by a certain degree of self-interest. However, academics and government officials have worked based on empirical data, providing a more accurate approximation of the number of these 'foreign' limited companies.[24] The German government, responding to an official question in Parliament, estimated the number of English companies set up in Germany between January and August 2005 to be around 3,200.[25] A more detailed survey was compiled by several German academics whose estimates, however, diverged significantly. One short study calculated by way of extrapolation that the total number of English limited companies in Germany amounted to 30,300 in December 2005 and to 46,000 in November 2006.[26] Another – more detailed – study by Wilhelm Niemeier offers various calculation methods and suggests a number of between 7,100 and 7,600 at the end of 2005, based on data collected from German registration sources.[27] However, Niemeier points out that, presumably, the real number is significantly higher, since not all foreign companies in Germany fulfil their duties to register a branch in Germany and to apply for a trade concession.[28] Furthermore, he stresses the fact that those studies analysing data from the Companies House (the British company register) come to a different outcome. A similar approach is put forward in a study by Horst Eidenmüller.[29]

Not only the German, but also the English-speaking academic literature has tried to quantify this German interest in a foreign legal form. In a first, impressionistic overview, John Armour arrived at a figure of over 500 'German' English companies at the end of 2004.[30] One of the major studies that followed the methodology of collecting data from the English Companies House and then filtering out those companies apparently conducting business exclusively in other countries is the study conducted by Becht, Mayer and Wagner, which had been discussed as a working paper since 2006 and was published in 2008.[31] This detailed study counts a total of 41,499 'German' English companies set up between 1997 and 2006.[32] Of course, the study does not take into account the number of firms that

23 On 1 January 2012, there were 1,071,908 GmbHs registered in Germany, see Kornblum 2012, p. 729.

24 See Deakin 2006, p. 450; Hirte 2006, § 1 para. 35.

25 Reply by the Federal Government to the question by the deputies Otto Fricke, Dr Max Stadler, Jens Ackermann, further deputies and the FDP parliamentary party (Drucksache 16/134) of 16 December 2005, Bundetags-Drucksache 16/283.

26 Westhoff 2007; building on Westhoff 2006.

27 Niemeier 2006.

28 Niemeier 2006, p. 2242.

29 Eidenmüller 2007, p. 170.

30 Armour 2005, p. 386. This data was identified by searching Companies House for companies with largely German-language names, but ending with the word 'Limited'.

31 Becht, Mayer & Wagner 2008.

32 Becht, Mayer & Wagner 2008, p. 248, table 3, panel B.

were wound up during the same period.[33] Arguably, this number is relatively high, since 'foreign' English companies suffer from an increased risk of being shut down during the period of their early existence.[34]

Graph 1. Newly Set Up English Private Limited Companies Doing Business Exclusively in Germany[35]

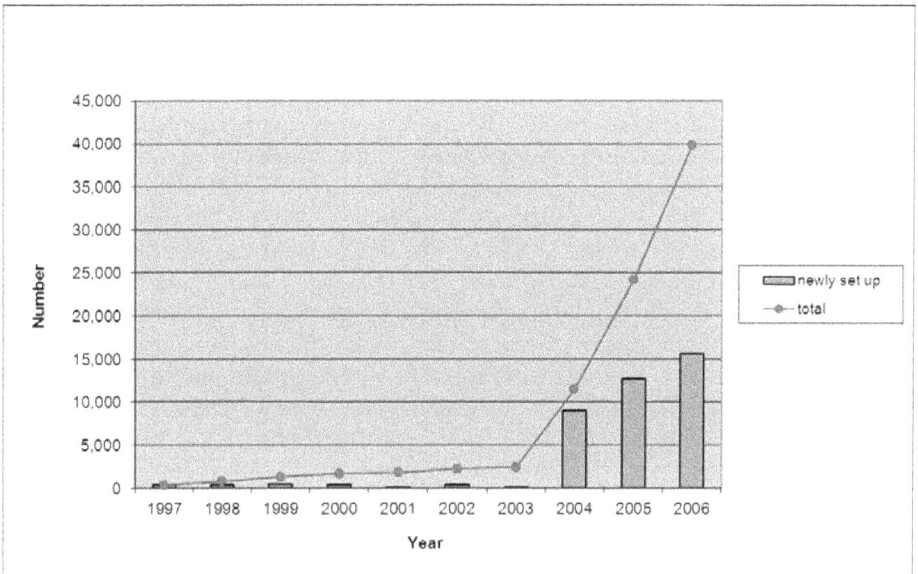

Source: adapted from Becht et al. (n 31 above).

The study by Becht et al goes beyond merely calculating the number of 'foreign companies' incorporating in England. It also analyses the *reasons* for the high number of these foreign companies. The study shows that amongst the main reasons are the substantial differences regarding minimum capital requirements, set-up costs and set-up speed.[36] Facilitated by the famous *Doing Business* reports from the World Bank, the differences between countries have become comparable and transparent.[37] Other aspects might include the rules of company organisation, including the co-determination rights of employees.[38] A partly different author team complemented this perspective by studying the costs of branching in the respective

33 See Niemeier 2006, p. 2244.
34 Niemeier 2006, p. 2241.
35 The 'total' number is only the sum of the previous numbers and does not take into account the number of companies that were wound up over the period.
36 Becht, Mayer & Wagner 2008, p. 250.
37 See <http://www.doingbusiness.org/>.
38 Cheffins 1997, p. 442.

destination country: that is, the factual and administrative costs of setting up a branch of the English company in the various destination jurisdictions.[39]

2.3. *National Lawmakers' Responses*

The national lawmakers responded to the challenge posed by English company law that was triggered by the *Centros / Inspire Art* case law.

In France and Spain, new, deregulated forms of limited liability companies were introduced soon after *Inspire Art*. Since 2003, it has been possible in France to found the *Société à Responsabilité Limitée* (SARL) within twenty-four hours and with a nominal minimum capital of EUR 1 (previously, the minimum capital for the SARL had been EUR 7,500).[40] The formalities of incorporation were reduced to a minimum—even applications for registration via the internet became possible. Founders can also seek the assistance of a *Centre de Formalités des Entreprises*. The French reform legislation included further facilitative measures in other areas: the newly-founded companies enjoy certain tax and social contribution reductions within the first years of their existence and may use the private address of the founder as the corporate seat even where this would otherwise be contrary to rental contracts or general city planning legislation. In sum, the main purpose of this new legislation is to encourage small start-up enterprises that have their real seat and their main field of activity in France, to choose the French legal form.[41] Largely similar legislation has existed in Spain since April 2003[42] with the adoption of the *Sociedad Limitada Nueva Empresa* (SLNE) as a special form of the traditional *Sociedad de Responsabilidad Limitada* (SL or SRL).[43] In contrast to French law, the SLNE must have a minimum nominal capital of EUR 3,012.[44] Like the new French SARL, the *nueva empresa* is designed to encourage and support small and medium sized start-up enterprises located in Spain.[45] One special feature is a quick set-up procedure: according to Article 134 of the amended version of the *Ley de Sociedades de Responsabilidad Limitada*, the SLNE can be founded within forty-eight hours.[46] Arguably, these two 'early' reforms have already significantly reduced the business exits in these two countries, as compared to other EU countries.[47] In the meantime, France has already adopted a second reform. After the 2003 reform concerning the

39 Becht, Enriques & Korom 2009.

40 Drury 2005, p. 729. From the French literature, see Massart 2002; de Vendeuil 2003.

41 The new form of SARL has not been introduced with a view to attract incorporations from abroad.

42 Ley 7/2003 of 1 April 2003, de la Sociedad Limitada Nueva Empresa por la que se modifica la Ley 2/1995, de 23 de marzo, de Sociedades de Responsabilidad Limitada, BOE núm 79, de 2 de abril, Sec 1, 12679.

43 Irujo 2004.

44 The new legislation also fixes a maximum nominal capital of EUR 120,200.

45 Irujo 2004, p. 761.

46 Irujo 2004, p. 763.

47 Becht, Enriques & Korom 2009, p. 252.

SARL, the *Société par Actions Simplifiée* (SAS) was reformed in 2008.[48] The SAS is a legal form between the SARL and the *Société Anonyme* (SA), the latter being the French public limited company. Amongst the various amendments to the SAS, the most remarkable element of the reform was without doubt the waiving of the previous minimum capital requirement of EUR 37,000.[49] One of the explicit goals was again the desire to make the French company legal form more attractive and competitive.[50]

Other countries have followed suit. In the Netherlands, a fundamental review of the private limited (BV) law has been conducted over the last years. The legislation was debated for several years and came into force on 1 October 2012.[51] The reform provided for more freedom for entrepreneurs in that businesses will have more options in their articles of association to depart from the default provisions of law on matters such as voting rights, board member appointment and shareholder resolutions. Most importantly, in most cases the earlier minimum capital of EUR 18,000 for BVs is no longer required. Furthermore, the set-up speed for businesses, which was in urgent need of reform, as this was an important ground for Dutch entrepreneurs to seek incorporation abroad, is set to be improved.[52]

Similarly, Germany has adopted a major company law reform.[53] At first, it was uncertain whether the country would take the Spanish route of adopting a new legal form alongside the existing ones,[54] or rather follow the French/Dutch example of reforming the existing legal forms. Finally, a compromise was found: the existing *Gesellschaft mit beschränkter Haftung* (GmbH, private limited liability company) was reformed and at the same time, a variant of the GmbH was introduced. Whereas the existing GmbH still requires the minimum capital of EUR 25,000, the new younger

48 Loi no 2008-776 du 4 août 2008 de modernisation de l'économie, Journal officiel de la République française 2008, No 0181, 12471. See: <www.modernisationeconomie.fr/>.

49 On this, Mortier 2008; Barbièri 2008; Massart 2008.

50 Mortier 2008, p. 2233.

51 Wet vereenvoudiging en flexibilisering Nederlands bv-recht ('Wet Flex BV').

52 Drury 2005, p. 730, 740, pointing to the facts of Case 79/85 *DHM Segers v Bestuur van de Bedrijfsvereniging voor Bank- en Verzekeringswezen, Groothandel en Vrije Beroepen* [1986] ECR 2375.

53 Gesetz zur Modernisierung des GmbH-Rechts und zur Bekämpfung von Missbräuchen (MoMiG) of 23 October 2008, Bundesgesetzblatt 2008, I 2026. From the (already) vast literature, see Goette 2008; Hirte 2008; Teichmann 2010.

54 Various suggestions were made to this end: the Bavarian idea of a *Kaufmann* (single trader) with limited liability (<www.justiz.bayern.de/imperia/md/content/stmj_internet/-ministerium/ministerium/gesetzgebung/gesetzentwurf_kaufmann_mbh_16_05_2007.pdf>) or the North Rhine-Westphalian suggestion of a 'Basis-GmbH' (BGmbH) (<www.justiz.nrw.de/JM/justizpolitik/gesetzgebung/gesetzgebungsvorhaben/gmbh_recht/inhalt_gesetzentwurf/gesetzentwurf.pdf>). The Green Party developed the concept of a 'Personengesellschaft mit beschränkter Haftung (PmbH)' (partnership with limited liability), see Berninger & Schnittker 2006. Finally, an academic came up with the 'Leipzig draft' of a Kommanditgesellschaft with limited liability (KmbH), see Drygala 2006.

brother of the GmbH, the *Unternehmergesellschaft* ('UG'—start-up company),[55] is integrated into the existing GmbH statute and can be set up without minimum capital.[56] However, the new code imposes some restrictions: the UG is not allowed to fully distribute its profits until its level of capital has reached the threshold of the regular GmbH (EUR 25,000).[57] One principal concern of the German reform is to facilitate and accelerate the establishment of a business. Thus, for instance, model articles of association are made available for standard set-ups, without having to consult a public notary. Furthermore, the set-up process is accelerated. Table 1 shows the timeline of developments for the German reform; this specific information will be of importance at a later stage.

Table 1. Steps of the German MoMiG law reform[58]

Step	Date
First[59] rumours about reform activity by German government[60]	31 August 2004
First (unpublished) government draft, proposing to abolish minimum capital for private limited liability companies[61]	30 November 2004
Rumour that government could increase rather than reduce minimum capital[62]	March 2005
First government drafts, proposing to reduce minimum capital to EUR 10,000[63]	April-June 2005
Drafts were not adopted - early General Election changes government	18 September 2005
First new proposal to reform the GmbH, proposing a minimum capital of EUR 10,000[64]	29 May 2006

55 The full name of the legal form is 'Unternehmergesellschaft (haftungsbeschränkt)'.
56 Section 5(1) of the new GmbH-Gesetz (GmbHG, act on the private limited liability company).
57 Section 5a of the new GmbH-Gesetz.
58 See on this also Fleischer 2010, paras. 116-117.
59 There had been prior discussions to reform abusive practices, but they did not intend to reform minimum capital requirements. See Hirte 2003.
60 (Then) Minister of Justice Brigitte Zypries speech at IHK Gießen-Friedberg, 'Rechtspolitik für Unternehmen und Anleger - Voraussetzung für Innovation und Wachstum', Sommerempfang der IHK Gießen-Friedberg am 31. August 2004 in Karben.
61 Draft is unpublished. See Jahn 2005; Priester 2005, p. 1318.
62 Faigle 2005.
63 Referentenentwurf eines Gesetzes zur Neuregelung des Mindestkapitals der GmbH (MindestkapG), Stand 15. April 2005; Gesetzentwurf der Bundesregierung eines Gesetzes zur Neuregelung des Mindestkapitals der GmbH (MindestkapG) of 1 June 2005.

Step	Date
Amended government proposal, introducing the *Unternehmergesellschaft*, a GmbH variant without minimum capital[65]	25 July 2007
MoMiG law adopted and in force	23 October and 1 November 2008

But it is not only continental Europe that is responding to international developments, as the UK itself also attempts to further modernise its company law. One of the explicit ambitions of the new Companies Act 2006 was to make the UK even more competitive in an ever more globalised and interlinked environment.[66] To be sure, it has not been the objective of the UK lawmakers to actively 'export' their company law to the rest of Europe. Rather, the goal of the 2006 reform was to 'maintains the UK's position as one of the most attractive places in the world to set up and run a business'[67] and 'to promote growth, competitiveness and jobs'.[68] Moreover, the company law reform in the UK started well before the ECJ handed down its judgment in *Centros*. Nevertheless, the UK seems eager to take up the global challenge and to safeguard its leading position in Europe.[69]

Not all countries have embraced this general tendency, however. One of the counter-examples is Austria, where no comparable reform has been implemented and the minimum capital requirement remains unchanged at EUR 35,000. There were discussions over the past years to follow the general trend,[70] but no reform step has yet been taken. One of the main reasons for the government's reluctance in recent years seems to have been the potential loss of tax revenue, since the

64 Referentenentwurf eines Gesetzes zur Modernisierung des GmbH-Rechts und zur Bekämpfung von Missbräuchen (MoMiG) of 29 May 2006.

65 Gesetzentwurf der Bundesregierung Entwurf eines Gesetzes zur Modernisierung des GmbH-Rechts und zur Bekämpfung von Missbräuchen (MoMiG) of 25 July 2007, Bundestags-Drucksache 16/6140.

66 Department of Trade and Industry, *Company Law Reform – White Paper* (London, The Stationery Office 2005, Cm 6456) 9.

67 *Ibid.*, 8. See on this already Company Law Review Steering Group, *Modern Company Law for a Competitive Economy*, 1998, at 5.1; Company Law Review Steering Group, *Modern Company Law for a Competitive Economy - The Strategic Framework*, 1999, Ch. 2.

68 Department of Trade and Industry, *Company Law Reform – White Paper* (London, The Stationery Office 2005, Cm 6456) 9.

69 This, too, can be a form of (defensive) regulatory competition. The *White Paper* (*supra* n. 66) notes that 'Increasingly, businesses can make choices as to where to incorporate, and recent legal judgments are tending to make such cross-border incorporations easier.' See also already Company Law Review Steering Group, *Modern Company Law for a Competitive Economy - The Strategic Framework*, 1999, 5.6.12.

70 On the reform discussion, see Bachner 2008; Dommes *et al.* 2005.

minimum corporation tax depends on the company's share capital.[71] More recently, the government has reinvigorated its attempts to reform Austrian company law, with a plan to reduce minimum capital to EUR 10,000.[72]

2.4. *Responsive Lawmaking and Defensive Competition*

In sum, the Court's case law has created a level playing field for entrepreneurs in the European corporate market. The ECJ case-law has facilitated the usage of foreign legal forms. EU Member States are responding to the success of UK company law by so-called 'responsive lawmaking'. Now that EU Member States have to recognise each other's companies, some Member States are enacting corporate law preferred by their shareholders (especially entrepreneurs), managers or both, and are thus luring companies away from other Member States which have a less attractive company law system. Nevertheless, it is unclear to what extent Member States have incentives to engage in regulatory competition. Some authors suggest that the European development after *Centros* and *Inspire Art* may in some ways resemble the US developments in connection with the 'Delaware effect'[73] in corporate law in the nineteenth century.[74] Others stress the difference between the EU and the US situations.[75] In contrast to the US, Member States in the EU cannot raise franchise taxes from in-state incorporations.[76] Hence, any incentives they might have will be of a more indirect nature - such as benefits for domestic legal services industries. The reform attempts described above are indications that Member States try to prevent a loss in market share for their domestic legal products, i.e. they do engage in 'defensive regulatory competition'. But it is questionable whether Member States also have incentives to offensively reform and market their own legal products, i.e. engage in 'offensive regulatory competition'.[77]

71 See Kürzel 2012, <http://fiduzia.blogspot.co.uk/2012/08/gmbh-reform-in-osterreich-warten-auf.html>.

72 See Ergebnisse der Regierungsklausur in Laxenburg, 9 November 2012, p 4, <https://www.bka.gv.at/DocView.axd?cobId=49364>.

73 At the end of the nineteenth century, the states of New Jersey and Delaware, concerned about entrepreneurs' decisions as to the place of their companies' incorporation, adopted modernised statutes on incorporation. Eventually, Delaware's statute made it the leading state for incorporations in the United States from the 1920s onwards, presently serving as the state of incorporation for nearly half of the corporations listed on the New York Stock Exchange and as the major destination for reincorporations. See Romano 1993, p. 6.

74 See for example, Kirchner, Painter & Kaal 2005; Martin & Alogna 2007.

75 Kieninger 2004, p. 769; Bratton, McCahery & Vermeulen 2009.

76 Council Directive 2008/7/EC of 12 February 2008 concerning indirect taxes on the raising of capital, *OJ* 2008, L46/11.

77 Klöhn 2012. However, there is one element in the German law reform, which could be categorised as 'offensive regulatory competition', namely the change in the law that now allows the German GmbH to have its head office abroad. See new § 4a GmbHG which gave up the requirement to have the head office or a place of business in Germany.

Table 2. Company Law Reforms in Several EU Countries 2003–2008

Feature / Country	**Legal Form**	**Pre-reform**	**Post-reform**	**Alteration in %**
Minimum Capital (in EUR)				
Denmark	Anpartselskab (ApS)	16,800	16,800	0
France	Société à Responsabilité Limitée (SARL)	7,500	1	- 99
Germany	Gesellschaft mit beschränkter Haftung (GmbH)	25,000	25,000 / 1	0 / - 99
Netherlands	Besloten Vennootschap (BV)	18,000	1	- 99
Spain	Sociedad de Responsabilidad Limitada (SRL)	3,010	3,012	+ 0.07
Set-up Costs (in EUR)				
Denmark	ApS	6,715	0	- 100
France	SARL	450	310	- 13
Germany	GmbH	1,500	n.a.	
Netherlands	BV	1,750	n.a.	
Spain	SRL	600	450	- 25
Set-up speed (in days)				
Denmark	ApS	23	6	- 74
France	SARL	10	7	- 30
Germany	GmbH	16-18	n.a.	
Netherlands	BV	10	n.a.	
Spain	SRL	47	2	- 96

Source: adapted from Bratton et al (n. 75 above); Becht et al (n. 31 above); <www.doingbusiness.org; www.gruenderstadt.de/Infopark/spanische_slne.html>

3. Assessment

Thus far this paper has revealed that there is ample evidence that: (i) liberal ECJ case-law has granted companies the opportunity to register in a Member State of their choice while conducting their entire business in another; and (ii) EU Member

States are indeed responding to this phenomenon by amending their corporate laws to remain attractive in the face of competition from other jurisdictions.

In considering the merits of these two developments, there are a number of questions. What is the *impact* of the various law reforms on the continent? Has this legislation been *successful* in convincing entrepreneurs to choose domestic rather than English law? Scholars have begun to explore the merits of law reform for entrepreneurship generally,[78] but the present study is more interested in the particular effect of the German law reform: we study a new sample of incorporations motivated by the *Centros* case-law. We can thereby test the claim that law reform as part of defensive regulatory competition is 'successful' in reducing arbitrage. If, as Becht *et al.* have shown, corporate mobility is driven by costs of regulation and companies have moved to the UK because of a more attractive legal environment, we would expect this effect to be reduced if not eliminated by ensuing law reform on the continent. And as some commentators indeed claim, the German law reform has been 'successful' in fending off the invasion of foreign company law forms.[79]

To test this claim, we study a sample of companies formed between 2004-11 in a 'Centros style' structure between the UK and Germany. That is, these companies are set up in the UK by German entrepreneurs, but operate in Germany. If the hypothesis is right, the entering into force of the German law reform in November 2008 should reduce the number of incorporations in the UK.

In a second step, we test the claim further by comparing the results to another jurisdiction, Austria. The reason is straightforward: since there has been no comparable law reform in Austria, but instead minimum capital has remained unchanged at EUR 35,000, we would expect foreign companies in Austria unchanged.

We advance the following hypotheses: (1) The *de facto* abolition of minimum capital in Germany following the entering into force of the MoMiG reform law in November 2008 should lead to a significant reduction in the formation numbers of English limited companies in Germany; (2) as no comparable reform has been done in Austria, we hypothesise that no comparable reduction takes place there.

4. German Data and Results

In order to test these hypotheses, we extract data from the English Companies House via the commercial FAME Database. This database contains data on all UK incorporated companies. We limit the time period to the years 2004-2011. This is for the following reason: the *Centros* trilogy of cases was completed by the end of

78 Braun *et al.* 2013.

79 Dierksmeier 2011, p. 210; Österreichische Notariatskammer (Austrian Notary Chamber), 'Österreichs Notare unterstützen raschere und kostengünstigere Unternehmensgründungen', press release of 22 March 2013, available at: <www.ots.at/presseaussendung/-OTS_20130322_OTS0139>.

2003.[80] As explained above, European businesses and entrepreneurs have a reliable legal framework for incorporation a *Centros*-type company only from this moment on. Since we are not interested in the early years, where the arbitrage opportunities first arose, we concentrate on the years following 2004 where the impact of the case-law has been most strongly felt. Moreover, the extension of the dataset through to 2011 gives us the opportunity to study the effects of the law reform in Germany, which entered into force in November 2008. In extending the period of study through to 2011, we also have a much broader view than most other studies carried out before, which end earlier.[81]

The crucial question in all previous studies has been how to filter out those companies that fulfil the '*Centros* criteria', i.e. are set up in the United Kingdom but have their head office in Germany. No official register or search criterion exists to identify this specific target group. Studies in the past years have all chosen different strategies and proxies to reach their desired outcome. We apply the following filters to the database: (1) the company is incorporated in the United Kingdom; (2) at least one director is German; and (3) the company shares its registered office with at least 100 other companies. While criteria (1) and (2) may seem self-explanatory, criterion (3) needs further elaboration. As emphasised above, it is well-known that most the 'foreign incorporations' that are of interest here are facilitated and managed by so-called incorporation agencies.[82] These agencies help entrepreneurs by offering them the complete package of administering the incorporation process for a flat fee. This service is in high demand as (usually legal illiterate) entrepreneurs do not just face problems with the legal framework of their home country, but that of another country as well. Incorporation agencies help by setting up the company and registering it, and some even stay on board by accompanying it over the years with respect to filing returns, taking care of accounting and other administrative work.[83] These agencies follow one pattern: they usually register all companies at the same address - with the effect that all companies which have been set up by them have an identical registered office, although their operations are located at entirely different places.[84] We use this piece of information as a proxy to filter out those companies that are set up by foreign entrepreneurs. Admittedly, this proxy is not perfect - but no other filter criterion seems to produce better results.[85]

All of these steps applied, we receive a sample of 48,103 'German' incorporations between 2004 and 2011 in the UK. Tables 4a and 4b list some summary statistics. In short, virtually all of these companies were private companies limited by shares (99.83%). Another interesting finding is that by

80 The *Inspire Art* decision was handed down on 30 September 2003.

81 For example, the Becht et al study covers the period from 1997 to 2006 only.

82 See above text to notes 21-22.

83 In many instances, the incorporation agencies even formally act as the company's 'secretary' under English law.

84 See above text to notes 21-22.

85 In fact, other studies run the risk of being over-inclusive. Our approach certainly might be under-inclusive, see on this below text on note 88.

February 2012, roughly 72% of these companies were dissolved or in default, and only 18% of them were active and running, suggesting a high rate of entrepreneurs who later discontinued their business activity – be it because of business failure, or simply because the company was struck off the register but the business continued elsewhere.[86]

Table 3a. UK incorporations operating exclusively in Germany 2004-11 by company type

	Total	Ltd	Plc	Company ltd by guarantee	Unlimited	LLP	Other
#	48,103	48,022	18	12	1	4	44
%	100	99.83	0.04	0.02	0.00	0.01	0.09

Table 3b. UK incorporations operating exclusively in Germany 2004-11 by company status

	Total	active	dormant	in default	dormant + default	in liquidation	dissolved
#	48,103	8,474	3,472	919	391	40	34,807
%	100	17.62	7.22	1.91	0.81	0.08	72.36

Further, we sort the sample according to date of incorporation and develop a graph. Analysis of the dates of incorporation reveals an important finding: the data confirm that the first years post *Centros/Inspire Art* saw a strong increase in incorporations, and that this trend has been reversed since 2006, the peak being in March 2006. Since then, numbers have been falling continuously – in March 2006, we count 1322 incorporations, and they have fallen to just 49 incorporations in December 2011. Graph 2 illustrates the trend by splitting up the number of incorporations over time to monthly rates.[87] As long as the two studies overlap, we compare our figures to the data from the Becht et al study. As one might expect, the

86 See on this below section 6.3.
87 This confirms the recent findings by Niemeier 2013, p. 307.

present figures are lower, but similar; further, the ratio between the two studies remains almost stable - which increases the confidence in our results.[88]

Graph 2.

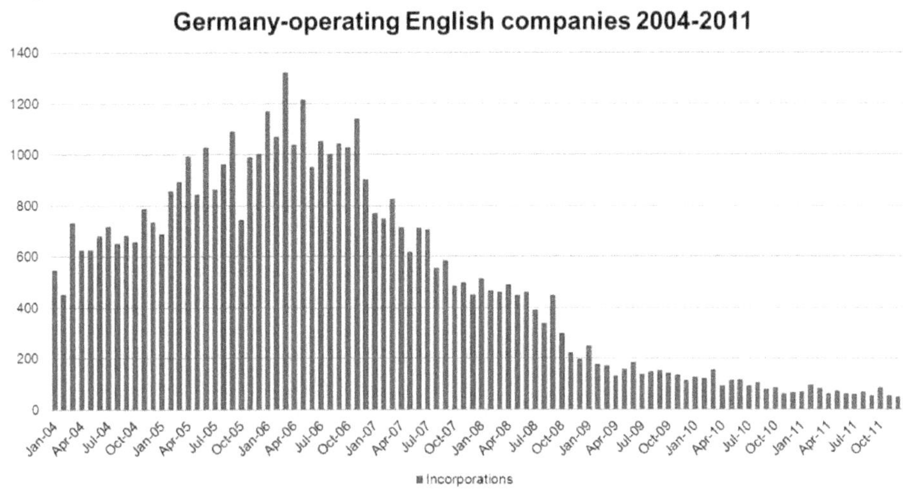

In the next step, we aim to exclude other potentially relevant factors. This relates in particular to the general economic downturn which, as generally acknowledged, started in 2007 and eventually led to a recession all across Europe. In order to exclude a potential bias of the data because of the general economic situation, we compare our figures in relation to *all company formations* in the United Kingdom over the same period. The purpose is to find out how large the share of 'German-based' UK incorporations *in relation to* the overall rate of company formation was over the time period studied. The result confirms our earlier finding: seen as a sub-category of the overall incorporation activity in the UK, 'German' company formations climb at first and then steadily fall. They start with 2.19% in January 2004 and climb up to a maximum value of 4.11% in December 2005, from where they fall steadily to a value of 0.13% in December 2011. Graph 3 thus shows a similar tendency as graph 2 by depicting the sample in relation to all UK incorporations between 2004-2011.

88 For the years 2004, 2005 and 2006, Becht et al find (in their second dataset) 9,038/12,777/15,633 companies, respectively. The ratio to the number of incorporations presented here fluctuates between 1.14 and 1.21 (7,900/10,958/12,940).

Graph 3.

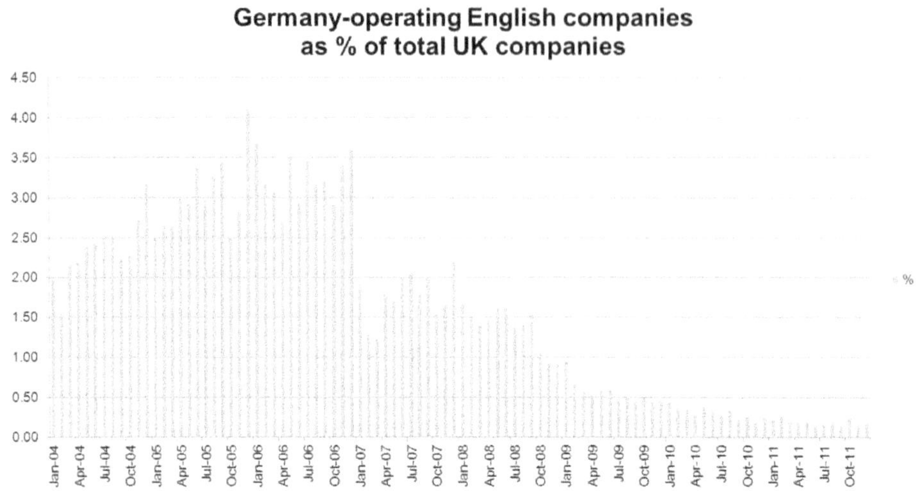

Finally, the same calculation is carried out with regard to all *German* incorporations over the same period of time. After all, the entrepreneurs are active in the German market and have to choose between the German GmbH and the English private limited company. This additional step will also exclude any bias due to the idiosyncrasies of the English market. The German data comes from a comparable database to the one used above: *Orbis* provides comprehensive firm-level data for companies worldwide. Unfortunately, the database does not allow for a monthly breakdown so that we can only extract yearly incorporation data. Using private company formations for Germany (GmbH), we aim at confirming the above findings in relations to the overall rate private company formation in Germany. The result confirms both findings made above: seen as a sub-category of the overall incorporation activity in Germany, figures for German entrepreneurs choosing an English limited company are increasing in the first years of the time period studied. English limited companies accounted for 15.23% of the formation numbers of private companies in Germany in 2004. This figure climbed up to a maximum value of 21.46% in 2006, whereby the value for 2006 was only slightly higher than the value for 2005 (20.30%). The figures show a stark decline over the following years until they end at 1.13% in 2011. Graph 4 thus confirms both previous illustrations, albeit in a more coarse calibration, due to the lack of monthly data.

Graph 4.

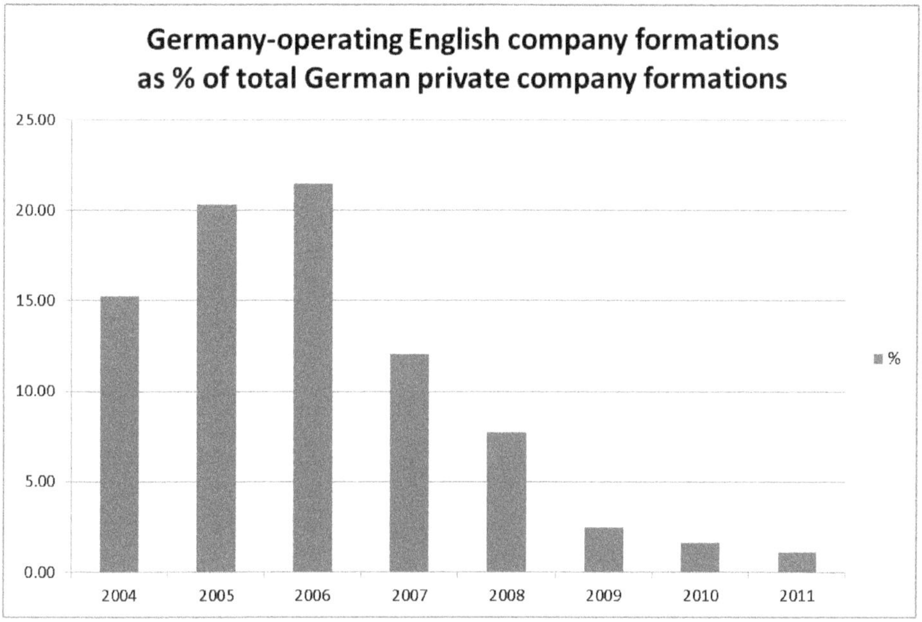

What does this mean for our hypothesis? The important finding is that the numbers seem to fall way before the German law reform took effect. Without claiming any causality or statistical significance, the finding is nevertheless intuitively clear: a peak in *Centros*-type incorporations in early 2006 at least questions the claim that the German law reform from November 2008 was causal for the decline of English limited companies in Germany. In fact, the change in the law itself seems to have had little effect at all: by November 2008, the incorporation rate had already reached the figure of only 300 per month (down from a peak value of 1322 in March 2006) and the rate of decline has even further slowed down since then.[89]

One possible counter-argument will immediately come to mind: *anticipation* of law reform. Arguably, entrepreneurs knew that law reform would be coming and would have an incentive to wait until the German reform law takes effect. However, this argument is to be dismissed, and this for two reasons. Firstly, we describe above the various and complicated steps of the German law reform process.[90] Looking at the timeline, it becomes clear that in March 2006, entrepreneurs will most certainly have been aware of the impending law reform. However, at the time, the state of the discussion was to lower minimum capital requirements to EUR 10,000 only – the complete abolition of minimum capital requirements being

89 The average monthly growth/decline rate was +0.38% in 2006, -4.99% in 2007, -5.16% in 2008, -3.00% in 2009, -1.94% in 2010 and +1.03% in 2011.

90 See above, table 1.

proposed much later, in July 2007.[91] Whereas the proposed move from EUR 25,000 to EUR 10,000 is certainly substantial, it will probably not induce entrepreneurs to wait with starting their business idea for months of uncertainty. Secondly, consider the early years of rising incorporation numbers. We noted above that first rumours about a law reform emerged already in the second half of 2004.[92] If an anticipation effect existed, we would expect the growth in incorporations to slow down already at this point in time and accordingly much earlier than what the figures tell us. It is inconsistent with the anticipation effect that foreign incorporations continued to rise for 18 months after the government discussed legislative action, including a draft from November 2004 which proposed to abolish minimum capital requirements altogether.[93] Graph 5 illustrates this line of thought by mapping the legislative process on the real data.

Graph 5.

In conclusion, the data presented here suggest that the German law reform which came into effect was not, at least not only, the relevant reason for the decline in English private limited companies set up by German entrepreneurs to operate in Germany, nor was there any significant anticipation effect of the law reform. We can thereby make a first cautious statement to question the claim of a 'successful' German law reform in a sense that it claims to have reduced the number of foreign incorporations in Germany.

91 *Ibid.*
92 *Ibid.*
93 *Ibid.*

5. Austrian Data and Results

In order to test the reliability of these findings, the second part of this study evaluates a second sample of foreign incorporations, this time for Austria. The contrast between Germany and Austria is extremely striking and revealing for the current study, since both countries have had an experience with English-incorporated companies.[94] It is even more useful as a comparative measure to test the validity of our initial thinking above, and this is for the two following reasons.

First, Austrian company law bears a remarkable similarity to its German counterpart. It is not only that both countries share a common history, culture and language, but specifically the law on business organisation has common roots.[95] Accordingly, not only legal concepts in Germany and Austria are very similar, but corporate forms have a very similar twin across the border, with even the same technical names: for example, the German *Gesellschaft mit beschränkter Haftung* (GmbH) corresponds to the Austrian *Gesellschaft mit beschränkter Haftung* (GesmbH).[96]

Secondly, and importantly for the question under consideration here, in contrast to the German MoMiG law reform enacted in 2008, the Austrian private company has *not* been reformed in the wake of the *Centros* case law. So different from most other continental legal systems described above, Austria has not seen a reaction prompted by the invasion of English private limited companies, at least not yet.[97] To be sure, there has been ample discussion regarding such a reform, yet no legal action has been taken.[98] The lack of any reform legislation over the sample period makes Austria a phenomenally interesting case to study: in Austria, the minimum capital for private companies amounts to EUR 35,000 (which is even higher than the German pre-reform amount of EUR 25,000).[99] This amount has not been changed in Austria over the past years. If the hypothesis described above is correct, we would expect to see no decline in English companies in Austria - since

94 On Austria, see Dommes *et al.* 2005; Kalss & Adensamer 2006, § 20.

95 Generally Doralt & Diregger 2008, paras. 194 *et seq.* Specifically for the GmbH see Kalss & Eckert 2005, p. 54 *et seq.*

96 Both company forms were adopted around the turn of the 20th century: the German GmbH originates in 1892, the Austrian counterpart is from 1906.

97 Very recently, the government has proposed to finally reform its company law, with a plan to reduce minimum capital to EUR 10,000. See Begutachtungsentwurf eines Gesellschaftsrechts-Änderungsgesetzes 2013 (GesRÄG 2013), available at: <http://justiz.gv.at/internet/html/-default/2c9484853d643b33013d8d8493ae52be.de.html>. The Austrian notaries support the proposal but want to add the German approach of requiring companies to save additional capital until they have reached the traditional minimum capital level. See Österreichische Notariatskammer (Austrian Notary Chamber), 'Österreichs Notare unterstützen raschere und kostengünstigere Unternehmensgründungen', press release of 22 March 2013, available at: <www.ots.at/presseaussendung/OTS_20130322_OTS0139>.

98 On the reform discussion, see Bachner 2008; Dommes *et al.* 2005.

99 See Austrian GmbH law, § 6(1).

the market need for a cheap-cost alternative is as big as it was just after *Centros*.[100] We would therefore expect the developments in both Germany and Austria to diverge: the German law reform, allegedly having fought back the invasion of English companies, would have led to a decline in foreign companies, whereas Austria did not react and should, accordingly, not see a comparable decline.

Consequently, in the same methodology as described above for Germany, we go on to collect data for Austria. Accordingly, we extract data via FAME for the same timeframe, 2004-2011. Corresponding filtering criteria are applied in the same way to limit them to *Centros*-style companies operating in Austria.[101]

The results are depicted in Graph 6. In summary, we count a total of 3,585 'Austrian' incorporations over the years 2004-11. Strikingly, the development is very similar to the German story: the formations continue to grow until spring 2006, and from then seem to steadily fall. The peak value in April 2006 is 148 incorporations per month, although this value appears to be an outlier, compared with 98 incorporations for March 2006 and 60 incorporations for May 2006. The lowest value in December 2011 amounts to a mere 13 incorporations.

Graph 6.

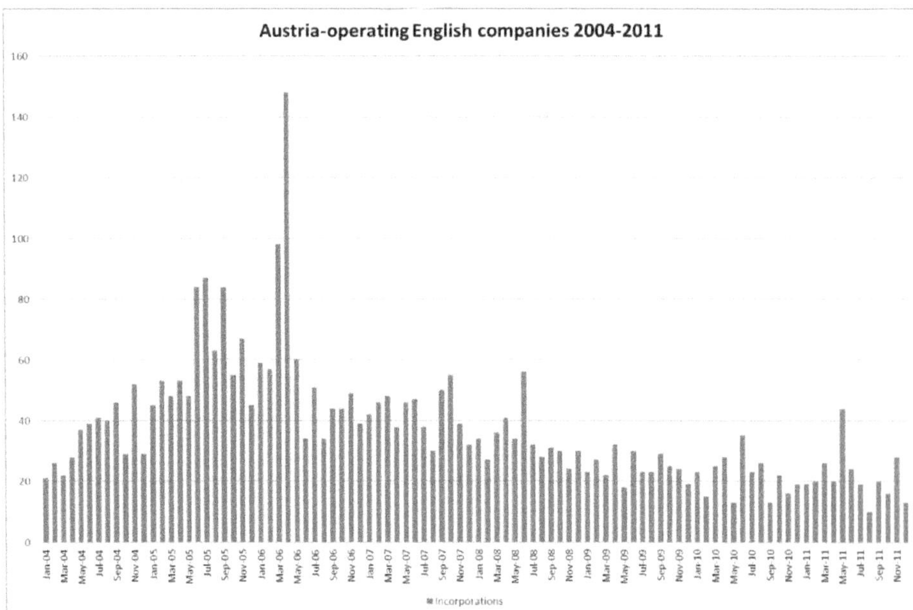

100 See above end of section 3.

101 One adjustment is made, however: since the size of the Austrian economy in relation to the German economy is roughly 1:10, we apply this factor to our filter criterion. Consequently, we are looking for firms where the registered office corresponds to that of at least 10 (and not 100) others.

One major finding from this is that the German and Austrian developments seem to have been quite similar: both increase substantially over the first years and begin to fall in spring 2006. This finding appears to be in a somewhat uneasy tension with our hypothesis. If English incorporations operating in Austria declined in the same way as in Austria, the logical consequence is that the German law reform has certainly not caused (at least not exclusively) the German development.

As a caveat, there is a possibility that Austrians, too, may have been using the (reformed) German UG since it came into force. For an Austrian entrepreneur, a low-cost legal form similar to the one he is familiar with must seem attractive and maybe even preferable over the English legal form. The Austrian entrepreneur could easily register such a German UG without any language difficulties and, particularly if he lives in the border region, in geographical proximity. As explained above, the German GmbH (and UG) does not any more require a head office or even place of business in Germany.[102] So we might expect Austrian entrepreneurs wishing to escape from domestic minimum capital requirements to opt for the German UG rather than the British Limited. This would mean that the German law reform could have similar effects on the Austrian market as it would in Germany. Our current data do not allow us to verify this hypothesis. Even if this assumption were correct, however, we would expect to see an effect on the Austrian incorporation activity much later than the observed peak and downward trend in early 2006. Due to initial legal uncertainty, such a spill-over effect would probably even come with a greater time delay.

As with Germany, we subsequently test our findings within the general market environment of both the UK and Austria, excluding a general downward trend in the market; and as with Germany, relative rather than absolute figures show the same effect (see graphs 7 and 8).

102 New § 4a GmbHG. See *supra* n. 77.

Graph 7.

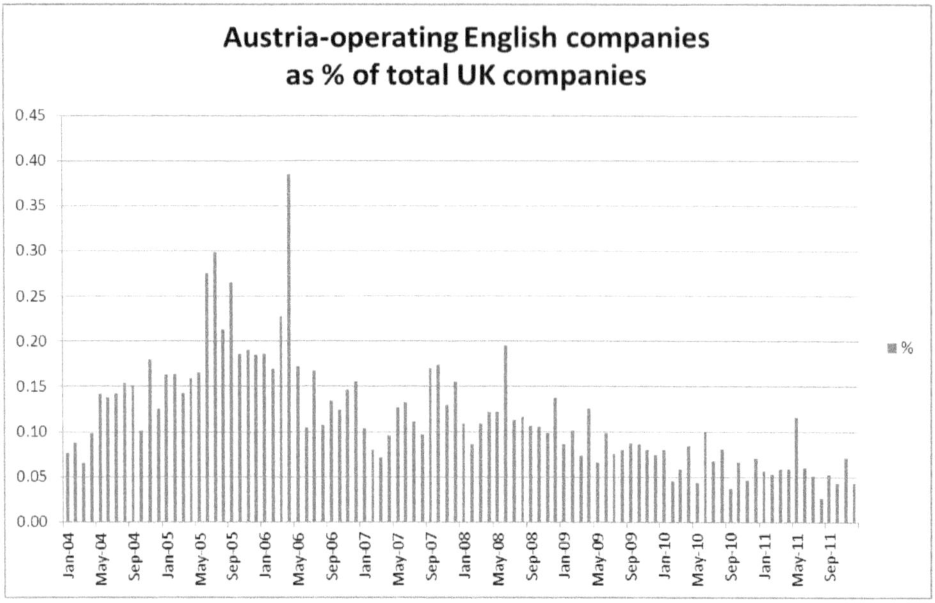

Graph 8.

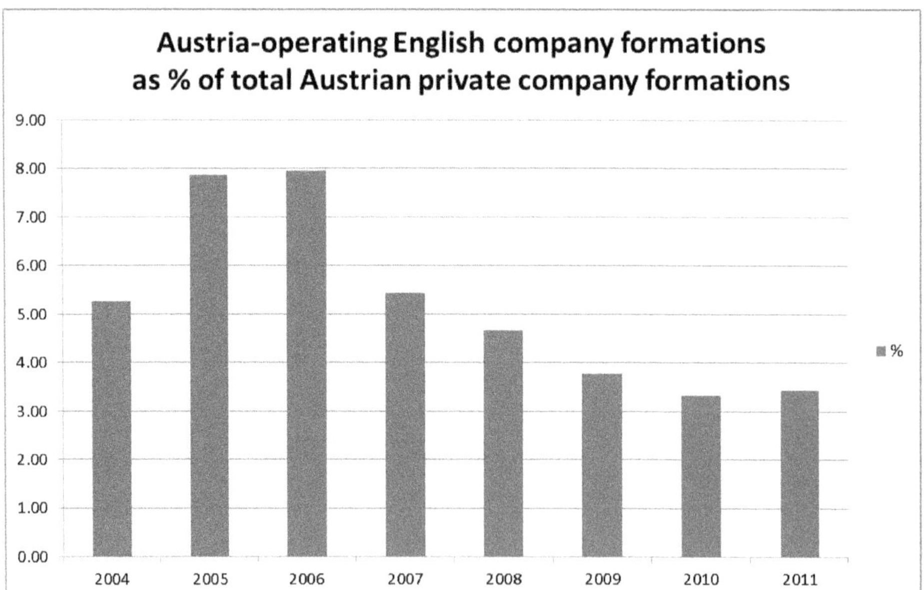

6. Analysis

After studying and discussing the data for both Germany and Austria, this section attempts to synthesize the findings and provide a number of explanations for the results.

First, the empirical data analysed here have revealed the following: (1) foreign English incorporations in Germany show a strong increase between 2004 and early 2006, and an equally strong decrease between early 2006 and 2011. (2) The data for Austria show a similar picture, although the Austrian slope appears not as steep as the one for Germany.

This double finding is dramatic in its combination: it brings us to the conclusion that the German law reform from November 2008 was not 'effective' as is claimed. This conclusion rests on two pillars: first, the German figures were declining well ahead of the German law reform taking effect and, secondly, the counter-example of Austria shows that British incorporations are disappearing even in a similar jurisdiction where minimum capital has not been reformed. Far from establishing empirical proof in the mathematical sense, the more modest approach undertaken here is limited to a more intuitive understanding of the figures. To a lawyer's mind, the data produced here put at least a question mark behind the claim of a 'successful law reform'.

What, then, might be possible explanations for the striking development in Germany? I limit myself to five conjectures, all of which have probably contributed in some form or another to the development.

6.1. *Restrictive Attitude in Lawmaking and Case-law*

The first observation is that German lawmakers, courts, and public authorities have become increasingly restrictive over the years in their attitude towards foreign-incorporated companies. Under the banner of combating abusive practices, this has led to a number of attractive features of foreign incorporations disappearing.

Consider the developments in German case-law. Initially, German courts were surprisingly open and friendly towards English companies. Naturally, the European Court of Justice in *Überseering* directly overruled German case-law, but *Centros* and *Inspire Art*, for example, did not directly concern problems of German law. In any case, the highest German civil court, the *Bundesgerichtshof (BGH)*, in 2003 already confirmed that it would no longer apply the infamous real seat theory to EU-based companies, thus accepting foreign incorporations by unreservedly applying the law of the registered office.[103] This was extended in 2005 to a second seminal BGH judgment, confirming that liability questions of both shareholders and of directors would not be considered according to German, but rather according to English law; in other words, the choice of foreign law was uncompromisingly

103 BGH, judgment of 13 March 2003 (VII ZR 370/98), BGHZ 154, 185; BGH, judgment of 2 June 2003 (II ZR 134/02), NJW 2003, 2609.

accepted.[104] These (and other[105]) cases paved the way for a high increase in English incorporations operating in Germany.

This liberal attitude shifted to a more restrictive trend from early 2006 onwards, in particular in order to prevent abusive practices and to close loopholes. Several aspects deserve to be mentioned.

First, the courts clarified that the strict insolvency filing obligation principles under German law and the corresponding liability provisions would apply to foreign-incorporated companies operating in Germany. The *Landgericht Kiel* handed down its seminal judgment on this question in April 2006, which has remained the standard authority on this issue for the coming years.[106] It was eventually confirmed by other courts[107] and by the legislature in the 2008 MoMiG law reform.[108] Following this line, setting up a foreign company would not help firms to escape from German insolvency law and in particular the strict filing obligations under German law.

The next instance was the extension of the German prohibition system for disqualified directors to directors of foreign companies. This had presented a loophole in the early years of the *Centros* era: German businessmen who had been disqualified in Germany (i.e. were banned from exercising the position of a director) simply set up an English company in order to circumvent this provision - the German disqualification system only prevented them from becoming a director of a *German* company.[109] It was the *Oberlandesgericht (OLG) Jena* in March 2006, which was the first German court to apply this system by analogy to directorships in foreign companies, such as the English limited company.[110] This decision was subsequently confirmed by the BGH[111] and eventually codified in the MoMiG reform.[112] Again, this shift in attitude made English incorporations less attractive to German businessmen, since one of the interesting loopholes had now been closed.

104 BGH, judgment of 14 March 2005 (II ZR 5/03), ZIP 2005, 806.

105 Lower instance case-law includes BayObLG (Bavarian Supreme Court), judgment of 19 December 2002, 2 Z BR 7/02, BayObLGZ 2002, 413; OLG Frankfurt (Court of Appeal, Frankfurt), judgment of 23 May 2003 (23 U 35/02), OLGR Frankfurt 2003, 447; LG (Regional Court) Hannover, judgment of 2 July 2003 (20 T 39/03), ZIP 2003, 1458; Kammergericht (Court of Appeal, Berlin), judgment of 18 November 2003 (1 W 444/02), NJW-RR 2004, 331. Even the fiscal judiciary concurred, see Bundesfinanzhof (Federal Finance Court), judgment of 29 January 2003 (I R 6/99), BFHE 201, 463.

106 LG Kiel, judgment of 20 April 2006 (10 S 44/05), EuZW 2006, 478. The court found that *Centros*-type companies had their Centre of main interests (COMI) in Germany and thus applied the German filing obligation via Art. 4 of the European Insolvency Regulation 1346/2000.

107 Kammergericht, judgment of 24 September 2009 (8 U 250/08), ZIP 2009, 2156.

108 MoMiG (n 53), Art. 1 No. 43 and Art. 9 No. 3 (introducing new § 15a InsO).

109 See GmbHG § 6(2) in the version prior to November 2008.

110 OLG Jena, decision of 9 March 2006 (6 W 693/05), ZIP 2006, 708. Technically, this concerned the registration of the English company's branch in Germany.

111 BGH, decision of 7 May 2007 (II ZB 7/06), BGHZ 172, 200.

112 MoMiG (n 53), Art. 1 No 7 and Art. 3 No 5.

The German courts went on to clarify more open questions in a way that was increasingly restrictive towards foreign-incorporated companies. In a seminal decision from February 2007, the BGH clarified that German principles of estoppel liability (*Rechtsscheinhaftung*) would apply to *Centros*-type foreign companies.[113] Similarly, a 2010 decision confirmed that German criminal law, in particular the rules on embezzlement, would apply to such a company.[114] And finally, German courts took the view that jurisdiction for intra-company disputes according to Article 22(2) of the Brussels I Regulation was not in Germany, but rather in the UK.[115] The effect of the latter judgment was that shareholders and directors of a UK-incorporated but Germany-based company can bring intra-company litigation only in the UK, which makes it excessively more costly for entrepreneurs domiciled in Germany.

Interestingly, not only in Germany, but also the UK itself contributed to this trend. The reform of English company law with the Companies Act 2006 led to two important aspects that fit into the line of arguments presented here. First, the Act extended the reach of the English system of directors' disqualification to cover directors disqualified abroad. This move is an almost mirror image of the German initiative described above: each of the two systems had somehow been limited to their own domestic firms and directors.[116] In the 2006 reform, the UK expanded the scope of the English directors' disqualification system to cover potential directors who had been disqualified abroad.[117] This would neatly complement the German trend and catch all those who are disqualified in Germany and choose a British company as a second attempt. Secondly, the CA 2006 introduced a ban on sole 'corporate directors' under English law. Whereas previously, the directors of a company could be any other (including legal) person, the new law stipulates that at least one of the directors has to be an individual.[118] The old system had been prone to abuse: in particular, control structures are difficult to trace in companies which exclusively have corporate directors. Those intending to commit fraud may use a company with corporate directors to help obscure the identities of the persons involved. As the discussions around the introduction of the CA 2006 pointed out, this 'can be a particular problem with the corporate directors of companies established in overseas jurisdictions with poor records of transparency and corporate law enforcement.'[119] English company law thereby explicitly refers to the

113 BGH, judgment of 5 February 2007 (II ZR 84/05), NJW 2007, 1529.
114 BGH, judgment of 13 April 2010 (5 StR 428/09), ZIP 2010, 1233.
115 OLG Frankfurt, judgment of 3 February 2010 (21 U 54/09), ZIP 2010, 800; confirmed by BGH, judgment of 12 July 2011 (II ZR 28/10), BGHZ 190, 242.
116 Davies & Worthington 2012, p. 10-14; in more detail Walters & Davis-White 2009, Ch. 16. To be sure, English law allowed disqualification of directors of foreign companies, see Company Directors Disqualification Act 1986 s 22(2).
117 See CA 2006, section 1184. No secondary legislation has been made to date.
118 CA 2006, section 155(1). The provision came into effect on 1 October 2008, but did not apply to existing companies until 2010.
119 Hansard, HC Standing Committee D, 2nd Sitting, col.494 (6 July 2006).

usage of English legal forms through foreign businesspersons and intentionally eliminates another loophole potentially subject to abuse.

In sum, we see on both sides of the Channel activities by lawmakers, courts, and authorities to address lacunae that were felt to be unacceptable, thereby making the use of foreign companies to run a business at home less attractive.

6.2. *Acceptance and Reputation Problems*

The second aspect that may help us understand the decline of English companies in Germany relates to psychological acceptance problems in the market. It is well-known that the English company form, when used by domestic entrepreneurs, went through a series of reputational problems, which further increased over time. The 'Limited', as it was called in the German public discourse, was characterised as a cheap and dishonest vehicle, used by businesses with apparently dubious objectives.

The core of truth in this is that, as we have seen above, the rate of *Centros*-type companies in Germany ceasing to operate has been very high.[120] This has sometimes been misinterpreted as a high insolvency rate.[121] Another emotional side of the debate relates to the fact that minimum capital is still seen as a legitimate and useful element of corporate law by many in continental Europe.[122] Although it has increasingly been acknowledged that minimum capital is largely unsuitable as a creditor protection tool,[123] many see it at least as a 'threshold of seriousness'.[124] If in such an environment suddenly the opportunity arises to 'circumvent' rules which are generally seen as useful, those who make use of it will automatically be regarded as dishonest.

It is worth noting that this negative public perception has been further fuelled by interest groups who campaigned against foreign company forms for thoroughly rational motives. For example, this is true for public notaries, whose duties include an advisory role for and certification of the incorporation of a domestic GmbH; accordingly, they stand to lose income if start-ups switch to foreign company forms.[125] Lawyers who have been working all their life on German company law suddenly face the problem of being confronted with a new legal system which they do not understand; the logical reaction of many is to speak against it.[126] Similar

120 See above table 3b.
121 As explained above, the high rates of companies that are 'dissolved' does not necessarily mean insolvency, it can be interpreted as companies that are struck off the register but may continue their business elsewhere.
122 See *inter alia* the volume by Lutter 2006.
123 Amour 2006.
124 Eidenmüller, Grunewald & Noack 2006, p. 30; Pentz, Priester & Schwanna 2006, p. 46, 72; Miola 2006, p. 517 *et seq*., 551.
125 See the account at Becht, Enriques and Korom 2009, p. 186 *et seq*.
126 See the contributions by lawyers Happ & Holler 2004; Müller 2006; Römermann 2006.

motives hold true for registration authorities and judges.[127] It has even been suggested that German lawyers ought to be liable if they choose an English company form instead of a German one.[128]

6.3. *Underestimation of Costs*

Reportedly, many entrepreneurs underestimated the costs that would be involved in running a foreign company. This behavioural misconception may help explain the initial popularity of the British legal form in Germany and its subsequent decline.

At first glance, the formation of a *Centros*-type English company with operations in Germany was promulgated since it would allegedly be cheaper than its German counterpart. This may have appeared thus at first glance - when comparing minimum capital figures as well as set up speed and costs.[129] These, however, have to be contrasted with additional costs of running a foreign company - language, certification and translation costs, information costs for legal advice, double accounting obligations (for main company and branch), to name just a few.[130]

Moreover, the true hidden costs for running an English company are that English law is substantially more demanding than German law when it comes to continuous disclosure obligations and filing obligations of documents.[131] This applies in particular to the filing of annual accounts, which have to be submitted to the Companies House in English, thus usually producing translation costs for continental businesses. Non-compliance may trigger serious consequences in the form of civil penalties on the company and criminal liabilities on the directors.[132] The registrar of companies operates a very tough enforcement system indeed, using computer-generated default notices proceedings with cumulative daily default fines and strike-off notices (producing over 95% compliance rates on first due date).[133] Many foreign entrepreneurs concerned will have been very surprised to experience the vigour of enforcement of these reporting obligations, which is much stricter than in most other jurisdictions.[134] If the Registrar has reason to believe that a company is not carrying on business or is not in operation, he may initiate a procedure with a view of striking the company's name off the register, an inexpensive way of

127 See, for example, the article by registration judge Ries 2009.
128 Dierksmeier 2005 explains potential liability issues for German lawyers.
129 See above table 2 (pre-reform figures).
130 For example, English company documents frequently have to be translated and certified for the registration authority supervising the German branch of the company.
131 See generally Ringe & Otte 2012, paras. 259 *et seq*.
132 See Davies and Worthington 2012, p. 21-35.
133 See, for concrete details and compliance rates, Company Law Review Steering Group 2000, URN 00/1335) 13.50-13.53.
134 This development had partly been anticipated by the English company law review. See Company Law Review Steering Group 1999, 5.6.13.

dissolving inactive companies without any substantial assets.[135] Striking-off may also be used where liquidation cannot be carried out due to a lack of resources for the liquidation procedure.[136]

It is plausible to partly explain the decline of foreign incorporations over 2006-08 in both Germany and Austria by this strict disclosure regime and its enforcement. Some of the foreign entrepreneurs may have realised the high costs of disclosure and translation for the first time after their first year of operation and, subsequent hereto, did not think the continuance of their business worthwhile. In the case of non-compliance, they may have been either deterred from continuing by the high penalties imposed on them or they will have been deleted from the register (by 'striking-off') for not complying with the disclosure obligations.

Looking at the time scale, the filing of accounts must be carried out within ten (now nine) months after the end of the company's financial year.[137] Taking into account the company's first business year and the subsequent ten-month window means that the annual accounts have to be filed for the first time at the latest 22 months after the company was incorporated.[138] Add another six months for the striking-off procedure, and we can expect many companies being struck off the register after 28 months. These dramatic consequences will then slowly become known to the German market. The big wave of companies that were incorporated in the early years 2003-2005 inevitably arrived at this moment sometime between 2005 and 2008 and may account for a drop in interest in the English legal form.

In short, running a business with a foreign legal form creates additional costs which many entrepreneurs will not have been aware of or will have underestimated. Many will have found out about this over time, which explains the initial soaring of company formations and the subsequent decline.

6.4. *Diffusion Theory*

In an attempt to present the previous points in a more formal context, the pattern that we observe in the present study can be understood as an account of 'diffusion theory'. This theory, borrowed from organisational management science and from sociology, is a research discipline that seeks to explain how, why and at what rate new ideas, innovations and organisational concepts spread through companies.[139] The theoretical literature essentially advances two sets of explanations regarding the process leading to the adoption of new practices. The first has its origins in traditional rational choice economics and stresses the importance of cost effectiveness and the likelihood of diffusion amongst peers, and focusses on the

135 CA 2006, ss 1000-1011. The most common starting point for initiating such a procedure is indeed non-compliance with the duty to file annual accounts or annual returns, see Davies & Worthington 2012, paras. 33-56.

136 CA 2006, s 1001.

137 Companies Act 1985, section 244; now Companies Act 2006, section 442.

138 Zimmer & Naendrup 2007, p. 792 *et seq.*; Wegen & Schlichte 2006.

139 The theory goes back to Rogers and his 1962 book (Rogers 1995).

growing level of general information about the value of a diffusing innovation.[140] By contrast, more sociology-based accounts tend to emphasize growing levels of social pressure towards conformity: in particular, they assume that organisations frequently imitate other organisations in order to appear legitimate and that with increasing institutionalisation the adoption of practices is therefore frequently driven by a desire to appear in conformance with social norms.[141] More recently, this literature has been extended to analyse the processes of change and its sophistication within a diffusion process[142] and the implications of contestation in diffusion processes.[143] Specifically, scholars show that social consensus of contestation and negative press reporting about a specific organisational practice (here: golden parachutes in executive compensation) can have a negative impact on its adoption and ultimately lead to its decline.[144]

These elements of organisational theory can help explain both the rise and the decline in English company forms on the continent. In the early years post *Centros*, the English limited company enjoyed a positive image, suggesting an innovative and cheap innovation of business organisation. Both rational choice considerations and social advantages supported its popularity: entrepreneurs would imitate each other, presumably due to both social norms and expected lower costs. This changed with increasingly negative reporting about the foreign legal forms, prompted by unknown disadvantages, high compliance and enforcement costs and to reputational problems due the fact that many dubious entrepreneurs made use of the unconventional legal form.[145] In particular, increasingly negative publicity in the German media and practitioner-oriented legal journals about the pitfalls of using English company forms may have contributed to a shifting social consensus on the integrity of using foreign legal forms.[146]

6.5. *Law Reform*

It is *not* the claim of this paper that law reform has not contributed to the decline of the English company form in continental Europe. Rather, this may well have been the case, but to a significantly lesser extent than previously accepted.

Law reforms (and their anticipation) certainly play a role. This is surely the case in Germany, where the reform of the GmbH has led to a dramatic increase in

[140] Strang & Macy 2001; Sturdy 2004.
[141] DiMaggio & Powell 1983; Scott 1995; Sturdy 2004; Tolbert & Zucker 1996.
[142] Ansari, Fiss & Zajac 2010.
[143] Fiss, Kennedy & Davis 2012.
[144] *Ibid.*
[145] See on this above sections 6.2. and 6.3.
[146] Compare, for example, the extremely positive 2003/04 press articles by Behm 2003 (suggesting that the German GmbH could soon be a phase-out model) and Behm 2004 (suggesting that already every fourth German company formation uses an English legal form) with the 2007 article Schulz-Trieglaff 2007 (describing that the English limited company bears high hidden costs).

popularity for the new GmbH variant, the *Unternehmergesellschaft (haftungsbeschränkt) (UG)*. First studies show that the UG has been well accepted by market participants: they report roughly 70,000 formations between November 2008 and February 2012.[147] It is undeniably the case that those entrepreneurs seeking to incorporate their business without minimum capital will find the UG easier and more accessible to them. The other interesting question is whether *Austrian* entrepreneurs might make use of the German UG to any meaningful extent in the same way as they did with English companies - the UG, being based on German law, might be a more attractive and accessible company form also to them.[148] This is, however, a subject matter beyond the scope of the present study.[149]

Austria did not reform its own company law, as discussed above. There is one other interesting piece of law reform that deserves attention, however. Austria reformed its taxation law in early 2006 in order to charge a minimum corporation tax on British limited companies that would be equal to that of an Austrian GesmbH. This is due to the peculiarities of the Austrian corporate taxation system: the payable corporation tax depends on the amount of the legal capital of the respective company.[150] The problem was that most *Centros*-type companies simply had no subscribed share capital of meaningful value (i.e. only £1 or £100 instead of EUR 35,000 and thus - absent profits - did not have to pay an equivalent corporation tax. A reform coming into effect in February 2006 closed this perceived 'discrimination' of the domestic company by treating foreign companies as if they had a minimum capital equalling that of the domestic GesmbH.[151] This move may well have contributed to the loss in attractiveness of English companies in Austria as described above.[152] To be sure, this reform is very different in character to the one described above: the Austrian law reform simply removed a tax incentive to run a business from the UK that solely existed due to the structure of its own taxation laws. As such, it is not a response to a more competitive foreign law.

7. Conclusion

In conclusion, this paper offers insights into the effects of lawmaking within a setting of regulatory competition. It questions the traditional assumption that the German 2008 law reform, abolishing minimum capital for closed corporations, caused a reduction in the number of foreign firms set up by German entrepreneurs. Rather, as we have seen, a number of other reasons may be responsible for the decline: in particular, the closing down of loopholes that had made the English

147 Miras 2012; Kornblum 2012 (ca. 64,000 at 1 January 2012). See also Bayer & Hoffmann 2012a; Bayer & Hoffmann 2012b.

148 The website <www.ugstattltd.at/> offers German UGs to Austrian entrepreneurs.

149 See above section 5.

150 Körperschaftsteuergesetz 1988, § 24(4).

151 Abgabenänderungsgesetz 2005 (AbgÄG 2005), Bundesgesetzblatt für die Republik Österreich no 161 of 30 December 2005. See on this question Dommes *et al.* 2005, p. 539.

152 See above section 5.

limited company so attractive to some German entrepreneurs. Further, German start-ups underestimated the costs involved with running a foreign company and complying with disclosure obligations that are strictly enforced. They also encountered high acceptance and reputation costs at home. All of these problems in their combination can be framed in terms of diffusion theory, highlighting the sociological aspects of subscribing to innovations or new organisational concepts.

What are the implications? It would certainly be too much to conclude that the German law reform was superfluous, wrong or without effect. As emphasised earlier, the new UG legal form has certainly had its share in making the English limited company less attractive. But the paper at least cautions against overemphasising the importance of the MoMiG reform. The implications developed here may however well be of interest to lawmakers in general, and to the Austrian government in particular. As mentioned above, Austria is currently still debating whether to reform its company law. The data shown in this paper may well put the importance of this project into perspective.

Overall, I firmly believe that the effects of the defensive regulatory competition observed thus far have been positive. Lowering minimum capital requirements, reducing administrative burdens, and speeding up the incorporation process are positive elements of an 'entrepreneurship culture'. Where EU Member States adopt reform statutes reducing start-up burdens, this gives businesses and investors the necessary legal framework for swift and uncomplicated practical implementation of entrepreneurial ideas and is thus beneficial for all.

Looking further ahead, an increasingly burgeoning amount of tools for cross-border movement has become available,[153] and even the plans for the adoption of the Fourteenth Company Law Directive on the cross-border transfer of the registered office of limited companies are currently being revived.[154] If cross-border mobility were to eventually become reality for existing companies (as opposed to start-ups), the entire debate around free movement of companies and regulatory competition would enter into an entirely new dimension.

On start-up competition, the final point is that there is still a solid number of German entrepreneurs who prefer an English company over the (reformed) German equivalent.[155] It is submitted that the great wave of amateurs is over and that this is now the hour of the experts - sophisticated entrepreneurs, who make a rational comparison between the two regimes, taking into account the true costs of running a foreign business, and who resist any emotional or social pressure to the contrary.

153 Especially the (Tenth) Cross-Border Merger Directive and the European Company Statute (see *supra* n. 15 and n. 16).

154 Consultation on the cross-border transfers of registered offices of companies (January-April 2013), available at: <http://ec.europa.eu/internal_market/consultations/2013/seat-transfer/index_en.htm>.

155 The last months of my sample show formation numbers of between 50 and 80 per month.

Bibliography

Ansari, Fiss & Zajac 2010
Ansari, A., Fiss, P.C. & Zajac, E., 'Made to Fit: How Practices Vary as they Diffuse', *Academy of Management Review*, 2010, Vol. 35(1), p. 67-92.

Armour 2005
Armour, J., 'Who Should Make Corporate Law? EC Legislation Versus Regulatory Competition', *Current Legal Problems*, 2005, Vol. 58(1), p. 369-413.

Armour 2006
Amour, J., 'Legal Capital: An Outdated Concept?', *European Business Organization Law Review*, 2006, Vol. 1, p. 5-27.

Armour & Ringe 2011
Armour, J. & Ringe, W.-G., 'European Corporate Law 1999-2010: Renaissance and Crisis', *Common Market Law Review*, 2011, Vol. 48, p. 125-174.

Bachner 2008
Bachner, T. (ed.), *GmbH-Reform – Erleichterte Gründung, Gläubigerschutz, Insolvenz-prophylaxe*, Vienna: Linde, 2008.

Barbièri 2008
Barbièri, J.F., 'La SAS revisitée par la LME', *Bulletin Joly Sociétés*, 2008, Vol. 7, p. 560-561.

Bayer & Hoffmann 2012a
Bayer, W. & Hoffmann, T., Neue Daten zur Unternehmersgesellschaft', *GmbH-Rundschau*, 2012, R051.

Bayer & Hoffmann 2012b
Bayer, W. & Hoffmann, T., 'Unternehmergesellschaften in der Insolvenz', *GmbH-Rundschau*, 2012, Vol. 21, p. 289-290.

Becht, Enriques & Korom 2009
Becht, M., Enriques, L. & Korom, V., '*Centros* and the Costs of Branching', *Journal of Corporate Law Studies*, 2009, Vol. 9, p. 171-199.

Becht, Mayer & Wagner 2008
Becht, M., Mayer, C. & Wagner, H., 'Where Do Firms Incorporate? Deregulation and the Cost of Entry', *Journal of Corporate Finance*, 2008, Vol. 14(3), p. 241-256.

Behm 2003
Behm, M., 'Lieber 'limited' als beschränkt', *Financial Times Deutschland,* Hamburg, 30 September 2003, p. 14.

Behm 2004
Behm, M., 'Gründer bevorzugen Ltd. statt GmbH', *Süddeutsche Zeitung*, Munich, 8 September 2004, p. 18.

Berninger & Schnittker 2006
Berninger, M. & Schnittker, H., 'Eckpunktepapier zur Schaffung der Gesellschaftsform einer Personengesellschaft mit beschränkter Haftung' (June 2006).

Bratton, McCahery & Vermeulen 2009
Bratton, W.W., McCahery, J.A. & Vermeulen, E.P.M., 'How Does Corporate Mobility Affect Lawmaking? A Comparative Analysis', *American Journal of Comparative Law*, 2009, Vol. 57, p. 501-549.

Braun *et al.* 2013
Braun, R., Eidenmüller, H., Engert, A. & Hornuf, L., 'Does Charter Competition Foster Entrepreneurship? A Difference-in-Difference Approach to European Company Law Reforms', *Journal of Common Market Studies*, 2013, Vol. 51(3), p. 399-415.

Cheffins 1997
Cheffins, B.R., *Company Law: Theory, Structure and Operation*, Oxford, Oxford University Press, 1997.

Company Law Review Steering Group 1998
Company Law Review Steering Group, *Modern Company Law for a Competitive Economy*, London: DTI, 1998.

Company Law Review Steering Group 1999
Company Law Review Steering Group, *Modern Company Law for a Competitive Economy – The Strategic Framework*, London: DTI, 1999.

Company Law Review Steering Group 2000
Company Law Review Steering Group, *Modern Company Law for a Competitive Economy: Completing the Structure*, London: DTI, 2000.

Davies & Worthington 2012
Davies, P.L. & Worthington, S., *Gower and Davies' Principles of Modern Company Law*, 9th edn., London: Sweet & Maxwell, 2012.

Deakin 2006
Deakin, S., 'Legal Diversity and Regulatory Competition: Which Model for Europe?', *European Law Journal*, 2006, Vol. 12(4), p. 440-454.

de Vendeuil 2003
de Vendeuil, S., 'Les dispositions de droit des sociétés de la loi numéro 2003-721 du 1er août 2003 pour l'initiative économique', *La Semaine Juridique Entreprise et Affaires*, 2003, p. 1401-1405.

Dierksmeier 2005
Dierksmeier, J., 'Die englische Ltd. in Deutschland - Haftungsrisiko für Berater', *Betriebs-Berater*, 2005, Vol. 28, p. 1516-1522.

Dierksmeier 2011
Dierksmeier, J. 'Kapitalgesellschaften aller Länder willkommen! Die deutsche GmbH im internationalen Wettbewerb der Rechtsformen 2010', in: Ebke, W. *et al.* (eds.), *Das deutsche Wirtschaftsrecht unter dem Einfluss des US-amerikanischen Rechts*, Frankfurt: Verlag Recht und Wirtschaft, 2011, p. 205-217.

DiMaggio & Powell 1983
DiMaggio, P. & Powell, W., 'The Iron Cage Revisited: Institutional Isomorphism and Collective Rationality in Organizational Fields', *American Sociological Review*, 1983, Vol. 48(2), p. 147-160.

Dommes *et al.* 2005
Dommes, S. *et al.*, 'The English Private Company Limited in Austria - Questions Regarding Company Law', *Steuer und Wirtschaft International*, 2005, p. 477-491.

Doralt & Diregger 2008
Doralt, P. & Diregger, C., 'Einleitung', in: Goette, W. & Habersack, M. (eds.), *Münchener Kommentar zum Aktiengesetz*, 3rd edn., Munich: C.H. Beck, 2008, paras. 194 *et seq*.

Drury 1999
Drury, R.R., 'Migrating Companies', *European Law Review*, 1999, Vol. 24, p. 354-372.

Drury 2005
Drury, R.R., 'The "Delaware Syndrome": European Fears and Reactions', *Journal of Business Law*, 2005, p. 709-744.

Drygala 2006
Drygala, T., 'Für eine alternative Rechtsform neben einer reformierten GmbH—Leipziger Entwurf einer Kommanditgesellschaft mit beschränkter Haftung (KmbH)', *Zeitschrift für Wirtschaftsrecht (ZIP)*, 2006, p. 1797-1805.

Eidenmüller 2007
Eidenmüller, H., 'Die GmbH im Wettbewerb der Rechtsformen', *Zeitschrift für Unternehmens- und Gesellschaftsrecht (ZGR)*, 2007, Vol. 36, p. 168-211.

Eidenmüller, Grunewald & Noack 2006
Eidenmüller, H., Grunewald, B. & Noack, U., 'Minimum Capital in the System of Legal Capital', in: Lutter, M. (ed.), *Legal Capital in Europe,* Berlin: de Gruyter, 2006, p. 17-42.

Faigle 2005
Faigle, P., 'Härtere Auflagen für Existenzgründer - Justizministerium erwägt eine Verdopplung des Stammkapitals für GmbH', *Berliner Zeitung,* Berlin, 17 March 2005, p. 14.

Fiss, Kennedy & Davis 2012
Fiss, P., Kennedy, M.T. & Davis, G.F., 'How Golden Parachutes Unfolded: Diffusion and Variation of a Controversial Practice', *Organization Science,* 2012, Vol. 23(4), p. 1077-1099.

Fleischer 2010
Fleischer, H., 'Einleitung', in: Fleischer, H. & Goette, W. (eds.), *Münchener Kommentar zum GmbHG,* Munich: C.H. Beck, 2010, paras. 116-117.

Gerner-Beuerle & Schillig 2010
Gerner-Beuerle, C. & Schillig, M., 'The Mysteries of Right of Establishment after Cartesio', *International & Comparative Law Quarterly,* 2010, Vol. 59(2), p. 303-323.

Happ & Holler 2004
Happ, W. & Holler, L. '„Limited" statt GmbH? Risiken und Kosten werden gern verschwiegen', *Deutsches Steuerrecht,* 2004, p. 730-736.

Hirte 2003
Hirte, H., 'Die organisierte „Bestattung" von Kapitalgesellschaften: Gesetzgeberischer Handlungsbedarf im Gesellschafts- und Insolvenzrecht', *Zeitschrift für das gesamte Insolvenzrecht (ZInsO),* 2003, p. 833-844.

Hirte 2006
Hirte, H., 'Die „Limited" mit Sitz in Deutschland - Abkehr von der Sitztheorie nach Centros, Überseering und Inspire Art', in: Hirte, H. & Bücker, T., *Grenzüberschreitende Gesellschaften,* 2nd edn., Cologne/Berlin/Munich: Carl Heymanns Verlag, 2006, p. 2-59.

Hirte 2008
Hirte, H., 'Die „Große GmbH-Reform" – Ein Überblick über das Gesetz zur Modernisierung des GmbH-Rechts und zur Bekämpfung von Missbräuchen (MoMiG)', *Neue Zeitschrift für Gesellschaftsrecht,* 2008, Vol. 20, p. 761-766.

Irujo 2004
Irujo, E.J.M., 'Eine spanische „Erfindung" im Gesellschaftsrecht: Die „Sociedad limitada nueva empresa" – die neue unternehmerische GmbH', *Recht der Internationalen Wirtschaft*, 2004, Vol. 10, p. 760-766.

Jahn 2005
Jahn, J., 'Ein-Euro-GmbH soll erlaubt werden' *Frankfurter Allgemeine Zeitung*, Frankfurt, 9 February 2005.

Kalss & Adensamer 2006
Kalss, S. & Adensamer, N., 'Ausländische Gesellschaften in Österreich', in: Hirte, H. & Bücker, T. (eds.), *Grenzüberschreitende Gesellschaften*, 2nd edn., Cologne/Berlin/Munich: Carl Heymanns Verlag, 2006, p. 660-715.

Kalss & Eckert 2005
Kalss, S. & Eckert, G., *Zentrale Fragen des GmbH-Rechts – Entwicklung, Perspektiven, Materialien*, Vienna: Linde, 2005.

Kieninger 2004
Kieninger, E.M., 'The Legal Framework of Regulatory Competition Based on Company Mobility: EU and US Compared', *German Law Journal*, 2004, Vol. 6(4), p. 741-770.

Kirchner, Painter & Kaal 2005
Kirchner, C., Painter, R.W. & Kaal, W.A., 'Regulatory Competition in EU Corporate Law After *Inspire Art:* Unbundling Delaware's Product for Europe', *European Company and Financial Law Review*, 2005, Vol. 2, p. 159-206.

Klöhn 2012
Klöhn, L., 'Supranational Legal Entities and Vertical Regulatory Competition in European Corporate Law: The Case for Market-Mimicking EU Corporate Forms', *Rabels Zeitschrift für ausländisches und internationales Privatrecht*, 2012, Vol. 76(2), p. 276-315.

Kornblum 2012
Kornblum, U., 'Bundesweite Rechtstatsachen zum Unternehmens- und Gesellschaftsrecht (Stand 1.1.2012)', *GmbH-Rundschau*, 2012, p. 728-735.

Kürzel 2012
Kürzel, G., 'GmbH-Reform in Österreich – Warten auf Godot?', 9 August 2012, available at: <http://fiduzia.blogspot.co.uk/2012/08/gmbh-reform-in-osterreich-warten-auf.html>.

Lowry 2004
Lowry, J., 'Eliminating Obstacles to Freedom of Establishment: The Competitive Edge of UK Company Law', *Cambridge Law Journal*, 2004, Vol. 63(2), p. 331-345.

Lutter 2006
Lutter, M. (ed.), *Legal Capital in Europe,* Berlin: de Gruyter, 2006.

Martin & Alogna 2007
Martin, D. & Alogna, F.G., 'New Delaware', *Wall Street Journal,* New York, 20 December 2007.

Massart 2002
Massart, T., 'Une grande réforme à petit budget: la SARL au capital de un euro', *Bulletin Joly Sociétés,* 2002, Vol. 12, p. 1361-1366.

Massart 2008
Massart, T., 'La modernisation de la SAS ou comment apporter moins pour gagner plus', *Bulletin Joly Sociétés,* 2008, Vol. 7, p. 632-640.

Miola 2006
Miola, M., 'Legal Capital Rules in Italian Company Law and the EU Perspective', in: Lutter, M. (ed.), *Legal Capital in Europe,* Berlin: de Gruyter, 2006, p. 515-558.

Miras 2012
Miras, A., 'Aktuelle Fragen zur Unternehmergesellschaft (haftungsbeschränkt)', *Neue Zeitschrift für Gesellschaftsrecht*, 2012, p. 486-490.

Mortier 2008
Mortier, R., 'La modernisation du droit des sociétés', *La Semaine Juridique Entreprise et Affaires*, 2008, Vol. 41, p. 2233-2239.

Müller 2006
Müller, K.J., 'Die englische Limited in Deutschland – für welche Unternehmen ist sie tatsächlich geeignet?', ***Betriebs-Berater***, 2006, p. 837-843.

Munari & Terrile 2002
Munari, F. & Terrile, P., 'The *Centros* Case and the Rise of an EC Market for Corporate Law', in: Ferrarini, G., Hopt, K.J. & Wymeersch, E. (eds.), *Capital Markets in the Age of the Euro: Cross-Border Transactions, Listed Companies and Regulation,* The Hague: Kluwer Law International, 2002, p. 558-560.

Niemeier 2006
Niemeier, W., 'GmbH und Limited im Markt der Unternehmensrechtsträger', *Zeitschrift für Wirtschaftsrecht (ZIP)*, 2006, p. 2237-2250.

Niemeier 2013
Niemeier, W., 'What Kinds of Companies will a "One-Euro-EPC" Generate? Market Data and Observations from the German "Laboratory"', in: Hirte, H. & Teichmann, C. (eds.), *The European Private Company – Societas Privata Europaea (SPE),* Berlin/Boston: de Gruyter, 2013, p. 293-349.

Paschalidis 2012
Paschalidis, P., *Freedom of Establishment and Private International Law for Corporations*, Oxford: Oxford University Press, 2012.

Pentz, Priester & Schwanna 2006
Pentz, A., Priester, H.J. & Schwanna, A., 'Raising Cash and Contributions in Kind when Forming a Company and for Capital Increases', in: Lutter, M. (ed.), *Legal Capital in Europe*, Berlin: de Gruyter, 2006, p. 42-75.

Priester 2005
Priester, H.J., 'Die deutsche GmbH nach 'Inspire Art' - brauchen wir eine neue?', *Der Betrieb*, 2005, p. 1315-1319.

Rickford 2004
Rickford, J., 'Current Developments in European Law on the Restructuring of Companies: An Introduction', *European Business Law Review*, 2004, Vol. 15(6), p. 1225-1258.

Ries 2009
Ries, P., '„Rule Britannia": Betrachtungen zur SPE aus der Sicht eines deutschen Registerrichters', *Neue Zeitschrift für Gesellschaftsrechts (NZG)*, 2009, Vol. 27, p. 1052-1054.

Ringe 2005
Ringe, W.-G., 'No Freedom of Emigration for Companies?', *European Business Law Review*, 2005, Vol. 16(3), p. 621-642.

Ringe 2011
Ringe, W.-G., 'Sparking Regulatory Competition in European Company Law: The Impact of the Centros Line of Case Law and its Concept of "Abuse of Law"', in: de la Feria, R. & Vogenauer, S. (eds.), *Prohibition of Abuse of Law: A New Principle of EU Law?*, Oxford: Hart Publishing, 2011, p. 107-125.

Ringe 2013
Ringe, W.-G., 'Corporate Mobility in the European Union - A Flash in the Pan? An Empirical Study on the Success of Lawmaking and Regulatory Competition', *European Company and Financial Law Review*, 2013, Vol. 10, p. 230-263.

Ringe & Otte 2012
Ringe, W.G. & Otte, S., 'Gesellschaftsrecht', in: Triebel, V., Illmer, M., Ringe, W.G., Vogenauer S. & Ziegler K. (eds.), *Englisches Handels- und Wirtschaftsrecht*, 3rd edn., Frankfurt: Verlag Recht und Wirtschaft, 2012, p. 26-28.

Rogers 1995
Rogers, E., *Diffusion of Innovations*, 4th edn., New York: Free Press, 1995.

Römermann 2006
Römermann, V., 'Die Limited in Deutschland - eine Alternative zur GmbH?', *Neue Juristische Wochenschrift (NJW)*, 2006, p. 2065-2070.

Roth 2000
Roth, W.H., 'Case Note on *Centros*', *Common Market Law Review*, 2000, Vol. 37, p. 147-155.

Roth 2003
Roth, W.H., 'From *Centros* to *Ueberseering*: Free Movement of Companies, Private International Law, and Community Law', *International and Comparative Law Quarterly*, 2003, Vol. 52(1), p. 177-208.

Schön 2006
Schön, W., 'The Mobility of Companies in Europe and the Organizational Freedom of Company Founders', *European Company and Financial Law Review*, 2006, Vol. 3(2), p. 122-146.

Schulz-Trieglaff 2007
Schulz-Trieglaff, K., 'Ltd. schützt nicht vor Verbot', *Frankfurter Allgemeine Zeitung*, Frankfurt, 30 October 2007, p. 31.

Scott 1995
Scott, W.R., *Institutions and organizations*, London: Sage, 1995.

Siems 2007
Siems, M., '*SEVIC*: Beyond Cross-Border Mergers', *European Business Organization Law Review*, 2007, Vol. 8, p. 307-316.

Strang & Macy 2001
Strang, D. & Macy, M.W., 'In Search of Excellence: Fads, Success Stories, and Adaptive Emulation', *American Journal of Sociology*, 2001, Vol. 107(1), p. 147-182.

Sturdy 2004
Sturdy, A., 'The Adoption of Management Ideas and Practices: Theoretical Perspectives and Possibilities', *Management Learning*, 2004, Vol. 35(2), p. 155-179.

Szabó & Engsig Sørensen 2013
Szabó, D. & Engsig Sørensen, K., 'Cross-Border Conversion of Companies in the EU: The Impact of the VALE Judgement' Nordic & European Company Law Working Paper, 2013, No. 10-33.

Teichmann 2010
Teichmann, C., 'Modernizing the GmbH: Germany's move in Regulatory Competition', *European Company Law*, 2010, Vol. 7(1), p. 20-24.

Tolbert & Zucker 1996
Tolbert, P. & Zucker, L., 'The Institutionalization of Institutional Theory', in: Clegg, S.R., Hardy, C. & Nord, W.R. (eds.), *The Handbook of Organization Studies*, London: Sage, 1996, p. 175-191.

Walters & Davis-White 2009
Walters, A. & Davis-White, M., *Directors' Disqualification and Insolvency Restrictions*, 3rd edn., London: Sweet & Maxwell, 2009.

Wegen & Schlichte 2006
Wegen, G. & Schlichte, J., 'GmbH oder EU-inländische Gesellschaft - die Qual der Wahl für Unternehmer und Berater in der Praxis', *Recht der Internationalen Wirtschaft*, 2006, Vol. 11, p. 801-806.

Werlauff 1999
Werlauff, E., 'Using a Foreign Company for Domestic Activities', *European Business Law Review*, 1999, Vol. 10(7/8), p. 306-313.

Westhoff 2006
Westhoff, A.O., 'Die Verbreitung der limited mit Sitz in Deutschland', *GmbH-Rundschau*, 2006, p. 525-528.

Westhoff 2007
Westhoff, A.O., 'Die Verbreitung der englischen Limited mit Verwaltungssitz in Deutschland', *GmbH-Rundschau*, 2007, p. 474-480.

Wymeersch 2000
Wymeersch, E., '*Centros*: A Landmark Decision in European Company Law', in: Baums, T., Hopt, K.J. & Horn, N. (eds.), *Corporations, Capital Markets and Business in the Law: Liber Amicorum Richard M Buxbaum*, Deventer: Kluwer, 2000, p. 629-655.

Xanthaki 2001
Xanthaki, H., '*Centros*: Is This Really the End for the Theory of the Siège Réel?', *Company Lawyer*, 2001, Vol. 22, p. 2-8.

Zimmer & Naendrup 2007
Zimmer, D. & Naendrup, C., 'For Whom the Bell Tolls - Folgen einer Nichtbeachtung englischer Publizitätsgebote durch in Deutschland aktive Limited Companies', *Zeitschrift für Unternehmens- und Gesellschaftsrecht (ZGR)*, 2007, p. 789-818.

Zypries 2004
Zypries, B., Minister of Justice, speech at IHK Gießen-Friedberg, 'Rechtspolitik für Unternehmen und Anleger - Voraussetzung für Innovation und Wachstum', Sommerempfang der IHK Gießen-Friedberg, Karben, 31 August 2004.

S. Rammeloo

CORPORATE MOBILITY IN THE EUROPEAN UNION - AN ANALYSIS OF RINGE'S EMPIRICAL RESEARCH ON THE SUCCESS OF LAW MAKING AND REGULATORY COMPETITION

1. Introduction

Freedom of establishment as enshrined in Articles 49 and 54 TFEU entails the right to set up companies and firms, as may subsidiaries and branches throughout the European Union. Since a number of cases having resulted in preliminary CJEU rulings[1] entrepreneurs in the EU are free to select 'foreign' legal business formats to govern their company affairs. Thus, a legal person may be set up according to the laws of EU Member State A, the company's headquarters (and, usually, the main, or as it may occur, even all economic activities) however being established in EU Member State B (*e.g.* a German business entrepreneur incorporating a UK Ltd., the headquarters of that Ltd. residing in German territory).

Ringe's research concentrates on English company law 'formats', notably the UK private limited liability company (Ltd.), being preferred over German company types ('regulatory competition') by German start-ups over the past decade and the effects of the 'response' thereto by German legislator ('law making'). Ringe starts his empirical research by observing that pursuant to CJEU judicature English limited companies were indeed very popular with German entrepreneurs in the first few years of the last decade but experienced a sharp decline from early 2006 onwards. In his view this temporal fixation casts justified doubts over the so far nevertheless hardly contested claim that the *posterior* German company law reform (November 2008) 'successfully fought off' the use of foreign company forms. He further notices that Austria shows a parallel development - the rise and fall of popularity of foreign, notably English private limited liability companies - quite remarkably a

1 In view of notably inbound migrations of exclusively company headquarters: Case C-212/97, *Centros Ltd v Erhvervs- og Selskabsstyrelsen,* ECR 1999, I-1459; Case C-208/00, *Überseering BV v Nordic Construction Company Baumanagement GmbH,* ECR 2002, I-9919; Case C-167/01, *Kamer van Koophandel en Fabrieken voor Amsterdam v Inspire Art Ltd,* ECR 2003, I-10155.

company law reform in Austria however being absent. Ringe perceives that there must be other, possibly complementary explanations for the paralleled and rather striking developments in both Germany and Austria. His findings are highly intriguing and give rise to a few side comments.

2. Side Comments

As a more or less preliminary remark: any attempt to trace motives underlying businessmen's *preference* to make use of a UK Ltd. rather than of a 'domestic' limited liability company type might be blurred by 'non-rational' and therefore concealed incentives that become known to the outer world on the off-chance only. In the ECJ *Segers* case, for instance, a Dutch businessman still opted for a UK 'Ltd.' to 'impress' the outer world ('fashionable'), as was shown by documents (*e.g.* the Opinion of AG Darmon) underlying this case. This 'incentive' to prefer a foreign business format rather than a Dutch 'BV' (i.e. a *Besloten Vennootschap*: the close corporation nearing the concept of a UK Ltd.) has been substituted since long for more 'rational' arguments, at least legally speaking: The UK Ltd. Has grown popular because of its swift formation procedure, the absence of minimum capital requirements, the high degree of 'institutional' autonomy for company incorporators and, the fact that no employee co-determination at board level is prescribed.

Meanwhile, it may not be overlooked that the use of any 'foreign' company law may further be attractive, not solely for legal but practical reasons, notably because of easy access (language). InAustria for example businessmen from Slovenia tend to take their 'domestic' s.r.o. with them rather than the UK Ltd. 'Explanations' for the *downfall* of the Ltd's popularity in Germany may be of a concealed nature as well. Ringe's empirical search for genuine reasons rather than mere academic allegations is a worthy attempt to explain the downfall of the UK Ltd.'s popularity in Germany. His research refutes legal fallacies, while at the same however provoking some comments.

1. The sharp decline of the UK Ltd's popularity may, if not explained, at least to a certain extent be foreshadowed by the then-upcoming law 2008 law reform (MoMiG), as from 2003 onwards the ECJ judgment in Inspire Art Ltd. caused many critical beholders in 'real seat' oriented EU Member States to advocate legislative defense walls against the 'invasion' of UK Ltds. The fact, however, that even *without* a company law reform Austria experienced a *similar* decline in the UK's popularity implicitly demonstrates the capability of 'domestic' law to 'neutralize' undesired legal effects of the use (or even abuse) of UK Ltds.
   In the interest of those doing business with the company this goal could be achieved by a well-known Private International Law device, namely restricting the scope of the proper law of the company by submitting internal and external liability grounds to the proper law of contract, tort, insolvency, etc. rather than to the proper law of the company (*cf.* further below).
2. 'If less could be more… could more perhaps be less…?' Ringe stresses the importance of the 2008 German MoMiG law reform. But even deregulation

operations have their (unforeseen) price, so it seems. In October 2012 the Netherlands at long last celebrated its own law reform in the area of close corporations ('Flex BV'). With a view to making it as attractive as the UK Ltd. The Dutch legislator firmly reduced mandatory rules for the BV and, simultaneously, introduced the so-called and almost unanimously praised 'off the rack' method of 'default' provisions. Still, from Spring 2013 onwards and as a direct consequence of the 'Flex BV' deregulation operation Dutch private companies tend to complain about *increased* transaction costs and 'choice stress.' What initially was considered to be a highly attractive characteristic of the UK Ltd. appeared to be counter-productive with respect to the Netherlands BV. There is, in other words, a rather strange bias when it comes to comparing the attraction for the business world of a 'deregulated' business format, domestic or 'foreign'.

3. Ringe refers to a study by Becht et al, which analyses *inter alia* the *reasons* for the high number of these foreign companies. The study shows that amongst the main reasons are the substantial differences regarding minimum capital requirements.
   One may well ask why company founders would prefer to set up a UK Ltd. rather than a 'domestic' company type for the reason that the former does not require a minimum incorporation capital. While taking into account that the minimum amount of issued and paid up capital in most legal orders dates back more than four decades and was never adjusted to inflation indexes, one may doubt the weight of that 'burden' to date, in particular where counterparts of the UK Ltd. in the awareness that 'the company doesn't possess money of its own' usually stipulate relief from company managers in private for company transactions (*e.g.* a mortgage on a manager's immovable in private). This device, which is commonly known as 'creditor self-help,' indeed does not altogether take away the privilege of limited liability of shareholders, nor does it create unlimited liability of company managers for all company transactions, but one may well wonder why businessmen do not prefer a relatively modest 'threshold' *e.g.* 18,000 (Netherlands) or even 35,000 EUR (Austria). The popularity of the UK may in other words also decrease because businessmen slowly but increasingly grow aware of the fact that swift formation procedures and the absence of capital requirements are 'compensated' by rights *in personam* as well as *rights in rem* protecting at least some of the company's counterparts.
   A matter closely related to the company's 'own' capital is that of the finance world: as Ringe correctly points out banks may feel reluctant to provide 'foreign' (i.e. non-German) companies with loans.
4. In view of the UK company law deregulation operation, Ringe observes the following: one of the explicit ambitions of the new Companies Act 2006 was to make the UK even more competitive in an ever more globalised and interlinked environment. To be sure, it has not been the objective of the UK lawmakers to actively 'export' their company law to the rest of Europe. Rather, the goal of the 2006 reform was to 'maintain(s) the UK's position as one of the most attractive places in the world to set up and run a business' and 'to promote growth, competitiveness and jobs'. Moreover, the company law reform in the UK started

well before the ECJ handed down its judgment in *Centros*. Nevertheless, the UK seems eager to take up the global challenge and to safeguard its leading position in Europe.

Speaking further about 'transactions costs': even where thanks to the 2006 Companies Act reform the company secretary is no longer a mandatory company officer, the popularity of the UK Ltd. may as well dwell because of the 'annual returns' i.e. the filing of documents at the companies registrar). Non-compliance with UK law may result in awkward situations such as deregistration by the registrar and therefore a loss of legal personality... and of the limited liability regime.

5 In addition to Ringe's research it is important to observe the following. So far, UK Ltds. often appear to be so-called single-member companies: there is just one shareholder (usually the sole founder of the company) who at the same time is also the company's single director. Disputes resulting from the company's internal 'resolution making process' or conflicting interests, etc., are hardly to be expected.

In case of two or more shareholders, however, any internal company dispute related to the resolution making process *cum annexis* would inevitably lead to court proceedings in exclusively the UK. Although so far not adjudicated under the regime of Article 22.2 Regulation 44/2001, which legal instrument is to be replaced January 10, 2015 by Article 24.2 of Regulation 1215/2012 on jurisdiction and recognition and enforcement of judgments in civil and commercial matters the exclusive *forum societatis* (i.e. matters concerning the company's, formation, dissolution and winding up, resolution making process, etc.), even if the company's headquarters and business center would be located in another EU Member State, would appear to be the UK.

6. Last but not least, Germany has shown itself to be fairly capable of handling undesired legal effects of the use of UK Ltds. by (German and foreign) businessmen: the Private International Law device of qualification or characterization, not of the legal relationship as a whole, but of the dispute at stake may justify the submission of liability grounds not under the proper law of the company, but under the proper law of contract law, tort law or insolvency law.

3. Conclusions

The surplus value of Ringe's contribution is that, first, while providing for striking empirical data on regulatory competition in European company law and the impact of national law reforms, it uncovers genuine incentives underlying business world's preference for 'foreign' limited liability company types rather than 'domestic' ones. Ringe unravels alleged explanations that have been put forward by academic writings many times over the past years for the decline in the use of limited liability companies incorporated under foreign (UK) laws. This is being done by comparing two highly equivalently elaborated legal systems, Germany and Austria, the first having amended its company laws for at least the private limited company (GmbH) under the MoMiG 2008), the latter not having amended its company laws. Ringe's observations give rise to some side-comments, as a matter of fact not contesting but rather underscoring the outcome of his research.

PART II

NORM-SETTING AND ENFORCEMENT

V. Mak

PRIVATE ACTORS AS NORM-SETTERS THROUGH CHOICE-OF-LAW: THE LIMITS OF REGULATORY COMPETITION

1. Introduction

This chapter discusses the position of private actors as norm-setters in European private law. It has become increasingly recognized that regulation of private law relationships in Europe is given shape not just through the imposition of rules in a command-and-control structure with the legislator as the ultimate source of rules, but is also often governed by self-regulation by private actors. Such rules are not automatically binding law, yet are often voluntarily adopted by actors in a particular trade or industry. That means that they create a new source of norms outside the traditional framework of state legislation.

Although self-regulation has many advantages - e.g. self-regulation can benefit from expert input by the industry, it offers flexibility, and can be very effective when it stays close to, and plays into the preferences of the actors it seeks to regulate[1] - it also poses challenges. Focusing on the function of self-regulation as a source of law in European private law, at least two aspects stand out. First, self-regulation escapes the 'normal' framework of democratic legitimacy and accountability of lawmakers that applies to state-based law-making. Second, looking at the substantive side of law-making, it is not immediately clear that self-regulation can ensure that fundamental aspects of the regulation of private law relationships in Europe are met, such as legal certainty or consumer protection.[2] The fragmentation of rules across levels of regulation leads to legal uncertainty. Further, consumer protection is under pressure when it is taken outside the reach of formal legislation.

This chapter focuses on the second problem, the proliferation of law-making actors, which creates legal pluralism in European private law. Although it has been

1 *Cf.* Baldwin, Cave & Lodge 2012, p. 139.
2 Both are recognized as core aims of the European market. See e.g. Art. 114 Treaty on the Functioning of the European Union (TFEU).

recognized that legal pluralism in European private law exists, scholarship has not come up with a consistent theoretical framework to approach the issues arising from it.[3] Multilevel regulation has been coined as a term to describe the situation where multiple actors, either public or private, at various levels of regulation engage in activities that will directly or indirectly have legal effects.[4] It provides an analytical tool for understanding the interplay of lawmakers in a multilevel legal order. It does not, however, give guidance on how legal pluralism can be handled so as to ensure legal certainty and consumer protection.

Current strategies for law-making in European private law do grapple with this problem, although none has come up with a conclusive answer. They approach legal pluralism mainly through the lens of harmonization. Top-down harmonization, a strategy adopted by the European legislature, often fails to succeed since it imposes new rules upon legal systems, which in many cases create 'legal irritants' in those systems and as a result are not taken up by the national system in the way that they were envisaged. The most prominent alternative, 'regulatory competition',[5] has also not achieved significant gains in the streamlining of regulatory action between the EU and national legislatures, or self-regulation. In particular, theory and evidence suggest that this strategy is insufficiently attuned to the choices of private (contracting) parties or of legislatures to actually achieve changes in private laws.[6]

The alternative framework through which I seek to approach the problem is that of 'managing' pluralism. Managing pluralism, a term coined by Paul Schiff Berman, denotes a jurisprudence 'that seeks to create or preserve spaces for productive interaction among multiple, overlapping legal systems by developing procedural mechanisms, institutions, and practices that aim to manage, without eliminating, the legal pluralism we see around us'.[7] It can be understood as finding mechanisms that enable coordination or discourse between law-making communities.[8] Berman applies this approach to other areas, but it seems a promising starting point for European private law too. The theory needs elaboration. Even more, before embarking on a search for a new strategy, it is important to establish in which respects existing strategies fall short; or in other words: in which respects improvement is needed. In this chapter, I seek to focus on the weaknesses of the existing strategies, in particular regulatory competition, to identify more clearly in which way they fail and in which respects a new strategy could improve on them.

3 *Cf.* Michaels 2013, p. 139.
4 On the distinction between multilevel governance and multilevel regulation see Chowdhury & Wessel 2012; and below.
5 Reich 1992; Smits 2002.
6 Vogenauer 2013. Although this view is not uncontested. See further below.
7 Schiff Berman 2012.
8 Notably, other than Adieh on whose work he builds, Berman also includes non-state actors in his framework for multilevel regulation.

The chapter is structured as follows. I will first discuss three examples of law-making involving private actors (section 2). This short exposé is meant to illustrate the ways in which private actors are involved in law-making and the nature of their involvement. After this introduction, I will seek to identify how law-making by private actors should be positioned within the concept of multilevel regulation (section 3), before considering in more detail why 'regulatory competition' - an existing strategy that would seem to include private actors in norm-setting - fall short of giving voice to normative choices made by private actors (section 4). The chapter wraps up with a brief conclusion (section 5).

2. Private Actors - Three Degrees of Interaction in Law-making

Looking at existing examples of law-making by private actors, broadly speaking three degrees of interaction with other regulators can be observed. They are, on a continuum starting with the highest content of actual regulation and ending with the lowest: co-regulation, self-regulation, and the 'regulatory function' of consumers. I will discuss them with some examples for illustration. It should be noted that in many cases private and public elements blur into one another, and that the grouping into categories is therefore mostly meant to give a schematic overview, rather than a more detailed analysis.[9]

2.1. *Co-regulation*

In various sectors of industry or commerce, regulation has become hybrid: it is given shape by public actors, including legislators as well as agents who have been assigned certain regulatory or enforcement powers, and by private actors. Instances where the legislative framework is provided by the EU or the national legislature, with specific details to be filled in by private actors, can be described as co-regulation.[10]

Examples of co-regulation are found in various sectors and in various legal systems. One of the most topical areas is financial regulation. Australia has adopted a regime by which the supervisory authority, the Australia Securities and Investments Commission (ASIC), requests the industry to propose rules for designated areas and gives formal approval to rules so developed. This could be regarded as co-regulation.[11]

In Dutch law, an example is provided by the regulation of mortgage credit. The original regulation for mortgage credit actually emerged in self-regulation, which shows that co-regulation can also come into being in a bottom-up manner rather than imposed by legislation.[12]

9 For such an analysis, see e.g. Cafaggi 2015.
10 Senden 2005, available at: <www.ejcl.org/91/art91-3.PDF>.
11 Williams & Conley 2014, p. 122-123.
12 See Mak (forthcoming).

These examples may not be representative for the entire field, however. Although they require the participation of private actors, it should be noted that many instances of co-regulation are in fact manifestations of top-down legislation. The legislature prescribes what needs to be done and the role of private actors is limited to filling in the details of this action. Further, even if examples of co-regulation exist, they are usually limited to very specific areas and in that sense not representative for the approach chosen by a legislator (or other regulatory body).

2.2. *Self-regulation*

Self-regulation has existed from the time that trade and commerce started to increase and specialisations became more common. Perhaps the earliest examples are the medieval guilds, which prescribed for different groups of traders or craftsmen – such as bakers, tailors, knife-makers, locksmiths, shoemakers – what rules they should adhere to if they wanted to be part of that community.[13]

More recent examples of self-regulation are sometimes not too far away from this medieval origin. For instance, regulation of professions still occurs often through self-regulation, in particular for so-called 'regulated' professions, i.e. professions for which one needs to have obtained a particular (national) qualification in order to have access to them. Examples of such, in the Netherlands but also in other European countries, are lawyers, doctors, accountants, architects, bailiffs, notaries, and tax advisers.[14]

Other cases of self-regulation can be encountered in the field of corporate governance. With the realization that corporations should take some responsibility for social or environmental issues, or the protection of human rights, companies are more and more seeking to introduce rules that can structure such 'corporate social responsibility'. To provide some guidance for these processes, a set of principles has been developed by John Ruggie as Special Representative of the UN, which were published as the 'UN Guiding Principles for Business and Human Rights'.[15] Although it is possible to translate some CSR duties into legal obligations, much of the field is still given shape through self-regulation or (within a business or group of companies) through corporate governance.[16]

2.3. *The 'Regulatory Function' of Consumers*

More recently, an image has emerged of the consumer as a regulatory actor of some sort. Chris Hodges identifies three aspects that indicate a change in market

13 See for a brief historical overview Cafaggi 2015, p. 108-113.

14 A database exists at EU level that lists regulated professions per Member State: <http://ec.europa.eu/internal_market/qualifications/regprof/index.cfm?action=regprofs>.

15 For the full text of the Principles, plus comments, see <www.business-humanrights.org/UNGuidingPrinciplesPortal/Home>.

16 *Cf.* Lambooy 2010; also available at: <https://openaccess.leidenuniv.nl/handle/1887/-16169>.

regulation, supporting the idea that the consumer can be regarded as an actor regulating market behaviour.[17] First, there seems to be a growing awareness that behavioural effects can be achieved by actors other than public enforcement bodies. Second, Europe is working towards a pan-European system for alternative dispute resolution in consumer cases (ADR or CDR) which, if it is achieved, will cover all business sectors. Thirdly, and perhaps most significantly, through these processes the aggregation of data from a wide range of consumer disputes becomes possible, which can provide a feedback loop to consumers as well as to the industry. They can accordingly decide to adjust their behavioural choices. The system in this way provides its own quality control.[18]

Although this type of market regulation is not, as yet, governed by actual regulation in the form of legislation or 'soft law' instruments, it is an important new influence on the behaviour of market actors. What it implies is that consumers could, like more established regulators, have an effect on the behaviour of other actors - in particular businesses.

Strictly speaking, this form of regulation therefore does not count as law-making. However, seeing that it targets the behaviour of private actors and may have an influence on that behaviour, it warrants mention as a potentially new source of norms deriving from private actors, besides the aforementioned co-regulation and self-regulation. Further, it may well be that regulation is at some point introduced to regulate consumer feedback - e.g. where it is untrue or harmful to businesses - or to regulate the way in which businesses deal with consumer feedback. Practice shows, for example, that some businesses manipulate consumer reviews on their websites in order to project a more positive image of their product.

3. Legal Pluralism and Private Actors

The input from private actors in regulation can be considered an additional source of law besides state-based legislation and case law. It is important to take stock of its position besides other sources of law to get a grasp on how it fits with strategies for law-making in European private law under consideration in this chapter.

The problem with rules made by private actors - I will for the sake of brevity refer to 'self-regulation' even where one could also include co-regulation - is in fact twofold. First, it cannot be fit into traditional categories or sources of 'law'. This problem applies to the international as well as to national examples of self-regulation. Self-regulation after all is a phenomenon that can escape (legal) boundaries. Industries can seek to regulate themselves 'globally' if their activities take place in multiple countries. An example, besides the ones already mentioned in the previous part, is self-regulation of data protection through Binding Corporate Rules.[19] Notwithstanding the continued growth of the global dimension of trade

17 Hodges 2014. Forthcoming in Leczykiewicz & Weatherill 2016.

18 Hodges 2014, p. 2.

19 Moerel 2012.

and industry, self-regulation can also occur locally, *e.g.* introduction of codes of conduct for national branches of trade or even regional. At both the national and the international level, however, it is doubtful whether it can be considered a source of 'law'. That is problematic since self-regulation is not legally binding, or at least not in most cases. Often, a state-regulator is necessary to enforce rules of self-regulation.[20]

Second, when we look at strategies to manage legal pluralism in European private law - or in other words: strategies for multilevel regulation - it can be seen that self-regulation is not taken into account. The strategy of top-down harmonization of laws only applies to legislation or regulation originating from the state or from governmental agents. The alternative, regulatory competition, in its current definition also does not take account of self-regulation. Like the top-down strategy, it only encompasses rules which are considered legally binding. There may however still be a possibility to expand the theory of regulatory competition also to include private actors if one broadens the notion of law-making that is uses.

I will elaborate on both points before, in section 4 of the chapter, considering wider critiques on the strategy of regulatory competition.

3.1. *Self-regulation as a Source of Law*

It is conventional knowledge that sources of law in most legal systems can be divided into a number of categories which, although there may be some variation between legal systems as to which sources are recognized and which value they are given, share commonalities. They would include a range of the following: (i) international Treaties and Conventions; (ii) legislation or statute law; (iii) documents preceding legislation or *travaux préparatoires*; (iv) case law, in common law systems given additional force through a doctrine of precedent; (v) customary law; (vi) general principles of law; and (vii) legal scholarship.[21]

Some variation exists. Common law systems for example place greater emphasis on case law as a source of legal development whereas, generally speaking, in civil law systems legislation is the primary source of law. That distinction is however not entirely clear-cut as common law systems have gradually introduced more and more statutory law and civil law systems often leave significant room for development of legal doctrines in the case law.[22] A further distinction is that statutory interpretation in common law systems takes a more narrow approach than in civil law systems. Preparatory works can only in very limited circumstances be

20 Brummer 2011.

21 See e.g. Art. 38 of the Statute of the International Court of Justice (ICJ) with regard to sources of international law.

22 For an example, see the Dutch rules on liability for road accidents. The apportioning of liability between drivers and non-drivers who are hurt in a road accident on the basis of Art. 6:101 of the Dutch Civil Code has been fleshed out in detail in a number of cases. In relation to children under 14 who are injured in such an accident, see HR 1 June 1990, NJ 1991, 720 (Ingrid Kolkman) and HR 31 Mai 1991, NJ 1991, 721 (Marbeth van Uitregt).

considered in the interpretation of statutes, whereas in civil law systems no restrictions apply to the consultation of the *travaux préparatoires* for the purpose of establishing the intent of the legislator.[23] Finally, legal scholarship has traditionally had a more limited role in English law than it has in, for example, German or French law.[24]

Self-regulation stands apart from these sources of law because it is - mostly - not regarded as binding law. In many instances, in order to enforce rules based on self-regulation, one needs to fall back on state law.[25] Rules created by private actors in those instances will only be enforced if the applicable national law prescribes that they should be enforced, for example as part of contract law or as trade custom or usage. It is not uncommon, for example, that rules developed by traders in a particular industry are regarded as (binding) trade usage, provided that the rules are widely known and widely observed in that particular trade. Effect is given to such usage in many national laws, as well as in some transnational sets of rules, such as the Vienna Convention on Contracts for the International Sale of Goods (CISG)[26] or the Common European Sales Law (CESL).[27]

Only in a limited respect is it possible to enforce rules of self-regulation without state intervention, for example where parties opt for arbitration. Even if arbitration in the final instance also comes down to a state system, either because recognition and execution of an arbitral decision requires state cooperation or because an arbitral decision is challenged before a national court, the decision itself can be self-standing where parties voluntarily subscribe to it and execute it. Court intervention, moreover, is limited for arbitral decisions.

In most cases, therefore, a party needs the backup of state law to enforce rules made through self-regulation. That can be a weak point of self-regulation in comparison to public regulation. I will not explore this weakness, nor the interplay between regulation and self-regulation in more detail in this chapter.[28] A more relevant issue is what the consequences are for the role of private actors in strategies for law-making in European private law.

3.2. *Private Actors and Strategies for Law-making in European Private Law*

The role of private actors in law-making in European private law seems to be restricted if we take account only of rules that are considered as 'law', i.e. rules that are legally binding. I will discuss the two most prominent strategies for law-making

23 Compare for English law *Pepper v Hart* [1992] UKHL 3; [1992] 3 WLR 1032; [1993] 1 All ER 42.

24 But see Braun 2006, who notes that English judges are increasingly referring to scholarship in their judgments.

25 Brummer 2011.

26 Art. 9 CISG.

27 The CESL has been adopted by the European Parliament and now awaits approval by the Council before it becomes law. Art. 67 of the CESL stipulates the requirements for trade usage to be used as a source for the interpretation of contracts.

28 For an analysis in a specific context see e.g. Pavillon 2012.

in European private law, top-down legislation and regulatory competition, to illustrate this limitation. Regulatory competition, however, could be re-defined so as to include private actors. I will explore this possibility briefly as an introduction to section 4.

First, top-down legislation. It seems quite natural that the role of private actors in this context is limited. As shown by the examples in section 1, co-regulation would be the only category of real involvement. Otherwise, law-making is the prerogative of the - democratically chosen - legislature.

Regulatory competition also does not include law-making by private actors, at least not directly. The theory of regulatory competition predicts that competition between laws can persuade state legislatures to adapt their laws to better fit the needs of the market. Whether such competition actually takes place and whether it leads to adaptation of laws is a hotly contested question in particular in contract law, as reflected in a recent debate between Rühl and Vogenauer.[29] I will discuss that question in section 4. With regard to private actors, it is important to note that the theory, as it is currently defined, only covers competition between binding laws that have been promulgated by state lawmakers. Self-regulation is not included as a source of law that takes part in the competition of rules.

Notwithstanding, private actors do have an indirect role as lawmakers in the 'law market' envisaged by regulatory competition. The first step in the process, namely, is that private parties make a choice of law.[30] Competition ensues when more parties start choosing laws of other countries as the applicable law to their contract. Private actors, representing the demand side of the market, therefore provide an essential element of the law market idea.

A more direct role may also be possible in limited circumstances. Since regulatory competition is concerned only with adaptations of binding law in response to market forces, it can only include law-making by private actors to the extent that it has an effect on binding legislation. Circumstances in which this can occur are for example where co-regulation - by which private parties create norms that are meant to fill in 'open' parts of state regulation - is converted into binding legislation. That can happen in cases where the state wishes to pull certain areas of regulation closer towards it, either because of an actual or a perceived failure of self-regulation or because of a change of policy, *e.g.* post-crisis. A recent example in Dutch law is the replacement of certain rules of self-regulation in the mortgage credit market by state regulation, which for the most part copied the initial rules.[31] In this way, law-making by private actors is still taken on board as a source of law in regulatory competition.

However, this remains a weak type of inclusion. One could also argue that is does not do justice to the role of self-regulation as a source of norms or rules besides

[29] See below, section 4.

[30] *Cf.* Rühl 2013.

[31] Temporary Rules on Mortgage Credit; Netherlands Government Gazette 2012, No. 26433. For amendments to these rules as of 1 January 2014, see *Parliamentary Papers II* 2013/14, 32847, No. 98.

other types of regulation. Whereas legally the nature of self-regulation is different from public regulation - i.e. it is voluntary in nature and not by default binding on parties - many private actors in practice often do not perceive this difference. To a business, rules are rules.[32] The duty of compliance officers in a firm is to ensure that rules are complied with and for them all rules, whether originating in legislation or in self-regulation, require monitoring. Thus, the distinction between binding and non-binding rules becomes blurred. Competition of rules could therefore in theory also include rules of self-regulation. Situations in which this may occur are where businesses have the option to sign up to a code of conduct for a particular branch (*e.g.* the codes of practice of the International Labour Organization (ILO)).[33]

Still, in many views this character of self-regulation in practice does not make it part of an official legal system. State regulation is still the primary source for the regulation of private law relationships. It is appropriate, therefore, to consider the possibilities for streamlining legal pluralism in European private law first from the perspective of current regulation. Out of the two strategies mentioned, the one that might give some space to private actors as norm-setters is regulatory competition between private laws. For the purpose of this discussion, I will focus on regulatory competition in contract law, taking into account also the applicable rules of private international law that define the limits for choice of law.

4. A Critique of Regulatory Competition in European Contract Law

Regulatory competition is based on the economic theory of jurisdictional competition, which goes back to Charlies Tiebout.[34] Fitting the economic model of a market, it assumes that law can be viewed as a product created by states - the supply side - and chosen by private actors - the demand side. The theory of regulatory competition, therefore predicts that under the right conditions a 'law market' can operate in which lawmakers compete for their law to be chosen by private actors. In recent years, the theory has gained support amongst legal scholars.[35]

Interestingly, it is largely unknown whether regulatory competition works in practice. Although some evidence exists that suggest a competitive regulatory effect in corporate law,[36] the practical application of the theory in other areas of private law, such as contract law, has not been established. In contract law, in fact, a recent debate in legal scholarship illustrates that the viewpoints on regulatory competition can be at opposite ends of the spectrum. Rühl has made a fervent argument in favour of regulatory competition in European contract law,[37] whereas Vogenauer

32 Self-regulation therefore is subject to some concerns that are similarly encountered with public regulation, such as compliance problems.
33 See <www.ilo.org/safework/info/standards-and-instruments/codes/lang--en/index.htm>.
34 Tiebout 1956; and see Rühl 2013, p. 64 and sources there cited.
35 See e.g. O'Hara & Ribstein 2009; Eidenmüller 2009; Eidenmüller 2011, p. 716–719; Smits 2010.
36 Though that effect may be limited; compare Bratton, McCahery & Vermeulen 2009, p. 385.
37 Rühl 2013.

proposes that there is little support for it on the basis of theory and empirical evidence.[38] Somewhat puzzling, with regard to empirical evidence, both authors rely largely on the same data – yet they arrive at different outcomes.

How to assess these two contrasting viewpoints? In my view, the arguments against regulatory competition are somewhat more persuasive, realizing however that much depends on the interpretation given to the empirical data that are available. It is worthwhile to also assess the arguments that both authors put forward from a broader perspective, including theoretical arguments concerning regulatory competition. Even if regulatory competition is not happening now or has not happened, the theory may help predict whether the concept does contains a basis for success in the future of European contract law.

As a prelude to the theoretical and empirical arguments, I recall briefly the main stages (or assumptions) that make up the theory of regulatory competition.[39] First, private parties are assumed to choose, within the limitations imposed by rules of private international law, the rules of private law that best fit their contract. Second, from this context, a process of competition between legal rules arises. Third, from this process the most favoured rule for a particular situation becomes clear. Fourth, countries have an interest in having their laws chosen as the 'applicable law' to a contract, for example because it creates income for the legal sector in their country.[40] Fifth, because of this interest in having their law chosen, countries will adapt their laws and seek to enhance their competitive advantage. Sixth, to increase the competitive advantage of their legal system, legislators will adopt the rule that has come up as 'most favoured' through the process of competition between rules. As a final step, this process of regulatory competition should lead to spontaneous harmonisation – i.e. not steered by the European legislature – of European private law.

Another (final) step identified by Rühl is that the outcome of successful regulatory competition would be that the law adapted in response to competition is chosen more often after the reform than it was before.[41] Although that would indeed be an acknowledgment that the 'best' rule had come up through the process of competition, it is in my view not a required step for proving that regulatory competition has taken place. The fact that legislators adopt the most favoured rule should be adequate proof that they have responded to the preferences of business and consumers in relation to contract law. To require additional evidence showing that the amended law is chosen more often than the old rules were before would perhaps only be useful in situations where it cannot be determined that the legislator's introduction of new rules was in response to regulatory competition, but nonetheless may have been. Unfortunately, very little data are available to support the occurrence of either situation in practice.

38 Vogenauer 2013.
39 See also Chirico & Larouche 2008, p. 487 *et seq.*
40 *Cf.* Vogenauer 2013.
41 Rühl 2013, n. 89.

4.1. *Regulatory Competition: Theoretical Arguments*

Theoretical arguments may provide ground to predict whether regulatory competition is likely to occur or not. Whereas the discussion between Vogenauer and Rühl deals only with business-to-business (B2B) contracts, for European private law it is important also to consider business-to-consumer (B2C) contracts. These (quantitatively) make up a large part of contracting in the EU and, moreover, they are the subject of the majority of EU legislative instruments in European contract law. I will discuss both in turn.

4.1.1. Business-to-business Contracts

From a theoretical perspective, regulatory competition faces challenges on the demand as well as on the supply side. I will here focus on the demand side since the main theoretical arguments seem to concentrate here. On the supply side, the political responses from legislators and the so-called 'battle of the brochures' seem to indicate that there is a willingness to consider regulatory competition in contract law.[42]

With regard to the demand side, an often heard statement is that contracting parties' choice of law reflects a 'homeward trend', meaning that parties are inclined to choose the law with which they are most familiar, i.e. the law of their own country.[43] That argument seems persuasive since many academics concede that the main prerequisites for regulatory competition on the demand side - full information on the quality of the available laws which is accessible at low cost - are often impaired.[44]

Interestingly, Rühl challenges this presumption. Her argument is that (i) even if not all, some contracting parties do consider the quality of the chosen law and (ii) for regulatory competition to work it is not required that *all* businesses and consumers engage in choice of law but it is sufficient that 'a substantial number of businesses and consumers respond to differences in legal rules on the basis of their quality'.[45] From the perspective of competition, that seems a valid way of reasoning. It has been suggested in other contexts that competition - with an eye to innovation - can sufficiently take place if a small number of top-players in the market engage in choice.[46]

The real problem then is to determine whether contracting parties make competitive choices on the basis of the *quality* of contract laws. That is eventually an empirical question (on which see part 4b below). In terms of predicting whether

42 Vogenauer 2013, p. 30 *et seq.*; Rühl 2013, p. 74 *et seq.*

43 And references in Rühl 2013, n. 14 and 18.

44 See for example Bratton, McCahery & Vermeulen 2009.

45 Rühl 2013, p. 68.

46 *Cf.* the 'informed minority' argument attributed to Alan Schwartz and Louis Wilde. See Schwartz & Wilde 1983 and Schwartz & Wilde 1985.

competition will happen it is nevertheless noteworthy that theory here suggests that parties do not decide on the basis of quality.

On the demand side, two problems emerge: homogeneity of preferences and lack of information.[47] The first point addresses the core nature of contracting. When parties negotiate to conclude a contract they basically seek to align their preferences in order to reach agreement. In most cases, this requires both parties to give or take a little. In terms of choice of law, this means that businesses will normally be interested in regimes that offer the greatest freedom to limit or exclude potential liability. Consumers, on the other hand, rationally would seek to pick a regime that is the most effective with regard to policing the limitation and exclusion of liability in contract law. In order to reach agreement, Vogenauer suggests, the compromise solution in theory should be somewhere in the middle.[48] A party will only be able to impose individual preferences if it has superior bargaining power.[49]

Second, regulatory competition can be hampered by a lack of information on the part of businesses and consumers at the moment of contracting. The parties will at this point be looking for a law that best suits their interests. However, it is virtually impossible - and also very costly - to obtain a full overview of all available laws that may be chosen as the applicable law to the contract. Further, parties' preferences may change over time and the law chosen at the time of contracting may therefore not be the most advantageous option for a dispute that arises at a later time.

Effectively, because of these problems, the choice of law that results will often not be the law that best fits the needs of the contracting parties in terms of quality. If quality is considered at all, then often in a superficial manner. Economic theory supports the idea that, rationally, parties with limited information or 'bounded rationality' seek to find a solution that enables them to choose at the lowest possible cost. Instead of aiming to find the most efficient law for their transaction, it has been suggested that parties operate on the basis of a 'hypothetical consensus test' advocated by the new institutional economics approach.[50] The question would then be whether the parties would be able to hypothetically agree on a solution whilst operating behind a Rawlsian 'veil of ignorance', i.e. without knowing whether under the chosen regime they would come out as winners or losers.[51]

Parties that make a choice of law on the basis of this hypothesis are likely to take into account the quality of their chosen law, however not on the basis of an actual analysis - which would be too costly - but on the basis of the *perceived* quality of the law. That may result in the choice for a neutral law that is often chosen in the trade or sector within which the parties operate.[52] Also, many contracting parties will be inclined to choose the law with which they are most familiar. That will in

47 Vogenauer 2013, p. 19-26.
48 *Ibid.*, p. 19.
49 *Ibid.*
50 *Ibid.*, p. 23.
51 Kirchner 2006, p. 39-41, 46 and 49-50; Rawls 1999.
52 Vogenauer 2013, p. 24-25.

most cases be the law of their own country, with the result that a 'homeward trend' can be observed in choice of law.

From a theoretical perspective, the predictions for successful regulatory competition in contract law therefore seem shaky. Rühl's suggestion is that, whilst these theoretical arguments may hold true for a large number of contracting parties, still a significant number of actors do make their choice of law on the basis of the actual quality of the available contract laws.[53] In theory, that could of course be true for the bigger market players with sufficient resources to research their legal options and with sufficient bargaining power to impose their choice on the other party.[54] Whether it is supported by empirical evidence is another question, to which I will come back in part 4b.

4.1.2. Consumer Contracts

For consumer contracts, we can add another line of argumentation. In these types of contracts, as with B2B contracts, parties are largely free to determine the content of the agreement and to determine which default rules apply through a choice of law. The main difference, of course, is that there are restrictions on this freedom. Consumer contract laws contain many mandatory rules aiming to empower consumers, *e.g.* through imposing information duties on traders, or to protect them against unfair terms or unsafe products.[55] Generally, traders cannot contract out of such duties or, if they do wish to diverge from the provisions laid down by law, they can only do so if it is not to the detriment of the consumer.[56]

A factor to take into account, further, is that the degree of consumer protection in contract law varies between systems. In many Western legal systems, the legislature will be hesitant to introduce regulation since intervention in contract law interferes with the functioning of a free market. The introduction of rules to protect consumers can be viewed as paternalistic.[57] Although in-between forms of regulation have become more popular – think for example of Sunstein and Thaler's theory of 'nudging' or 'libertarian paternalism' which seeks to offer an alternative somewhere between empowerment and hard paternalism[58] – the balance between freedom of contract and regulatory intervention is still often a hard one to strike, not least because the costs and benefits of consumer protection laws are often not easily determined.[59] In the EU, even if the TFEU and now also the Charter of Fundamental Rights prescribe that laws should pursue a 'high level of consumer

53 Rühl 2013, p. 68.
54 See Vogenauer 2013.
55 For the EU, see Council Directive 93/13/EEC of 5 April 1993 on unfair terms in consumer contracts, *OJ* 1993, L95/29; Council Directive 85/374/EEC on liability for defective products, *OJ* 1985, L210/29.
56 Compare Art. 7:6 Dutch Civil Code.
57 For an analysis, see Ogus 2010.
58 Thaler & Sunstein 2008; Sunstein & Thaler 2003, p. 1162.
59 *Cf.* O'Hara & Ribstein 2009, p. 134.

protection', the majority of current legislation allows Member States significant freedom in determining the exact level of protection in their national private laws. Most Directives are aimed at minimum harmonization, which allows Member States to give more protection in their national laws than prescribed by the Directive ('gold-plating'). Even if the Commission's practice with recent Directives has been to push towards full harmonization, the scope of this legislation is still very limited. The debate preceding the introduction of the Consumer Rights Directive - resulting in a very much toned-down version of full harmonization - illustrates that it is in fact very hard to achieve one level of consumer protection throughout the EU. Leaving aside whether it would be desirable to achieve a uniform level of protection, or whether it would be feasible in the light of political, socio-economic and cultural differences between the Member States, the divergence of levels of consumer protection between national contract laws must be taken as a given.

What this means for regulatory competition in consumer contract law is that competition, at least in theory, is possible. Parties can make a choice of law in favour of a system where they perceive the level of protection to be appropriate. In practice, such a choice will of course mostly be made by the trader rather than by the consumer.

The theoretical argument, however, is weakened by the fact that choice of law options are often limited for consumer contracts. EU rules of private international law, laid down in the Rome I Regulation, allow a choice of law but also add that the consumer remains entitled to the protection that he has under the law of the country where he has his habitual residence.[60] Moreover, EU legislation in the field of consumer law is more and more opting for a degree of full harmonization, which means that rules will be the same throughout Europe, at least within the scope of the respective Directives.[61]

The limitations to choice following from national laws or EU legislation can be regarded as answers to concerns that would arise if consumer protection was left entirely to the mechanism of the market. One could envisage for example a race-to-the-bottom scenario since traders have an incentive to opt for system with lowest level of consumer protection. Private international law rules of consumer protection can prevent this, and perhaps also future legislative initiatives at EU level (such as the CESL).

4.2. *Regulatory Competition: Empirical Evidence*

Does regulatory competition happen in European contract law? There are two points to consider in this respect. First, whether contracting parties' choices of law are made on the basis of the actual quality of the available contract laws. Only in

60 Rome I Regulation, Art. 6(2).

61 See e.g. Directive 2011/83/EU on consumer rights, *OJ* 2011, L304/64; Directive 2008/48/EC on credit agreements for consumers, *OJ* 2008, L133/66; Directive 2005/29 concerning unfair business-to-consumer commercial practices in the internal market, *OJ* 2005, L149/22.

that case can a competition of rules ensue that brings out the most efficient rule. Second, legislators should respond to the choices of law made in practice by adapting their laws to attract more parties to their contract laws.

With regard to the first point, evidence suggests that quality does play a role in the choice of contract law. However, what role that is, and how big that role is, is open to debate. Both Vogenauer and Rühl discuss data obtained from surveys of businesses in relation to their contracting practices. Those surveys are very diverse in geographical scope and methodology. They nevertheless indicate - as a first step - that choice of law in contracting does take place.[62]

Whether choice of law takes place on the basis of quality is another question. Looking at a number of surveys on contract law, Rühl deduces that quality does play a role in the choices that contracting parties make. In her overview:[63]

- Vogenauer and Weatherill (2005): asked businesses what characteristics of a contract law influenced their choice. 87 percent replied that the extent to which the law enabled trade was a driving factor, 79 percent pointed to predictability, 78 percent to fairness and 66 to flexibility of the contract law in question.
- Vogenauer and Hodges (2008): asked businesses which factors they took into account when choosing the governing contract law and allowed businesses to choose from a list of non-legal factors like language, procedural factors like the availability of certain dispute resolution schemes, and qualitative factors like fairness and predictability of outcomes as well as the quality of the contract law as such. Most of the respondents pointed to qualitative factors, notably the quality of the contract law as such.
- Study of the English Law Society (2010): asked what factors influenced a choice of law; 56 percent of the law firms pointed to the 'attractiveness of legal principles' and 57 percent to 'the ease of use of the legal system'.
- Study conducted by the Queen Mary International School of Arbitration (2010): found that the 'appropriateness of the law for the type of contract' mattered for 60 percent of the businesses.

62 See Vogenauer & Weatherill 2006, p. 105; Voigt 2008; Vogenauer (forthcoming 2016), Ch. 1, the same results also available at: <www.law.ox.ac.uk/themes/iecl/pdfs/-Oxford%20Civil%20Justice%20Survey%20-%20Summary%20of%20Results,%20Final.pdf>.

63 Rühl 2013, p. 71; with reference to the studies conducted by Vogenauer and Weatherill and by Vogenauer and Hodges mentioned in the previous footnote. Rühl also refers to The English Law Society, Firm's Cross-Border Work (2010), available at: <http://ec.europa.eu/justice/news/consulting_public/0052/contributions/224_en.pdf>; and Queen Mary International School of Arbitration, 2010 International Arbitration Survey: Choices in International Arbitration (2010), available at: <www.arbitration.qmul.ac.-uk/research/2010/index.html>.

Quality is of course a relative concept. Furthermore, broad questions regarding the 'flexibility' of a contract law or 'the ease of use of the legal system' may not be the most persuasive factors to indicate that choices are made on the basis of substantive differences in (the quality of) contract laws. Notwithstanding such considerations, one could accept on the basis of these studies that the characteristics of contract laws do – at least for some contracting parties – play a role in the choice of contract law. Even if, as Vogenauer emphasizes on the basis of the Clifford Chance study, only a limited number of contracting parties opt for a law other than the contract law of their country, that would not take away the fact that there is evidence of choice. Recognizing Rühl's point that regulatory competition does not require all businesses and consumers to engage in choice of law but only a sufficient number,[64] we may have the evidence here to support that competition is occurring. What number counts as 'sufficient' of course remains open to debate.

The second element is more problematic. It is not immediately clear from the available data that legislators have adapted their contract laws in response to competition between contract laws in practice. It is true that many contract laws in Europe have seen reform in the last 20 years. Examples are Germany, the Netherlands, and a number of the EU's newer Member States (Estonia, Hungary, Lithuania, Poland and Romania).[65] Whether these adaptations were in response to choices of law in practice, or whether they incorporated rules or approaches that had been favoured in practice, can however not be deduced from the available data.

The most convincing evidence that international competition played at least a part in the legislator's reform of contract law can be seen in the German *Schuldrechtsreform* of 2002. The parliamentary documents indicate that the reform – and its wide scope, going far beyond what was necessary to implement Directive 99/44 on consumer sales – was partly instigated by concerns raised by other countries that German contract law was outdated. Also, the wish to be at the forefront of new legislative initiatives in European contract law (such as the CESL) was a key consideration of the German legislator.[66] Those considerations indicate that international competition of rules was at least a factor in the German law reform process. Further texts explore in more detail the rules that were subject to this review.[67] However, whether this makes the German reform of contract law an example of regulatory competition is not that easy to answer. The main concern of the legislator appears to have been that the law (dating from 1900) was brought up to date with modern practice. Moreover, the ambition to be at the forefront of EU legislative action appears to be a political motivation, presumably with the aim to influence EU contract law in a direction that would be close to national German law, that has little to do with the preferences of parties in contracting practice. Had the legislator wanted to adapt the law in response to these preferences, it would

64 See above.

65 Rühl 2013, p. 77.

66 See Deutscher Bundestag 11 October 2001, Plenarprotokoll 14/192, 18758; Däubler-Gmelin 2001.

67 E.g. Ziegler & Rieder 2001; Zimmermann 2005.

have made more sense to seek to take up some of the characteristics of the most popular choices for non-home state law: Swiss or English law.[68]

In sum, it is not immediately obvious who is 'right' in this debate. I would assess Vogenauer's argumentation as stronger since one of the key elements to support that regulatory competition *has* in fact happened or *is* happening, namely the requirement that legislators adapt their laws to give them a competitive advantage, cannot with such precision be read from the parliamentary documents accompanying recent reforms of contract law. If any mention of 'marketability' of national private laws is made at all, the parliamentary documents normally do not link it expressly to an improvement of the quality of the law in comparison to other systems. Even where reference is made to an improvement of laws to make them 'fit for Europe' - an argument to which Rühl attaches much weight - that in my mind does not mean that national legislatures are working to make their laws of 'better' quality in comparison to other national laws. It only indicates that they are adapting their laws to comply with the requirements of European legislation. Sometimes legislatures take even further steps in this direction by extending European legislation to areas for which harmonization is not prescribed. That, however, is not regulatory competition.

5. Conclusion

The outlines of law-making strategies in European private law in which private actors are included have until now only barely been sketched. This chapter makes an attempt at defining the scope for law-making by private actors in relation to other law-making actors in a multilevel regulatory framework. Having focused mainly on regulatory competition, it can be seen that both the theory and the evidence on whether it is occurring in European contract law are debatable.

The real challenge is to find a way to 'manage pluralism' in European private law that can ensure fundamental goals such as legal certainty and consumer protection. Top-down legislation has drawbacks because it often creates legal irritants in national systems. Spontaneous harmonization through regulatory competition, as can be gleaned from the discussion in this chapter, may not happen if legislators do not adapt their laws in response to choices of law made by private actors. Until now, there is very little evidence that this occurs.

It is therefore time to look for new strategies to manage pluralism in European private law. My hope is that this chapter can at least serve to make more clear which challenges will need to be addressed.

68 Swiss and English law come out as popular choices in several of the empirical studies; see Vogenauer 2013, p. 36 *et seq*.

Bibliography

Baldwin, Cave & Lodge 2012
Baldwin, R., Cave, M. & Lodge, M., *Understanding Regulation: Theory, Strategy, and Practice,* Oxford: Oxford University Press, 2012.

Bratton, McCahery & Vermeulen 2009
Bratton, W.W., McCahery, J.A. & Vermeulen, E.P.M., 'How Does Corporate Mobility Affect Lawmaking? A Comparative Analysis', *American Journal of Comparative Law,* 2009, Vol. 57, p. 347-385.

Braun 2006
Braun, A., 'Professors and Judges in Italy: it Takes Two to Tango', *Oxford Journal of Legal Studies,* 2006, Vol. 26(4), p. 665-681.

Brummer 2011
Brummer, C., *Soft Law and the Global Financial System. Rule Making in the 21st Century,* Cambridge: Cambridge University Press, 2011.

Cafaggi 2015
Cafaggi, F., 'The Many Features of Transnational Private Rulemaking: Unexplored Relationships between Custom, Jura Mercatorum and Global Private Regulation', *University of Pennsylvania Journal of International Law,* 2015, Vol. 36(4), p. 101-159.

Chirico & Larouche 2008
Chirico, F. & Larouche, P., 'Conceptual Divergence, Functionalism and the Economics of Convergence', in: Prechal, S. & Van Roermund, B. (eds.), *The Coherence of EU Law: The Search for Unity in Divergent Concepts,* Oxford: Oxford University Press, 2008, p. 463-493.

Chowdhury & Wessel 2012
Chowdhury, N. & Wessel, R.A., 'Conceptualising Multilevel Regulation in the EU: A Legal Translation of Multilevel Governance', *European Law Journal,* 2012, Vol. 18(3), p. 335-357.

Dáubler-Gmelin 2001
Dáubler-Gmelin, H., 'Die Entscheidung für die so genannte Große Lösung bei der Schuldrechtsreform Zum Entwurf Eines Gesetzes zur Modernisierung des Schuldrechts', *NJW,* 2001, p. 2281-2289.

Eidenmüller 2009
Eidenmüller, H., 'Recht als Produkt', *JuristenZeitung,* 2009, Vol. 64, p. 641-653.

Eidenmüller 2011
Eidenmüller, H., 'The Transnational Law Market, Regulatory Competition, and Transnational Corporations', *Indiana Journal of Global Legal Studies,* 2011, Vol. 28(2), p. 707-749.

Hodges 2014
Hodges, C., 'The Consumer as Regulator', paper presented at the conference on 'The Image(s) of the Consumer in EU Law: Legislation, Free Movement and Competition Law' (Oxford, 27-28 March 2014).

Kirchner 2006
Kirchner, C., 'An Economic Analysis of Choice-of-Law and Choice-of-Forum Clauses', in: Basedow, J., Kono, T. & Rühl, G. (eds.), *An Economic Analysis of Private International Law,* Tübingen: Mohr Siebeck, 2006, p. 33-53.

Lambooy 2010
Lambooy, T., *Corporate Social Responsibility. Legal and Semi-legal Frameworks Supporting CSR,* Deventer: Kluwer, 2010; also available at: <https://openaccess.-leidenuniv.nl/handle/1887/16169>.

Leczykiewicz & Weatherill 2016
Leczykiewicz, D. & Weatherill, S. (eds.), *The Images of the Consumer in EU Law: Legislation, Free Movement and Competition Law*, Oxford: Hart, 2016.

Mak forthcoming
Mak, V., 'What is Responsible Lending? The EU Consumer Mortgage Credit Directive in the UK and the Netherlands', *Journal of Consumer Policy* (forthcoming).

Michaels 2013
Michaels, R., 'Why We Have No Theory of European Private Law Pluralism', in: Niglia, L. (ed.), *Pluralism and European Private Law,* Oxford: Hart, 2013, p. 139-159.

Moerel 2013
Moerel, L., *Binding Corporate Rules. Corporate Self-Regulation of Global Data Transfers,* Oxford: Oxford University Press, 2012.

O'Hara & Ribstein 2009
O'Hara, E. & Ribstein, L., *The Law Market,* Oxford: Oxford University Press, 2009.

Ogus 2010
Ogus, A., 'The Paradoxes of Legal Paternalism and How to Resolve Them', *Legal Studies,* 2010, Vol. 30(1), p. 61-73.

Pavillon 2012
Pavillon, C., 'The Interplay Between the Unfair Commercial Practices Directive and Codes of Conduct', *Erasmus Law Review,* 2012, Vol. 5(4), p. 267-288.

Rawls 1999
Rawls, J., *A Theory of Justice,* rev. edn., Cambridge Mass.: Belknap Press of Harvard University Press, 1999.

Reich 1992
Reich, N., 'Competition between Legal Orders: A New Paradigm of EC Law?', *Common Market Law Review,* 1992, Vol. 29(5), p. 861-896.

Rühl 2013
Rühl, G., 'Regulatory Competition in Contract Law: Empirical Evidence and Normative Implications', *European Review of Contract Law,* 2013, Vol. 9, p. 61-89.

Schiff Berman 2012
Schiff Berman, P., *Global Legal Pluralism. A Jurisprudence of Law Beyond Borders,* Cambridge: Cambridge University Press, 2012.

Schwartz & Wilde 1983
Schwartz, A. & Wilde, L.L., 'Imperfect Information in Markets for Contract Terms: The Examples of Warranties and Securities Interests', *Virginia Law Review,* 1983, Vol. 69, p. 1387-1485.

Schwartz & Wilde 1985
Schwartz, A. & Wilde, L.L., 'Product Quality and Imperfect Information', *The Review of Economic Studies,* 1985, Vol. 52(2), p. 251-262.

Senden 2005
Senden, L., 'Soft Law, Self-Regulation and Co-Regulation in European Union Law: Where do They Meet?', *Electronic Journal of Comparative Law,* 2005, available at: <www.ejcl.org/91/art91-3.PDF>.

Smits 2002
Smits, J., *The Making of European Private Law; Towards a Ius Commune Europaeum as a Mixed Legal System,* Antwerp: Intersentia, 2002.

Smits 2010
Smits, J., 'Legal Tourism: Contract, Marriage and Citizenship beyond the State' (lecture Oxford Institute of European and Comparative Law, Oxford University, 29 April 2010).

Sunstein & Thaler 2003
Sunstein, C.R. & Thaler, R.H., 'Libertarian Paternalism Is Not an Oxymoron', *University of Chicago Law Review,* 2003, Vol. 70(4), p. 1159-1202.

Tiebout 1956
Tiebout, C., 'A Pure Theory of Local Expenditure', *Journal of Political Economy,* 1956, Vol. 64(5), p. 416-424.

Thaler & Sunstein 2008
Thaler, R.H. & Sunstein, C.R., *Nudge,* New Haven: Yale University Press, 2008.

Vogenauer 2013
Vogenauer, S., 'Regulatory Competition through Choice of Contract Law and Choice of Forum in Europe: Theory and Evidence', *European Review of Private Law,* 2013, Vol. 21(1), p. 13-78.

Vogenauer 2016
Vogenauer, S., 'Perceptions of Civil Justice Systems in Europe and their Implications for Choice of Forum and Choice of Contract Law: an Empirical Analysis', in: Vogenauer, S. & Hodges, C. (eds.), *Civil Justice Systems in Europe: Implications for Choice of Forum and Choice of Contract Law* (Hart Publishing, Oxford forthcoming 2016), Ch. 1, the same results also available at: <www.law.ox.ac.uk/-themes/iecl/pdfs/Oxford%20Civil%20Justice%20Survey%20-%20Summary-%20of%20Results,%20Final.pdf>.

Vogenauer & Weatherill 2006
Vogenauer, S. & Weatherill, S., 'The European Community's Competence to Pursue the Harmonisation of Contract Law - An Empirical Contribution to the Debate', in: Vogenauer, S. & Weatherill, S. (eds.), *Harmonisation of European Contract Law: Implications for European Private Laws, Business and Legal Practice,* Oxford: Hart Publishing, 2006, p. 105-148.

Voigt 2008
Voigt, S., 'Are International Merchants Stupid? Their Choice of Law Sheds Doubt on the Legal Origin Theory', *Journal of Empirical Legal Studies,* 2008, Vol. 5(1), p. 1-20.

Williams & Conley 2014
Williams, C.A. & Conley, J.M., 'The Social Reform of Banking', *Journal of Corporation Law,* 2014, Vol. 93(3), p. 101-134.

Ziegler & Rieder 2001
Ziegler, B. & Rieder, M.S., 'Vertragsgestaltung und Vertragsanpassung nach dem Schuldrechtsmodernisierungsgesetz', *Zeitschrift für Wirtschaftsrecht,* 2001, Vol. 22, p. 1789-1799.

Zimmermann 2005
Zimmermann, R., *The New German Law of Obligations. Historical and Comparative Perspectives,* Oxford: Oxford University Press, 2005.

S. Rutten

PRIVATE NORM-SETTING IN FAMILY LAW, MORE SPECIFICALLY: PRIVATE NORM-SETTING AMONGST RELIGIOUS COMMUNITIES IN FAMILY LAW ISSUES[1]

This chapter deals with questions on marriage and divorce in situations where people possess strong affiliation to religious family values and at the same time possess affiliation to the formal state law. More specifically, the question will be raised if, how and to what extent a state law system should accommodate private norm-setting in order to enable people to rely on informal religious marriage laws.[2]

Throughout Europe, there are people and communities that observe a particular religious belief and respect the binding force of the rules, norms and values of that religious belief. Religions usually also provide rules directly affecting family law issues, such as rules on marriage and divorce. Not in all cases and not everywhere are these religious rules also formally respected and recognized by the national legal system. Where religious rules – and the same goes for cultural norms – do not have legal validity, they only operate at an informal level, within not legally recognized religious law, within the religious communities themselves. Marriages entered into according to the rules and rituals prescribed by a particular faith by adherents of that faith, continue to be a frequent occurrence. This holds true for all types of believers: Christians conclude their marriage in Church, Jews marry according to the laws of Judaism, Muslims marry in a mosque, or elsewhere, according to Islamic rites, to name but a few.

1 Rather than offering profound and elaborate scientific considerations, this article only reflects the lecture held at the Maastricht Conference: *The Citizen in European Private Law: Norm-Setting, Enforcement and Choice* at 18 October 2013.

2 Next to private norm-setting, there may be several other ways in which this dual loyalty is respected in law. See *inter alia* Nichols 2012.

1. Religious Marriages: Legal Validity

In the Netherlands, religious marriages are allowed, provided they are preceded by a civil marriage.[3] A religious marriage by itself has no formal legal validity. Only a civil marriage is valid under the law. In other countries, religious marriages are governed by law in various ways. Several other European States also require a religious marriage to be preceded by a civil marriage. Belgium, France, Luxemburg, Austria, Switzerland, and Turkey are amongst such States. Germany has abolished its prohibition against entering into a religious marriage prior to a civil marriage. Many other States allow religious marriages and only may require subsequent civil registration. In those situations an arrangement must be provided that guarantees that civil authorities will be informed about the religious marriage, *e.g.* by the religious authorities. Religious marriages in this sense are allowed in a couple of Southern European States, the United Kingdom, and a few Scandinavian countries.

2. Religious Marriages: Motives

In the Netherlands thorough research into the motives people have when entering into religious marriages, and more specifically motives Muslims have to conclude Islamic marriages, has been carried out by Prof. Annelies Moors.[4] From this and other research[5] it follows that people can enter into an informal marriage for various reasons, either being religious, cultural, practical or pragmatic ones.

Religious marriages are concluded because of people's religious conviction. Furthermore, because that is the only marriage that really counts for the partners, on account of it being the traditional one, and because it is the socially accepted one. It therefore opens the door to, and legitimizes sexual relations between the partners and makes it possible for people to live and travel together abroad. Sometimes the informal marriage has to be concluded in order to prevent a marriage with another partner or to protect the family honour. Those marriages often will be arranged by family members.

The existence of cultural marriages, like the Roma marriages, simply can be motivated by an existing tradition.

More practical reasons to conclude a religious marriage instead of a civil one, can be that people want to avoid the existence of a formal marriage and nevertheless have a socially legitimized relationship. The avoidance of a formal marriage might be motivated by practical reasons: preventing the loss of social security provisions (*e.g.* pension claims of the surviving spouse can be lost if he or she legally remarries), avoiding tax law implications or maintaining other financial claims (*e.g.* an alimony claim after divorce may be lost if a divorced spouse

3 See Art. 68 Book 1 of the Dutch Civil Code.

4 Moors 2014.

5 E.g. the studies of Haeri 1994; De Koning & Bartels 2004; Van der Leun & Eupen 2009; Quraishi & Vogel 2008; El-Solh & Mabro 1994.

remarries). Furthermore, informal marriages are concluded because of necessity if there is an impediment to enter into a formal marriage, *e.g.* a lack of documents, especially in cases of migrants who experience difficulties in getting the required documents abroad demonstrating their personal status.

Finally, informal marriages, even temporary marriages,[6] can be used as a trial period before taking the decision to enter into a formal marriage.

3. Benefits and Limits of Religious Marriages

An important argument to allow religious marriages is the recognition of the strong adherence people may have to the religious and social meaning of such a marriage. It enables people to choose a marriage, which highly can be considered as a private act, in the way they choose themselves. It thus also recognizes religious and cultural freedom, and the existence of religious and cultural diversity.

Objections advanced against attributing legal validity to religious marriages, are related to the aim of having legal certainty about existing marriages, acquiring a complete registration of marriages, and the protection of the future spouses. If marriages are not registered their existence can be disputed or even be unknown. Secret marriages, cultural marriages, and religious marriages without registration cannot be invoked against third parties and cannot profit from legal protection. The marital status opens the door to all kinds of rights, obligations, possibilities and prohibitions. It is therefore important both for the spouses themselves as well as for the government and public authorities to have a complete overview of existing marriages. The need to enter into a civil marriage or to register a religious marriage will presumably decrease if people primarily adhere to a religious marriage.

4. Social Effect of Religious Marriages

The fact is that religious marriages *do* exist. Regardless of whether these marriages enjoy official civil status, they represent a social or socio-religious reality. If a religious marriage has taken place, the parties are regarded by the religious community as a married couple. This can have all sorts of social consequences, such as how the two families, the family of the wife and the family of the husband, interact with each other; all kinds of unwritten socio-religious rules and expectations enter into force between parents-in-law and children-in-law; the couple may entertain a relationship, live together and have sexual intercourse. All kinds of rights, duties, and responsibilities will arise between husband and wife.

One therefore could conclude that leaving autonomy to the parties themselves regarding their marriage, would meet social reality.

6 Temporary marriages are still allowed in Iran and still occur amongst Iranian (often younger) people in migrant states.

If the relationship ends, the question arises as to how the marriage can be dissolved in such a way that the spouses are no longer considered to be married, not only in law, but also within their religious community and social environment.

5. Religious Divorce

If a formal legal marriage exists between the spouses, a legal divorce will be open to them. Within Europe, there is always the possibility of instituting legal proceedings to obtain a divorce under private law. In most countries, this is in fact the only way by which a marriage can be legally dissolved. States want or are obliged to guarantee the protection of the interests that are at stake in case of a divorce, such as children, financial claims and division of property. States provide for court proceedings that must be followed in order to obtain a divorce decision. However, the religious marriage will still remain to exist since it will not be dissolved by a civil divorce.

6. Religious Divorce: Competence of Religious Authorities

The question may be raised as to whether there should be a possibility to have religious marriages dissolved by religious authorities.[7] This question is particularly relevant when it is held that a divorce decision passed by the civil court does not automatically dissolve the religious marriage. Under private law, the couple is considered to be divorced in law, they are no longer registered as married by the civil administration, but they are still regarded as married within their social environment. After all, a religious marriage can only be dissolved by means of a religious divorce. As long as this has not taken place, their social environment will continue to consider the partners to be married. If the woman wishes a divorce, but her husband resists, she will remain his wife in the husband's eyes even after the divorce. Of course, not all religious believers experience these obstacles after divorce; for many believers a civil divorce will suffice and a religious divorce is not required. However, it still frequently happens that religious people are in need of obtaining a religious divorce.

In several European states, Christians may direct themselves to an ecclesiastical court, Jews to a rabbinical court or rabbinical authorities and Muslims to an imam, in order to try to find a way to dissolve or end their religious marriage. However, most states refuse to accept Islamic courts within their territory. The UK is an exception: in the UK Islamic councils have been established and are officially recognized.[8] These councils are open to Muslims, and Muslims can consult those councils to obtain an (unofficial) Islamic divorce.

7 About alternative dispute resolution by religious authorities in general, see *inter alia* Boyd 2007; Rohe 2011.

8 More about the Shariah Councils in the UK, see *inter alia* Bano 2004; Bano 2007, p. 1-25; Bano 2008, p. 283; Pearl 2003, p. 5-16; Wilson 2010, p. 46-65; Keshavjee 2014.

Believers may consult these private religious authorities in order to be sure that their marriage will be dissolved in accordance with the rules of their faith. The religious authorities may also provide for arrangements on other matters following the divorce, such as child allowance, custody, and maintenance payments.

7. Family Divorce and other Arrangements by Private Actors

Intervention and control by religious authorities is one of the means by which a family dispute can be resolved through 'private regulation'. Another example of private regulation is by empowering the parties to come up with solutions themselves. They can do this by concluding an agreement among themselves. Alternatively, they may seek the involvement and assistance of a third party, such as a mediator, a lawyer, a notary or even a religious authority. In such situations, the agreement between the parties will be arranged by or through the assistance of that third party.

The parties may agree on the establishment of a religious divorce themselves by including a clause to that effect in the marriage contract proper or, in the course of the marriage in a later contract.[9] Such a clause may entail that in case there is going to be a (civil) divorce, spouses will commit themselves also to cooperate in the establishment of a religious divorce. They may also agree on the consequences of a divorce, for example, in a divorce settlement, and make arrangements in the settlement that observe religious rules. They may e.g. agree on the payment of the nuptial gift or bride price, the Islamic *mahr*, or make arrangements concerning the upbringing of children according to a particular faith.

8. Benefits of Private Regulation

The desirability of solutions reached by the spouses themselves is also driven by a greater acceptance of such solutions and the expected lasting effect of such a solution. These solutions often better meet the religious and social needs of the individuals themselves and there is a greater chance that these solutions will be respected and complied by the parties concerned. Individuals themselves are permitted to determine which normative system will be followed: uniform state law, traditional religious law or a combination of both.[10] A divorce that takes place in accordance with religious rules offers and implies a socially accepted dissolution of the marriage. The ex-spouses are genuinely considered to be divorced, and have become free agents able to resume their own life, start a new family and continue their independent living autonomously.

9 *Cf.* Bix 2012, p. 65-66; Broyde 2012, p. 138-163.

10 See further on the advantages of consensual accommodation for people in multicultural societies who simultaneously belong to more than one membership community: Shachar 2001, p. 103-109.

9. Limits of Private Regulation by Religious Authorities

However, private regulation, seeking solutions that may be reached by private actors, also has its limits. As regards the competence of religious authorities, the principle of the separation between Church and State, a concept representing a fundamental value of a democratic society in several European countries, needs to be taken into account. Another concern is whether substantive fundamental rights of individuals, especially women, are safeguarded. There is great concern that if the competence to decide on divorce is left to religious authorities, this may put the fundamental rights of women (and children) at risk.[11]

Furthermore in reality, the formal legal system and the informal religious legal order do not entirely function in isolation. People often prefer to both adhere to their religious rules but at the same time feel obliged by and also protected by the formal law. It would not be appropriate to force people, only because of their religious observance to a religion and possibly against their will, to approach religious authorities to solve their problems. In secular legal systems where religious legal pluralism formally has not been recognized, recourse to the formal official secular law should always remain an option, for all citizens and on equal footing. Because of the existence of patriarchal family structures within certain minority communities, the risk to be coerced to go to religious dispute settlement authorities would or could lurk.

10. Limits of Private Regulation by Party Autonomy

The principle of party autonomy, and thus the freedom of family members to come up with solutions themselves by contract, is limited by the law. Under the Dutch Civil Code agreements governed by private law are valid in general, provided they do not contravene mandatory law, public policy, or good morals.[12] Fundamental rights are undoubtedly included in the concepts of both public policy and good morals. Family law agreements, like marital agreements, may, if governed by Dutch law,[13] be subjected to this general clause in the civil code if and as far as the nature of the marital agreement does not oppose its application.[14] Future spouses are free, in principle, to agree, for instance, on the *mahr*. This is on the other hand, the concept of good morals should prevent parents to agree upon methods of education

11 Bano 2007; Boyd 2004; Büchler 2011; Zee 2014, p. 1-18; Wilson 2012, p. 268-274; Wilson 2010, p. 55-56.

12 Art. 40 Book 3 of the Dutch Civil Code.

13 Whether the marital agreement will be governed by Dutch law or not will depend on the rules on private international law.

14 Art. 59 Book 3 of the Dutch Civil Code.

that would harm their children, like raising them as martyrs for Islam or not to provide them with the necessary health care.[15]

11. Restrictions of Private Regulation by Religious Authorities

Attributing far-reaching competences in family matters to religious authorities would imply certain risks. Religious authorities apply religious rules. Within such religious norm-setting there will be no, or virtually any, room to take into account non-religious, hence secular norms. Although the European Court of Human Rights and the Netherlands Supreme Court have accepted that fundamental rights should be respected to a certain extent within official religious practices and thus may 'intrude' into religions, in reality, given the freedom of religion, caution and hesitation still prevail in this respect. Whether a formula can be developed which sufficiently justifies leaving decision-making in family matters to religious authorities, still has to be examined very carefully and thoroughly.

12. Secular Law as Solution: Secular Law and Religious Perceptions Combined

Since it is unlikely that religious solutions will be the right answer in all circumstances, the formal legal system should always entail appropriate and just provisions. Since secular law will not always meet religious needs, while people may feel bound to religious values, secular law is challenged to come up with solutions to meet the dilemma's and frictions caused by a concurrence of the official legal order and informal religious normative orders. One of the ways in which this possibly could be achieved is by the acceptance of party autonomy, accepting that people are allowed to a rather large extent, to make arrangements, including family arrangements, themselves.

However, a couple of challenging questions present themselves to be answered in this respect. On the one hand there are questions concerning the limits of party-autonomy: what can be left to the discretion of individuals and what cannot? How to determine the limits?

Are the limits of party autonomy by referring to public policy, human rights, good morals and mandatory rules, defined correctly and sufficiently clearly? Parents are allowed to make arrangements for the baptism of their children, but are they also allowed to agree upon the circumcision of their sons? Are concepts like 'good morals', 'public order' and human rights suitable test criteria? And how to protect the limits if agreements are made in a private (religious) setting? Can and should secular law provide for civil sanctions if limits are exceeded?

15 However, there is a huge discussion whether compelled interference of public and medical authorities via health care can be considered as a justified infringement of the freedom of religion.

On the other hand questions come up concerning the effectiveness of agreements made in the private religious sphere.

If arrangements have been made in a marital contract being part of a religious marriage, should this be given civil effect? Will it be possible to reconcile the norms of the informal religious legal order and those of the official law and how to proceed in this respect? How to equip individuals in order to enable them to make private arrangements in which secular and religious norms are reconciled?

People might need some help in trying to achieve this and lawyers must give a thought to how they can be of help. If future spouses wish to make an agreement concerning the Islamic *mahr* (the Islamic bride price), which often only becomes claimable at the time of divorce, they should be informed about the relation between the *mahr* on the one hand and other financial arrangements, like alimony upon divorce and matrimonial property issues, according to national law on the other hand. Parties should in fact take account of both sets of rules, since both sets of rules might be applicable: one set via party agreement and one set *ex lege*.

However, practice shows that reconciling both sets of rules is easier said than done. Regarding the *mahr* for example, even *courts* in West European States are still struggling with how to qualify this – in their own legal system unknown – institute.[16] Thus, the complexity of the merger of informal religious and formal secular concepts within one legal order still must be overcome.

Coping all these challenges necessitates a good understanding of religious family law figures and their implications within the religious social order. It also requires creativity, comparative research and empirical research. As long as legal pluralism exists and reigns within one legal order, this challenge will continue to exist and will continue to ask for suitable solutions. Private norm-setting amongst people can be one of the instruments to contribute to this.

16 *Cf.* Mehdi & Nielsen 2011.

Bibliography

Bano 2004
Bano, S., *Complexity, Difference and Muslim Personal Law: Rethinking the Relationship between Shariah Councils and South Asia Muslim Women in Britain*, Warwick: University of Warwick, 2004, available at: <http://wrap.warwick.ac.uk/1205>/.

Bano 2007
Bano, S., 'Islamic Family Arbitration, Justice and Human Rights in Britain', *Law, Social Justice & Global Development*, 2007, Vol. 1, p. 1-25.

Bano 2008
Bano, S., 'In Pursuit of Religious and Legal Diversity: A Response to the Archbishop of Canterbury and the "Sharia Debate" in Britain', *Ecclesiastical Law Journal*, 2008, Vol. 10(3), p. 283-309.

Bix 2012
Bix, B.H., 'Pluralis mand Decentralization in Marriage Regulations', in: Nichols, J.A. (ed.), *Marriage and Divorce in a Multicultural Context*, New York: Cambridge University Press, 2012, p. 60-77.

Boyd 2004
Boyd, M., *Dispute Resolution in Family Law: Protecting Choice, Promoting Inclusion*, Report to the Minister responsible for Women's Issues, Toronto, Ontario, December 2004.

Boyd 2007
Boyd, M., 'Religion Based Alternative Dispute Resolution: A Challenge to Multiculturalism', in: Banting, B., Courchens, T.J. & Seidl, F.L. (eds.), *Belonging? Diversity, Recognition and Shared Citizenship in Canada*, Montreal: Institute for Research on Public Policy, 2007, p. 465-473.

Broyde 2012
Broyde, M.J., 'New York's Regulation of Jewish Marriage: Covenant, Contract, or Statute', in: Nichols, J.A. (ed.), *Marriage and Divorce in a Multicultural Context*, New York: Cambridge University Press, 2012, p. 138-163.

Büchler 2011
Büchler, A., *Islamic Law in Europe? Legal Pluralism and its Limits in European Family Laws*, Surrey: Ashgate, 2011.

De Koning & Bartels 2004
De Koning, M. & Bartels, E., *Over het huwelijk gesproken: partnerkeuze en gedwongen huwelijken bij Marokkaanse, Turkse en Hindoestaanse Nederlanders*, Amsterdam: Vrije Universiteit, 2004.

El-Solh & Mabro 1994
El-Solh, C.F. & Mabro, J. (eds.), *Muslim Women's Choices: Religious Belief and Social Reality*, Oxford: Bloomsbury Academic, 1994.

Haeri 1994
Haeri, S., *Law of Desire: Temporary Marriage in Iran*, London: Tauris, 1994.

Keshavjee 2014
Keshavjee, M.M., *Islam, Sharia and Alternative Dispute Resolution*, London: I.B. Thauris, 2014.

Mehdi & Nielsen 2011
Mehdi, R. & Nielsen, J.S. (eds.), *Embedding Mahr in the European Legal System*, Copenhagen: DJØF Publishing, 2011.

Moors 2014
Moors, A.C.A.E., *Waarom vrouwen 'islamitische huwelijken' aangaan. Wetgeving, seksualiteit en islam in Nederland en daarbuiten*, Utrecht: FORUM, 2014.

Nichols 2012
Nichols J.A. (ed.), *Marriage and Divorce in a Multicultural Context*, New York: Cambridge University Press, 2012.

Pearl 2003
Pearl, D., 'Dispute Settlement amongst the Muslim Community in the UK', in: Rutten, S. (ed.), *Recht van de Islam*, Maastricht: RIMO, 2003, Vol. 20, p. 5-16.

Quraishi & Vogel 2008
Quraishi, A. & Vogel, F.E. (eds.), *The Islamic Marriage Contract; Case Studies in Islamic Family Law*, Cambridge: Harvard University Press, 2008.

Rohe 2011
Rohe, M., 'Alternative Dispute Resolution in Europe under the Auspices of Religious Norms', RELIGARE Working Paper, 2011.

Shachar 2001
Shachar, A., *Multicultural Jurisdictions*, New York: Cambridge University Press, 2001.

Van der Leun & Eupen 2009
Van der Leun, J. & Eupen, A., *Informele huwelijken in Nederland: een exploratieve studie*, Leiden: Universiteit Leiden, 2009.

Wilson 2010
Wilson, J., 'The Sharia Debate in Britain: Sharia Councils and the Oppression of Muslim Women', *Aberdeen Student Law Review*, 2010, p. 46-65.

Wilson 2012
Wilson, R.F., 'The Perils of Privatized Marriage', in: Nichols J.A. (ed.), *Marriage and Divorce in a Multicultural Context*, New York: Cambridge University Press, 2012, p. 268-274.

Zee 2014
Zee, M., '*Five Options for the Relationship between the State and Sharia Councils; Untangling the Debate on Sharia Councils and Women's Rights in the United Kingdom*', *Journal of Religion and Society*, 2014, Vol. 16, p. 1-18.

F. van der
Velden

ENCHAINED MARRIAGES: IS THERE A WAY OUT?

1. Introduction

In October 2013, many were surprised by the news that two American rabbis forced at least 50 men at gunpoint to divorce their wives. As such, this is not an unusual behaviour: gunpoint marriages and gunpoint divorces are well known throughout American legal history. But seemingly not only in the United States, in July of that year a Karachi Muslim claimed that his in-laws forced him at gunpoint to divorce his wife by *talāq*.[1]

Why do people use criminal acts to force somebody to perform certain acts of family law? Is in their opinion such a family act of greater importance than non-criminal behaviour?

According to Jewish law, divorce is realised by the handing over of a divorce letter, the *get*, which the man 'by his own free will' has to transmit in the hands of his wife. According to Jewish law 'by his own free will' does not mean: 'at his own discretion', but 'obeying the Torah'. But as the Torah leaves the man wide discretion in the choice of whether or not to divorce his wife, it often means that for a long time the wife will be caged in a *de facto* dead marriage. Such a Jewish wife is called an *agunah*, an enchained woman. She is, in my view and that of many others, in a morally unacceptable position, especially since according to the Torah she, from her side, has barely any opportunity to end her marriage.

In Islamic law, divorce law is less uniform. *Shari'a* divorce law differs between the different schools of Islamic law, in which the Islamic world is divided intellectually and geographically. As in many if not all religions, in Islam men are much better off than women. Although all *Shari'a* schools allow a man to dissolve his marriage unilaterally by *talāq*, and fully at the man's discretion, many schools

1 See for the rabbi cases e.g. <www.nytimes.com/2013/10/11/nyregion/rabbis-accused-in-kidnapping-plot-to-force-men-to-grant-divorces.html?_r=0> and for the Karachi talaq-case <http://tribune.com.pk/story/575706/breaking-marriage-man-alleges-he-was-forced-to-give-divorce-at-gunpoint/>.

include a number of grounds for divorce that are open to the wife while others schools of Islam, like the Hanafi school that prevails in *e.g.* Pakistan, are really very restrictive in their options for women to divorce.

But why should we, as members of a secular society, make a fuss about religious law? The French revolution introduced the secular state principle with its separation of state and church. Since then state law should not interfere with religious law nor be bothered by religious law.

2. Separation of State and Religion

Already some centuries before the French Revolution, the Netherlands started to embrace the division between church and state and the religious tolerance entailed by this division. In the 16th century the Reformation brought a system of government that was no longer based on religious rules and principles, although for a long time the reformed church held a privileged position. In 1853 the division of church and state was formulated compactly and almost poetically in the Dutch Act on Religious Bodies. To quote: '*All religious bodies are, and shall remain, assured of the freedom to regulate that which concerns, in their own bosom, their religion and its exercise*'. However, for a long time the division of church and state was not an absolute one. For example, the Dutch government remained involved in the organization of religious bodies, and until 1972 the state had the constitutional obligation to pay the salaries and pensions of ecclesiastic officials. In 1972 the relationship between government and religion changed to a purely economic one: the state pays religious officials for religious services that it requests as for example the spiritual guidance in the armed forces, in prisons and in hospitals.

The fairly recent end of the involvement of the Dutch government in religious organizations, surprisingly, coincides with a new and, in a certain sense, unwanted involvement of our secular society in religious matters. More and more, secular law is being called upon to help in religious disputes.

To give some examples: Muslim believers have asked courts to decide their dispute on who in the community of their mosque is entitled to appoint the imam.[2] In 2001 Christian organizations asked the Dutch government to maintain a law in which the respect of Sunday as a religious day of rest and worship was guaranteed, so that employees need only work on Sundays in case of urgency or on a voluntary basis. And Jewish and Muslim women try to solve their problems under religious law like those of enchained marriages by filing a civil lawsuit.[3] Some Jewish lawyers

2 Landman 1992, p. 69 *et seq*.

3 Rb Rotterdam 8 December 2010, LJN BP396. After a civil divorce to which he consented a Muslim Pakistani refuses to religiously divorce his wife by pronouncing *talaq*, which according to the woman forces her socially to continue in an unwanted religious marriage. She successfully claims that keeping her tied to that religious marriage violates Arts. 8 and 12 of the ECHR and is thereby a tortious act. As the man's behaviour is judged illegal as an unacceptable behaviour against the wife, the man is ordered to cooperate in the realization of a religious divorce under constraint of a default fine.

even proposed to amend the Dutch civil code by providing that no Jewish man could start a civil divorce procedure before he had transmitted the *get* to his wife: civil law as a correction of religious law.[4]

From time to time civil society is demanded to allow religious law in the secular atmosphere, when Muslim circles ask the government to be allowed to live and to be judged according to the *Shari'a* rules on family matters: religious law as a replacement of civil law.

3. Religion and Human Rights

In a civil and secular society the existence of religious law is not a problem as long as it does not interfere with the basic rules of the secular law system, with human rights and democracy. A calendar of human rights was codified in the Universal Declaration of Human Rights 1948 and accepted worldwide.[5] Subsequently, human rights conventions were ratified that oblige its contracting States to protect citizens against interference with these rights.

Human rights in family matters are set out in Article 16 of the Universal Declaration of Human Rights as it states:

> '(1) Men and women of full age, without any limitation due to race, nationality or religion, have the right to marry and to found a family. They are entitled to equal rights as to marriage, during marriage and at its dissolution. (2) Marriage shall be entered into only with the free and full consent of the intending spouses, and (3) The family is the natural and fundamental group unit of society and is entitled to protection by society and the State'.

This provision is almost copied in Article 23 of the 1966 International Covenant on Civil and Political Rights and got a widely detailed elaboration in Article 16 of the 1979 Convention on the Elimination of All Forms of Discrimination against Women. In a more condensed way it can be found in Article 12 of the 1950 European Convention on Human Rights.

The Universal Declaration as well as the conventions mentioned also contain rules on the freedom of thought, conscience and religion. Article 18 of the Universal Declaration and Article 9 of the European Convention state in an almost identical way:

> 'Everyone has the right to freedom of thought, conscience and religion; this right includes freedom to change his religion or belief, and freedom, either alone or in community with others and in public or private, to manifest his religion or belief in teaching, practice, worship and observance'.

4 Information given to the author by dr. Al 2002.

5 The Universal Declaration of Human Rights, although not being a convention, is generally accepted as an instrument of international law.

There is no hierarchy between the different human rights, as is clarified in Article 9 of the European Convention with the words:

> 'Freedom to manifest one's religion or beliefs shall be subject only to such limitations as are prescribed by law and are necessary in a democratic society in the interests ... of the rights and freedoms of others'.

As a consequence of this lack of hierarchy, courts have to decide on a case-by-case basis on its application.

To give some examples.

1. A Muslima expressed her will to be cremated if she would die. After her death her Muslim family was upset and demanded the body so they could bury her according to Islamic law.
2. A Muslima wants to marry her Christian boyfriend, a marriage that is not allowed according to the *Shari'a,* and therefore is rejected by her family.
3. A Muslima requires a Dutch court to dissolve her marriage as it is permanently broken down in her opinion. In his defence the husband opposes that according to Hanafi Islamic law, to which he belongs, she is not entitled to such a request.
4. A deadly ill Muslim patient asked for euthanasia, which in his case was legally allowed. Muslim friends threatened the doctor to sue him for malpractice if he should help the patient, as in their view the *Shari'a* forbids Muslims to use euthanasia.

In all these cases the human right of everyone to decide himself or herself over his or her life and future, as laid down a.o. in Article 9 of the European Convention, has priority over the right of others to manifest their religion by obliging fellow Muslims to observe the *Shari'a* family law rules as they understand it to rule.

Therefore, allowing the Muslim community to replace the secular family law system of the Netherlands by *Shari'a* family law in cases of family contracts and disputes between Muslims is unacceptable. It contravenes the Netherlands' obligation under Article 18 of the Vienna Convention on the Law of Treaties to refrain from acts which would defeat the object and purpose of adopted treaties as the European Convention on Human Rights and the UN Conventions on Human Rights.

On the other hand, secular law should respect the freedom of its citizens to follow the rules of their religion by removing unnecessary legal obstacles to the manifestation of their religion. Limitations of these rights are only allowed in the cases prescribed in Article 9 of the European Convention on Human Rights. In this respect Dutch family law is not fully convention-proof as in its provisions on family law sometimes it limits the manifestation of religion without sufficient cause.

If *e.g.* after their divorce parents want to divide the rights and duties they have towards their children between the two of them in full conformity with *Shari'a* law so that the father represents the child in legal and financial affairs and the mother has the child's daily care, national Dutch law should not interfere as long as such division does not harm the child's welfare.[6] And if an adopted person of age converts to Islam and wants to annul his adoption as adoption is forbidden in Islam, the Dutch civil code should not be an obstacle to such annulment.[7]

4. Enchained Marriages in a National Setting

Let us go back now to our subject, the enchained marriages. In the western world secular law and religious law are separate entities. Family law demonstrates this difference most clearly. Only in a restricted number of cases would secular law interfere in religious family law rules: if this were needed for the protection of children's welfare or for the free exercise by men or women of their right to self-determination.

In secular legal systems religious marriages and religious divorces will not be recognized or enforced. Recognition and enforcement are decisions by which a state gives legal force to acts and documents deriving from a person or body having legal powers under foreign state law as if these acts and documents derive from such persons or bodies in its own state. In principle religious acts do not get recognition in a secular legal system.

This principle of a sharp dichotomy between secular and religious law has its weaknesses.

In a strictly national setting religious marriages and divorces have no legal value. Nevertheless being religiously bound to an unwanted religious marriage and thereby being barred to a new religious marriage, like the Jewish *agunah*, is an obstruction of the human right of self-determination and thereby a tortious act in the secular law system. In many cases this action on tort may help religiously enchained women to throw off these chains and start a new life.[8]

6 Art. 1:251, para. 2 of the Dutch Civil Code as a general rule gives the parents after divorce the same custody rights as they had during their marriage. Art. 1:251a, para. 1 CC allows the parents to propose a different ruling, which the court may accept if such ruling is necessary in the interest of the child.

7 Art. 1:231, para. 2 of the Dutch CC rules that the adoptee may ask for an annulment of his adoption only after two and within five years after his majority.

8 See e.g. for The Netherlands: HR 22 januari 1982 NJ 1982, 489, ECLI:NL:HR:1982:AG4319; Hof Amsterdam 31 augustus 1989, NJ 1990, 679, ECLI:NL:GHAMS:1989:AD0874; Hof Amsterdam 5 oktober 1989, NIPR 1990, 394, Migrantenrecht 1990, p. 26; Rb. Rotterdam 8 december 2010, RFR 2011/76; Rb. Amsterdam 10 april 2012, ECLI:NL:RBAMS:2012:BW3800; Rb. Overijssel zittingsplaats Almelo 24 december 2013, ECLI:NL:RBOV:2013:4269; Rb. Den Haag 21 oktober 2014, ECLI:NL:RBDHA:2014:14191, JPF 2015/25; Rb. Amsterdam 2 april 2014, ECLI:NL:RBAMS:2014:1644, JPF 2015/2. See e.g.: for France: Tribunal de la Seine 22 février 1957; Tribunal civil de Grenoble 7 mai 1958; Cour de Cassation 5 juin 1985, Cour de Cassation 15 juin 1988, Cour de Cassation 21 novembre 1990, Cour de Cassation 12 décembre 1994. See for Israel e.g. P. v. P. FamC 9877/02 Rishon LeZion (Stein) 2010.

→

5. Enchained Marriages in an International Setting

In an international setting the situation is more complex.

Although western legal systems are secular for a major part, a number of them have some constitutional bindings with a religious entity. The United Kingdom, Greece, Denmark, Norway and Malta have a state religion, some other states like Italy, Spain and Portugal have concordats with the Holy See by which the roman-catholic religion has special privileges in family law cases. In the Islamic world, with some exceptions, states have Islam as state religion, some even call themselves Islamic states. In those states family and inheritance law is directly based on Islamic law, as it is interpreted by the Islamic school prevailing in that state or by a subjective interpretation of that law.

As in these western and Arabic states secular and religious law are intertwined, religious marriages and divorces have an equal position as or are at the same time state law marriages and divorces and thereby part of the secular law system.

To be more explicit, in Morocco, Algeria and Tunisia, all belonging to the Maliki school of Sunni Islam, the wife has a number of options to judicially require a divorce, while in the other Sunni schools as in Shia Islam the wife's opportunities are restricted or even near to none. Pakistan belongs to the Hanafi Sunni school, which is most restrictive in allowing the wife to enter divorce proceedings. Often a Muslima who wants to divorce has only one feasible option, that is to offer her husband a financial compensation, the *khul'*. The amount of such *khul'* will be a matter of negotiation and at the end can be a substantial burden for her. If he accepts her offer, he will give her a repudiation as a compensation, if he refuses it or is not willing at all to discuss a *khul'*, she will have hardly any further option for a divorce. In these states courts have no means to divorce apart from those mentioned in the religious law.

6. All's Well that Ends Well?

Once residing in a secular state the wife will in most cases be entitled to a divorce conforming with the family law rules of that state. As this secular divorce will not be valid religiously and thereby not recognized by the state of origin, it creates a limping marriage: the wife is divorced in the state of residence (and in most other secular states), but still married in her religion and in her state of origin (and in many other Muslim states). This brings her in a difficult position, unwillingly enchained to the man she once married.

Here, again, secular law has to interfere in religious law in the interest of the wife's human right to equal rights as to the dissolution of marriages, as provided for in Article 16 of the Universal Declaration of Human Rights. Until now men have been fined to compensation as a non-cooperation to a religious divorce was judged to be a tortious act against the wife, since obliging her to stay in an unwanted marriage was an unlawful interference to the wife's right to determine her life according to her wishes.

However, compensation does not work in all cases: the husband may have no money to pay the fine or he may live in a state in which the court's decision is not recognised.

Especially in Muslim states secular decisions in family matters are not recognised since according to their law, Muslims are and remain subject to the *Shari'a*, wherever they may live.

So the question remains, are there other options available to help Muslim women to end their unwanted marriage? Until now no other workable solution has been found.

It is up to the legal profession, and in particular to the legal academics to find additional ways out of marriage for those who are until now the enchained women, not by way of gunpoint divorces as above mentioned or comparable criminal acts but by ways acceptable in a civil society.

Bibliography

Al 2002
Al, J.C., *Overzicht van het Joods huwelijks- en echtscheidingsrecht*, Nijmegen: Wolf Legal Publishers, 2002.

Landman 1992
Landman, N., *De institutionalisering van de islam in Nederland*, Amsterdam: VU Uitgeverij, 1992.

N. Creutzfeldt

AN INTRODUCTION TO ALTERNATIVE DISPUTE RESOLUTION (ADR) FOR CONSUMERS IN EUROPE[1]

This chapter discusses alternative dispute resolution for consumers in Europe. It is based on a presentation first given at 'The Citizen in European Private Law: Norm-setting, Enforcement and Choice' at Maastricht University, 18 October 2013.

Civil justice landscapes are shifting and changing. The courts - in most European Union (EU) member states known to be difficult to access - take a long time to process cases, are costly, and do not provide for appropriate access to justice for low-value consumer to business disputes. This chapter provides a snapshot overview of consumer ADR in Europe and is divided into the following parts: an overview of ADR and EU legislation; the vision for consumer ADR; courts and ADR; some national examples; and finally, a view to what happens next.

1. What ADR are We Talking about?

First of all it is important to clarify what kind of ADR this paper is talking about. ADR is not well known outside of litigation, and is fairly new in many EU jurisdictions. This means that there is a distinct 'ADR universe' that is developing alongside the national court systems. Alternative dispute resolution typically describes a multitude of techniques (arbitration, conciliation, mediation, and settlement, for example) that aim to assist in reaching an outcome for a dispute without involving a court. There are numerous approaches and techniques within ADR; this chapter is concerned with ADR for consumer disputes.[2] Consumer ADR is typically aimed at small value complaints about goods and services that would usually not make it into a courtroom.

There are different types of ADR, and models often differ between countries. The most common examples are ombudsmen, conciliation bodies, no fault

1 This work was supported by the Economic and Social Research Council [grant number ES/K00820X/1].

2 Hodges, Benöhr & Creutzfeldt-Banda 2012.

compensation schemes, dispute resolution boards, and dispute resolution systems as part of business codes of practice. All of these models are made up of a mixture of the techniques mentioned above. In our 2012 book on consumer ADR in Europe there is more detail on procedure and various ADR techniques.[3]

The current ADR landscape in the EU is varied and inconsistent. With the outlook to improve access to justice and encourage consumer confidence in the European single market, European legislation on consumer ADR and online dispute resolution (ODR) was passed in 2013 and had to be implemented by July 2015; the ODR regulation by early 2016.

2. European Legislation

One of the ambitions of the European Union (EU) single market is to encourage consumer confidence and cross-border trade. For this purpose, consumers need clear information on who to contact for help with resolving problems regarding purchased goods and services. These problems are best dealt with - after the consumer has first approached the complained-about business - by an ADR body, rather than going to court which is typically costly and time consuming.

The landscape of ADR bodies in the EU, however, has been identified as being far from coherent. Notable problems include gaps in ADR coverage of consumer sectors as well as different variants in member states; a lack of awareness of ADR bodies in general; and differences in quality of existing ADR bodies.

EU-wide regulations aim to remedy this situation by creating a level playing field of ADR bodies throughout the EU, and providing ADR representation for every consumer sector within a common set of quality standards. This is set out in detail in the consumer ADR directive 2013/11/EU,[4] and the regulation on online dispute resolution (ODR) 524/2013,[5] controlling cross-border disputes.

3. The 2013 ADR and ODR Legislation

The ADR directive and ODR regulation were passed at EU level in record speed (a year) and were to be implemented by July 2015 and January 2016 respectively. Generally speaking, the consumer ADR directive requires all EU member states to have full consumer sector ADR coverage by implementation date. The directive also provides guidelines and procedural requirements for ADR bodies to comply with. After the comprehensive ADR coverage is established, the ODR platform is designed to link all EU ADR bodies, and provide a single entry platform for cross-border consumer complaints.

3 *Ibid*.

4 Directive 2013/11, *OJ* 2013, L165/63 and amending Regulation (EC) No 2006/2004 and Directive 2009/22/EC (Directive on consumer ADR), *OJ* 2009, L110/30.

5 Regulation (EC) No 534/2013, *OJ* 2013, L159/11.

I will briefly outline the procedural requirements and quality criteria for an ADR identity set out in the ADR directive, followed by an overview of the ODR regulation.

Article 5 of the directive on Access to ADR entities and ADR procedures states that:

> 'Member States shall facilitate access by consumers to ADR procedures and shall ensure that disputes covered by this Directive and which involve a trader established on their respective territories can be submitted to an ADR entity which complies with the requirements set out in this Directive.'

The requirements, or quality criteria, of the ADR procedures are specified in Articles 6 to 11 of the consumer ADR directive: Article 6: *expertise, independence and impartiality*; Article 7: *transparency*; Article 8: *fairness*; Article 9: *effectiveness*; Article 10: *liberty* and Article 11: *legality*.[6] The directive determines that a competent authority should monitor these standards for ADR bodies. There is no clear indication as to how this body (or these bodies) is to be set up; it is up to the member states to determine their best approach at a national level.

In 2016, ideally following the establishment of bodies that satisfy the consumer ADR directive by all 28 EU Member States, an ODR platform will provide an entry point for all cross-border consumer complaints. This means that consumers will have a single point of access, to then be directed to the appropriate national ADR entity to help solve their specific complaint.

The set of specific problems arising from transnational online purchases is seen to obstruct the growth of the internal market, consumer satisfaction and trust in the market.[7] This new model will improve access to justice online.[8] ODR[9] developed out of ADR, and is built on the ADR model, in particular arbitration. Thus, ODR is effectively the merging of IT and ADR.

Common ODR methods for business to consumer disputes involve automated negotiation, assisted negotiation, mediation, arbitration and small claims court procedures. For both ADR and ODR alike there is no single method that would be applicable to all consumer complaints. This produces a variety of approaches and different methods across individual cases and member states. ODR is widely used by private online companies such as eBay, PayPal and Amazon.[10] Arguably, these companies would not have been as successful without the confidence-building support of a dispute resolution system to support the online trading system. This, in part, has informed the European Commission's adoption of ODR, as it wants to strongly support the development of digital trading within the EU.

6 It is outside of the scope of this chapter to discuss each criteria mentioned and too early to assess how they will be implemented and monitored for the ADR bodies.

7 Cortés 2010.

8 COM(2010) 245 A digital agenda for Europe.

9 Hörnle 2009; Cortés 2011.

10 Rule 2002.

The new legislation is simple and bold. It establishes a vision of capturing issues between consumers and businesses, solving them and using the information to improve practice and markets. If consumers can be taught to 'think ADR' whenever they encounter a problem, the problem can be brought to a resolution. Many problems will not be full 'disputes', but rather will revolve around communication of further information. But actual disputes can also be resolved quickly and cheaply if consumers can be led to think 'ADR' instead of 'courts' or 'lawyers'.

ADR systems have huge potential to deliver not only effective, cheap and quick solutions in business to consumer disputes, but also to provide valuable market information that will enhance competition, innovation and safety.[11] ADR systems thereby challenge the traditional role of the courts. Some may be concerned at this.[12] Others will support the development of a new relationship and function between the courts and private sector ombudsmen. One model would be that courts decide issues of law, and ombudsmen apply settled law to the facts of individual disputes. This should allow for a rational transfer of cases between courts and ADR providers.

ADR has the potential to reshape our civil justice system in the 21st century, by providing an easy and straightforward solution to an area of great consumer dissatisfaction.

4. The Potential of Consumer ADR

There are many benefits to establishing a high quality pathway to resolve largely unheard consumer complaints - not least the opportunity to restore trust in the system. A well-functioning ADR landscape will not only improve access to justice for those typically low-value consumer claims, but most importantly will allow the consumer access to that justice at little or no personal cost. An ADR procedure is usually much shorter and more predictable than a court procedure. The procedure should be accessible and user-friendly as well as providing consumers with advice. If ADR bodies have a standardised system of capturing their complaint data, they can feed this back to companies and regulators, thereby creating a culture of detecting and responding to emerging issues through regulation.

Within the many debates about ADR, one of the most important is that regarding the relationship between ADR bodies and the national courts.

11 Hodges 2014.

12 See the critical stance of Lindblom 2008; Eidenmueller & Engel 2013. Available at: <http://papers.ssrn.com/sol3/papers.cfm?abstract_id=2290654>.

5. Courts and ADR Bodies - Formal Decisions vs. Informal Resolution

The role of (both evolving and established) ADR schemes in national settings in Europe has led to some confusion about their relationship with the court system.[13] The main concern is that ADR potentially doubles the avenues for consumer redress and thereby weakens the court's jurisdiction in consumer matters. The debate therefore focuses on the relationship between existing and developing ADR pathways and the courts: Will ADR compete with the courts? Does ADR bring any added value to a legal system? How can a high level of procedural quality be established when ADR is aimed at being faster and more cost-efficient than courts?

The lack of empirical evidence on European ADR models makes it currently impossible to answer these questions. We can, however, identify the main focus of the current debate. Three central themes are highlighted here: 1) *Types of disputes*; 2) *objectives and criteria*; 3) *significance of litigation for an ADR approach*.

First, the *types of disputes* that are brought to an ADR body are low-value claims that would not typically be brought to a court. Consumers who bring complaints to court typically claim that the process is too costly, time consuming, and complex. ADR schemes are designed to resolve complaints (ideally) at no cost to the consumer and in a fast, efficient, and user-friendly manner.[14]

Second, assessment *objectives and criteria* differ between the *interest-based* ADR procedure and the *legally based* court procedure. This means that a court procedure and an ADR procedure have different objectives. While a court process is aimed at enforcing legal positions and thereby has the potential to enhance the conflict, ADR (at least those procedures without a binding decision, like mediation and conciliation) is aimed at reaching a decision for both of the involved parties. The ADR procedure and court procedure criteria differ in that the former does not require stringent application of established legal principles.

Matters of the law are traditionally not of primary concern in the ADR procedure. Although most European ADR schemes are expected to follow the principle of legality and review the law in relation to weighting the interest of the parties as stated in 98/257/EG,[15] the application thereof is inconsistent.[16] The most recent version of the ADR directive, however, makes the principle of legality

13 This notion of concern was very apparent at the first ADR conference 'Schlichten statt Klagen: Alternative Formen der Streitbeilegung', Germany in November 2012. Available at: <www.bmelv.de/SharedDocs/Standardartikel/Verbraucherschutz/Markt-Recht/-SchlichtenStattKlagen.html>.

14 Public Consultation on the use of ADR as a means to resolve disputes related to commercial transactions and practices in the EU summary of the responses received 2011; available at: <http://ec.europa.eu/consumers/redress_cons/Feedback_Statement_Final.pdf>.

15 98/257/EC Commission Recommendation of 30 March 1998 on the principles applicable to the bodies responsible for out-of-court settlement of consumer disputes; available at: <http://eur-lex.europa.eu/LexUriServ/LexUriServ.do?uri=OJ:L:1998:115:0031:0034:EN:-PDF>.

16 Alleweldt 2009, available at: <http://ec.europa.eu/consumers/redress_cons/adr_study.-pdf>, p. 16.

mandatory in Article 11.[17] Of course, one can argue that the law is not the only reference when finding a solution in an ADR procedure. Rather, it can be seen as a standard to enable the parties to evaluate their positions and provide the option of an informed decision for the evaluation of the ADR process. To clarify, the ADR approach consists of an initial rights-based approach to determine the remit, followed by a stage of a comprehensive interest-based approach.

The third theme is the *importance of litigation for the ADR approach*. Most ADR procedures are based on voluntary participation by companies.[18] At any point in the ADR process, there is the option to take the complaint to court.[19] In some cases, if there is no existing case law, an ADR scheme can refer the case to the courts; this is normally specified in the ADR schemes' procedural rules and in the most recent ADR directive. On the other hand, courts value the work of ombudsmen and their decisions.

To sum up, the development of ADR models has resulted because certain types of complaints are better suited for an informal procedure, rather than a formal route.

6. Is There a Demand for ADR?

How many consumers actually complain? The reality is that only half of people that encounter a problem complain to the company that caused the problem. Then, half of those who complain are satisfied with the solution offered by the company and many others give up. A very small percentage of cases reach a court, typically higher value complaints of around EUR 500 and above.[20]

The consumer scoreboard 2013[21] reported the following:

- A quarter (25%) of EU consumers reported that, in the past 12 months, they had had a legitimate cause for complaint when buying or using goods or services in their own country.
- More than eight out of ten (83.4%) consumers who experienced problems took action to address them. The most likely action following a problem is complaint to the retailer/provider (71.6% of consumers having experienced a problem), followed by complaint to the manufacturer (12.1%).

17 Directive 2013/11/EU of the European Parliament and of the Council on alternative dispute resolution for consumer disputes and amending Regulation (EC) No 2006/2004 and Directive 2009/22/EC (Directive on consumer ADR)

18 The exception are telecom and energy sectors, where joining a ADR scheme is mandatory.

19 Which complies with constitutional requirements that the pathway to the courts has to remain open to resolve a dispute.

20 Speech by Jacquelyn Minor at the annual consumer ADR conference in oxford 26/27 September 2013. Available at: <www.csls.ox.ac.uk/documents/TheFirstOxfordAnnual-ConsumerADRConference-summarynote.pdf>.

21 <http://ec.europa.eu/consumers/consumer_research/editions/docs/9th_edition_-scoreboard_en.pdf>.

- Only 4.4% of consumers (who had experienced problems) decided to complain to a public authority and the same percentage brought the issue to an alternative dispute resolution (ADR) body. The likelihood of taking the case to court is even lower (1.6%). Finally, in 16.6% of cases, consumers who experienced a problem decided not to take any action.

It is important to note that while consumers who seek the help of an ombudsman are generally happy with the procedure, the problem remains that most people are unaware of ADR bodies. More recent statistics from the UK energy sector reinforce this. During the first half of 2014 energy complaints have more than doubled (compared to the previous 6 months) to 22,671 – the highest they have ever been.[22]

Is this increase in complaints to do with consumers feeling more empowered and knowing their rights, or is it because the energy companies are not treating their customers fairly? The chief energy ombudsman says that these figures seem to be merely the tip of an iceberg:

> 'We as an ombudsman service only get about 5% of the complaints eligible to come to us so 95% of people have gone through the complaints process of the company, remain dissatisfied, but don't come to us.'[23]

This means that there remains a vast number of dissatisfied consumers that do not reach out to the ombudsman.

What does the other party in these disputes, the energy companies, have to say on the matter? A spokesman for energy UK stated that:

> 'The energy industry works hard to provide the best service for its customers but in an industry serving 27 million households sometimes things go wrong.'

To sum up, although ADR satisfies users' criteria (fast procedure, cheap, user-friendly and mostly free to the consumer) it is not used enough which results in too many consumers remaining dissatisfied with unresolved issues. An aspect of the new ADR legislation is to ensure that companies provide their customers with information about ADR bodies.

The following section will provide an overview of the various different approaches to ADR that member states take.

7. Some National Examples

Some ADR models are more developed than others.[24] This has a lot to do with the national specific legal structures and national cultures of disputing.[25] To

22 Energy Ombudsman interview 14 July 2014, BBC radio 4.
23 Lewis Shand Smith, Chief Energy Ombudsman UK, Interview with Sky News 14 July 2014.
24 Hodges, Benohr & Creutzfeldt-Banda 2012.
25 Creutzfeldt 2016, forthcoming.

demonstrate ADR diversity this part looks at some national specificities: the Swedish model, a special French approach, the Netherlands, the UK and Germany. This section provides a country summary, more detail and further country analysis can be found in our book on Consumer ADR in Europe (Hart 2012).

7.1. *Sweden: Nordic Complaint Boards*

In Sweden the consumer ADR system is comprehensive, developed, and widely used. Interestingly, the courts have almost no function for consumer to business disputes. A range of ADR Boards exist for specific types of injuries or sectors. The National Board for Consumer Disputes *Allmänna reklamationsnämnden* (ARN) is the comprehensive single entry point, which is a public authority that functions like a court. It is well-known and widely used. Nearly all of the ADR bodies are free to their users and the ARN is funded by the state.

7.2. *A Special Case of the French Médiateurs*

Consumer ADR in France has distinct national characteristics with the existence of in-house médiateurs. This specific type of in-house ADR raises the question of independence. For example, in the energy sector there are several médiateurs. The three energy providers have in-house médiateurs, additionally there is one independent national energy ombudsman. This makes four energy ADR bodies and the national energy ombudsman typically dealing with complaints about the other three médiateurs.

The existence of several ADR bodies for the same sector is technically allowed under the ADR directive but surely contributes to consumer confusion and ultimately can only undermine trust in the ADR model.

7.3. *The Netherlands*

The Netherlands achieves a consistently high adherence to its ADR model *de geschillencommissie* (DGS) because of its unique structure, in which trade associations agree terms and conditions with consumer associations, and then pay for and support the related sectorial DGS board. This guarantees that any decision will be paid for by the trade association. It is an attractive model, but does not offer a guarantee where the trader is not a member of a trade association.

The Dutch system has historically used the arbitration model but it is to pilot the addition of a mediation stage in 2014 in relation to disputes involving kindergarten. It will probably use a panel of external mediators, paid on an hourly basis. An alternative would be to use a module fee, so parties have full predictability of cost, although different fees might have to be set for different types of case. In contrast, the Dutch financial services ADR, *KiFiD*, has an initial phase that combines mediation and expert evaluation with decision-making in the form of the ombudsman, but this comes at a cost.

DGS is also to introduce a funnel or sieve system. The model might consider introducing a 'light' procedure, under which both parties would submit their positions and a single judge would look at the case (quickly) and email to both his/her suggested solution. The solution may not be binding, but could be accepted by both sides, thereby stopping the case from going further to the full Board.

7.4. *The United Kingdom*

The UK has a wide ADR coverage. Indeed, some sectors double up on ADR bodies, but there is no comprehensive sector coverage yet. There are some very well developed ADR models like the Financial Ombudsman Service or the Ombudsman Services.

In contrast, the UK Financial Ombudsman Service will soon have 3,500 staff. In 2012/13 its frontline customer-contact division received 2,161,439 initial enquiries and complaints; 508,881 new cases were referred to adjudicators and ombudsmen for further dispute-resolution work; 198,897 cases were resolved by adjudicators through mediation, recommended settlements and adjudications, and 24,332 cases were resolved by ombudsmen making formal decisions at the final 'appeal' stage of their dispute-resolution process.

Similarly, the UK Ombudsman Services (covering energy, and part of the communications and property sectors) had 156 full time equivalent employees on 31 March 2013, and responded to 122,589 new contacts during 2012/13, an average of 490 per working day. OS's use of the triage and mediation stages is introducing new efficiencies and achieving notably increased speeds in case resolution.

7.5. *Germany*

ADR in Germany is, from a comparative perspective, a prime example of the maxim that context is paramount. The concept of 'ADR' is frequently referred to in Germany, but has a particular meaning, essentially encompassing mediation associated with court proceedings, or arbitration. There are some limited examples of ADR that do not occur in the context of alignment to court proceedings, such as ombudsman procedures, but they are currently limited in both scope and usage. In this respect, the German ADR landscape is fairly undeveloped in most consumer sectors.

The Insurance Ombudsman model has been notably successful, and has been used as a template to create conciliation bodies in the transport sector and elsewhere. Complaint procedures also exist within various regulatory bodies, but have not been widely used. The current situation is that consumer ADR is at a relatively early stage, but is developing into a confused state of diversity in the types and coverage of ADR bodies. There is considerable variation in the caseload attracted by individual bodies, and some are simply not widely known about. This diversity in models can confuse consumers, who need a simple ADR structure that is easily understood.

After this very brief overview of the diversity of ADR development in European member states there is a huge challenge ahead to implement the consumer ADR directive for July 2015.

8. What Happens Next?

By July 2015 all member states have to implement the ADR directive into their national frameworks. As outlined above, this will be a challenge as the current ADR coverage varies significantly across the EU. Some member states will have to slightly adjust existing ADR models, while others will have to create ADR bodies from scratch.

Things to consider when designing an ADR body:

- there needs to be ADR for every goods or services consumer transaction, the gaps need to be filled;
- the key is to offer high quality dispute resolution that meets the quality criteria outlined by the consumer ADR directive;
- consumers and business need to be made aware of the existence of these ADR bodies;
- ADR needs to be equipped to fit the demands of the digital age and for the ODR regulation to be successfully implemented in 2016.

If this shift towards resolving grievances informally is implemented successfully then it could create a new way not only of enabling access to justice, but also of building consumer trust in the single market. It will certainly create a system in its own right for consumers.

However, there is also a risk of getting it wrong, confusing consumers and thereby providing the opposite effect of complete loss of trust. The role of private dispute resolution needs to be carefully monitored and quality ensured.

Based on what was discussed previously, some measures to take into account during the implementation process are:

- consumer perception is very important;
- no one ADR size fits all;
- diversity needs to be respected;
- who funds the ADR schemes?
- how can they be independent?
- rights based or interest based decisions?
- binding or non-binding decisions?

9. Conclusion

Although there are challenges ahead, the consumer ADR directive is here to stay. Hopefully it will be implemented by each member state diligently, with the aim of improving access to justice for consumers, rather than the aim of basic compliance to the minimum standards of the legislation. ADR could be the route to justice with fair and just outcomes that build consumer trust. The current ADR landscape of diversity does not encourage trust; rather it provides too many options and thereby creates confusion for its users. Therefore, the consumer ADR directive poses the unique challenge of establishing a trusted ADR brand that is easily identified and accessed, and that produces fair outcomes. Streamlining and simplifying access and thereby building a trusted and fair route to justice for consumer to business complaints could be achieved.

Within the debate about civil justice systems and ADR we need to think about the wider contextual question. For example, what do we want legal systems to do? How should disputes get resolved? How do we maximise compliance with the rules? How do we identify non-compliance quickly? And once non-compliance is identified, what consequences are appropriate?

Bibliography

Alleweldt 2009
Alleweldt, F., *Study on the use of Alternative Dispute Resolution in the European Union,* 2009, Civic Consulting, available at: <http://ec.europa.eu/consumers/-redress_cons/adr_study.pdf>.

Cortés 2011a
Cortés, P., 'Developing Online Dispute Resolution for Consumers in the EU: A Proposal for the Regulation of Accredited Providers', *International Journal of Law and Information Technology*, 2010, Vol. 19(1), p. 1-28.

Cortés 2011b
Cortés, P., Online Dispute Resolution for Consumers in the European Union, Oxon: Routledge, 2011.

Creutzfeldt 2014
Creutzfeldt, N., 'How Important is Procedural Justice for Consumer Dispute Resolution? A Case Study of an Ombudsman Model for European Consumers, *Journal of Consumer Policy,* 2014, Vol. 37(4), p. 527-546.

Creutzfeldt 2016
Creutzfeldt, N., 'What Do We Expect from an Ombudsman? Narratives of Everyday Engagment with the Informal Justice System in Germany and the UK', *International Journal of Law in Context,* 2016, forthcoming.

Eidenmüller & Engel 2013
Eidenmüller, H. & Engel, M., 'Against False Settlements: Designing Efficient Consumer Rights Enforcement Systems in Europe', EUI Conference on 'The transformation of Enforcement' in Florence (27-28 June 2013). Available at: <http://papers.ssrn.com/sol3/papers.cfm?abstract_id=2290654>.

Hodges 2014
Hodges, C., 'Consumer Redress: Ideology and Empiricism', in: Purnhagen, K. & Rott, P. (eds.), *Varieties of European Economic Law and Economic Law and Regulation. Festschrift for Hans Micklitz,* Berlin: Springer, 2014, p. 793-821.

Hodges, Benöhr & Creutzfeldt-Banda 2012
Hodges, C.J.S., Benöhr, I. & Creutzfeldt-Banda, N., *Consumer ADR in Europe,* Oxford: Hart Publishing, 2012.

Hörnle 2009
Hörnle, J., *Cross-Border Internet Dispute Resolution,* Cambridge: Cambridge University Press, 2009.

Lindblom 2008
Lindblom, P.H., 'ADR - The Opiate of the Legal System? Perspectives on Alternative Dispute Resolution Generally and in Sweden', *European Review of Private Law,* 2008, Vol. 1, p. 63-93.

Rule 2002
Rule, C., *Online Dispute Resolution For Business: B2B, E-Commerce, Consumer, Employment, Insurance, and other Commercial Conflicts*, San Francisco: John Wiley & Sons, 2002.

C. Cauffman

CRITICAL REMARKS ON THE ADR DIRECTIVE

1. Introduction: The Aims of the ADR Directive

The Alternative Dispute Resolution Directive (the ADR Directive)[1] aims to increase the consumer's access to justice. This is of course an honourable aim. The EU has a vast track record of creating directives which oblige Member States to offer a certain minimum level of consumer protection.[2] Recently, it has moved to adopt consumer directives that introduce full harmonization[3] as well as directly applicable regulations.[4] This should ensure an identical level of consumer protection for

1 Directive 2013/11/EU of 21 May 2013 on alternative dispute resolution for consumer disputes and amending Regulation (EC) No 2006/2004 and Directive 2009/22/EC, *OJ* 2013, L165/63. The ADR Directive is accompanied by the ODR Regulation (Regulation 524/2013 of 21 May 2013 on online dispute resolution for consumer disputes and amending Regulation (EC) No 2006/2004 and Directive 2009/22/EC, *OJ* 2013, L165/1). The latter provides for the establishment of an ODR platform which offers consumers and traders a single point of entry for the out-of-court resolution of online disputes, through ADR entities which are linked to the platform. See Recital 12 of the ADR Directive.

2 See e.g. Council Directive 85/577/EEC of 20 December 1985 to protect the consumer in respect of contracts negotiated away from business premises, *OJ* 1985, L372/31; Council Directive 93/13/EEC of 5 April 1993 on unfair terms in consumer contracts, *OJ* 1993, L095/29; Directive 97/7/EC of the European Parliament and of the Council of 20 May 1997 on the protection of consumers in respect of distance contracts, *OJ* 1997, L144/19.

3 See e.g. Directive 2011/83/EU of the European Parliament and of the Council of 25 October 2011 on consumer rights, amending Council Directive 93/13/EEC and Directive 1999/44/EC of the European Parliament and of the Council and repealing Council Directive 85/577/EEC and Directive 97/7/EC of the European Parliament and of the Council, *OJ* 2011, L304/64; Directive 2005/29/EC of the European Parliament and of the Council of 11 May 2005 concerning unfair business-to-consumer commercial practices in the internal market and amending Council Directive 84/450/EEC, Directives 97/7/EC, 98/27/EC and 2002/65/EC of the European Parliament and of the Council and Regulation (EC) No 2006/2004 of the European Parliament and of the Council ('Unfair Commercial Practices Directive'), *OJ* 2005, L149/22.

4 See the ODR Regulation mentioned in footnote 1.

consumers throughout the EU. When the mechanisms available to enforce these rights are not available to consumers because of high cost or complicated procedures, these consumers' rights however remain highly theoretical. In the past, the EU already tried to overcome this problem through the Injunctions Directive[5] under which Member States need to appoint institutions or organisations capable of bringing actions aimed at the cessation of illegal conduct towards consumers. However, these cessation actions only have a preventative aim: preventing future illegal conduct towards consumers. They provide no solution for the *ex post* resolution of disputes between an individual seller and an individual consumer.

In this context, the ADR Directive aims to provide individuals and traders with access to a simple, fast and low-cost method of dispute resolution. This should result in a high level of consumer protection boosting consumers' confidence in the internal market and should contribute to the proper functioning thereof.[6] Whether it will reach these aims remains to be seen. Some of the weaknesses of the ADR Directive will be discussed below.[7]

2. The Weaknesses of the ADR Directive

A first weakness of the ADR Directive is that it leaves it to the Member States to determine whether the participation of traders in ADR procedures is mandatory.[8] This has the potential to undermine the envisaged level playing field for traders and is not conducive for consumer confidence in cross-border trade, which may ultimately be harmful for the internal market, contrary to the aims of the Directive.[9]

Secondly, the ADR Directive allows Member States to choose between ADR entities which propose or impose a solution or bring parties together with the aim of facilitating an amicable solution or a combination of these mechanisms.[10] This too may lead to an uneven level playing field within the internal market. This effect is reinforced by the combination of this freedom of choice with the Directive's rules on the extent to which an ADR outcome needs to comply with the applicable rules of substantive consumer law.

Where ADR bodies *impose* solutions, they are bound by the principle of legality.[11] This means that their solutions may not deprive the consumer of the protection he is entitled to by the mandatory provisions of the law of the Member

5 Directive 98/27/EC of the European Parliament and of the Council of 19 May 1998 on injunctions for the protection of consumers' interests, *OJ* 1998, L166/51.
6 Art. 1 *juncto* Recitals 4 and 5 of the ADR Directive.
7 For a critical view on the ADR Directive, see also Eidenmüller & Engel 2013; Eidenmüller & Engel 2014; Meller-Hannich, Höland & Krausbeck 2014; Rühl 2015, in print and <http://ssrn.com/abstract=2632117>; Wagner 2014; Weber 2015.
8 Recital 49 ADR Directive.
9 *Cf. supra* section 1.
10 Recital 21 ADR Directive.
11 Art. 11 ADR Directive.

State where he is habitually resident.[12] However, since the ADR bodies are not courts, they may not make preliminary referrals to the Court of Justice in case they are uncertain about the interpretation of rules of consumer law based on EU law.[13]

Where an ADR body merely *proposes* a solution, this solution may be less beneficial to the consumer compared to what he would obtain as a result of a court procedure.[14] It seems that it may even be less beneficial than the minimum he is entitled to under the substantive rules of EU consumer law. Equally, where the ADR body only brings parties together with the aim of facilitating an amicable solution there is nothing that prevents a solution that is less beneficial than the solution the consumer is legally entitled to. It is true that the consumer may refuse to accept the solution proposed by either the ADR body or the trader and bring court proceedings.[15] Article 9(2)(b)(ii) ADR Directive even seems to leave open the possibility for the consumer to accept the proposal and afterwards seek redress through court proceedings, without specifying the impact of this on the accepted proposal and vice versa. In any case, the whole idea of the ADR Directive is to provide the consumer with an alternative means of dispute resolution because court proceedings are generally too slow, too costly and too complicated for small consumer claims. So practically, the inferior proposed solution may be the consumer's only practicable option.[16] By allowing Member States to provide only for ADR bodies that propose solutions which do not necessarily need to meet the requirements of substantive consumer law, the EU seems to facilitate the creation of what has been called the distinction between the 'law in the books' and the 'law in action'.[17] Based on the harmonized rules of substantive consumer law, consumers in the EU have certain minimum rights, but in practice they may have to accept an inferior solution.

One could argue the following: without an ADR body that proposes a solution, the consumer who has low value claims does not obtain any remedy at all. Compared to this, an ADR body proposing a solution means progress, even if that solution does not deliver exactly what the consumer is entitled to under hard core law. I agree that ADR bodies which are not bound to apply the law may, in the short term, result in benefits for consumers compared to the current situation where court proceedings are not suited to deal with low value consumer claims. However, I am afraid that in the long run the disadvantages for the internal market will outweigh these benefits. These disadvantages result from an uneven level playing field for traders, legal uncertainty for cross-border consumer transactions and the creation of a 'law in action' that differs from the 'law in the books', created by the substantive rules of consumer law. Would both the consumers' and the EU's

12 *Ibid.*
13 *Cf.* Wagner 2014, p. 178; Weber 2015, p. 281.
14 *Cf.* Wagner 2014, p. 177.
15 See Art. 9(2) ADR Directive.
16 *Cf.* Rühl 2015 (SSRN), p. 17.
17 Pound 1910, p. 15.

interests not be better served with amendments to the national courts' systems in order to make it better suited to deal with consumer cases?[18]

This is all the more the case since the risk contained in the ADR Directive for the creation of a separate body of 'law in action' that differs from the 'law in the books' is only the most obvious in cases where the ADR body is only able to propose solutions instead of imposing them. As mentioned above, even with regard to ADR bodies that impose solutions, the ADR Directive only ensures that the consumer does not get less than he is entitled to under the mandatory rules according to the applicable law. The Directive does not guarantee the application of contractual rules that are more beneficial to the consumer, or by contrast, prevent the application of standards of consumer protection that are more consumer friendly than the rules contained in Consumer Rights Directives based on maximum harmonisation.

The ADR Directive also seems to fall short in offering the normal guarantees for the proper administration of justice.[19] Although the Directive purports to offer guarantees relating to the expertise of the members of the ADR bodies, their independence and impartiality, the value of these guarantees is questionable. The natural persons in charge of ADR do not need a university degree in law. It is sufficient that they 'possess the necessary knowledge and skills in the field of alternative or judicial resolution of consumer disputes, as well as a general understanding of law'.[20]

Although the Directive provides a list of requirements in order to guarantee the independence and impartiality of the natural persons in charge of ADR,[21] it is not opposed against them being 'employed or remunerated exclusively by a professional organisation or a business association of which the trader is a member', provided they have 'a separate and dedicated budget at their disposal which is sufficient to fulfil their tasks'.[22] Provided that the additional requirements of Article 6(3) ADR Directive[23] are complied with, Member States may even consider procedures before dispute resolution entities as ADR procedures where the natural

18 *Cf.* also Eidenmüller & Engel 2014, p. 261-298.

19 *Cf.* Eidenmüller & Engel 2014, p. 288-294.

20 Art. 6(1)(a) ADR Directive. Critical on this point also Eidenmüller & Engel 2013, p. 1707; Eidenmüller & Engel 2014, p. 288; Meller-Hannich, Höland & Krausbeck 2014, p. 36-37.

21 Art. 6 ADR Directive. It is required, for example, that the natural persons are appointed for a term of office of sufficient duration to ensure the independence of their actions, and are not liable to be relieved from their duties without just cause; that they are not subject to any instructions from either party or their representatives; that they are remunerated in a way that is not linked to the outcome of the procedure.

22 Art. 6(4) ADR Directive. Critical also Wagner 2014, p. 174.

23 E.g. that the natural persons in charge of dispute resolution are nominated by, or form part of, a collegial body composed of an equal number of representatives of consumer organisations and of representatives of the traders and are appointed as result of a transparent procedure.

persons in charge of dispute resolution are employed or remunerated exclusively by the individual trader.[24]

Similarly, the ADR Directive purports to ensure transparency, requiring ADR entities to make clear and understandable information on a whole list of elements (for example their contact details, the natural persons in charge of ADR, the method of their appointment and the length of their mandate) publicly available on their websites as well as on a durable medium upon request, and by any other means they consider appropriate.[25] However, the ADR Directive does not require the decisions of the ADR bodies to be published.[26] There is only a duty to make public annual reports containing generalised information on, for example, the number of disputes received and the types of complaints to which they are related; the percentage share of ADR procedures which were discontinued and, if known, the reasons for their discontinuation; the average time taken to resolve disputes, as well as any systematic or significant problems that occur frequently and lead to disputes between consumers and traders; such information may be accompanied by recommendations as to how such problems can be avoided or resolved in future, in order to raise traders' standards and to facilitate the exchange of information and best practices.[27] In the absence of the publication of the individual decisions, however, this does not seem sufficient to guarantee the transparency of their decisions, or the predictability of the outcomes of cases brought before them.

3. Conclusion

To conclude, the ADR Directive pursues an honourable aim, trying to provide consumers and traders with access to a simple, fast and low-cost method of dispute resolution. In the short term, it will probably improve the position of consumers compared to the *status quo ante*. However, it does not guarantee consumers the remedy they are entitled to. It institutionalises a system that does not meet the standards for the proper administration of justice and it may jeopardise the efforts made for the harmonization of the substantive rules of consumer protection and the creation of a level playing field for traders in the internal market in the long term. An EU measure aimed at amending the existing court procedures in the Member States in order to make them better suited to deal with low value consumer claims would have been preferable.

24 Art. 2(2)(a) ADR Directive. Critical also Meller-Hannich, Höland & Krausbeck 2014, p. 37; Wagner 2014, p. 174; Weber 2015, p. 280-281.

25 Art. 7(1) ADR Directive.

26 *Cf.* Rühl 2015 (SSRN), p. 17.

27 Art. 7(2) ADR Directive.

Bibliography

Eidenmüller & Engel 2013
Eidenmüller, H. & Engel, M., 'Die Schlichtungsfalle: Verbraucherrechtsdurchsetzung nach der ADR-Richtlinie und der ODR-Verordnung der EU', *Zeitschrift für Wirtschaftsrecht*, 2013, p. 1704-1710.

Eidenmüller & Engel 2014
Eidenmüller, H. & Engel, M., 'Against False Settlement: Designing Efficient Consumer Rights Enforcement Systems in Europe', *Ohio State Journal on Dispute Resolution*, 2014, Vol. 29, p. 261-296.

Meller-Hannich, Höland & Krausbeck 2014
Meller-Hannich, C., Höland, A. & Krausbeck, E., '"ADR" und "ODR": Kreationen der europäischen Rechtspolitik. Eine kritische Würdigung', *Zeitschrift für Europäisches Privatrecht*, 2014, p. 8-38.

Pound 1910
Pound, R., 'Law in the Books and Law in Action', *American Law Review*, 1910, Vol. 44, p. 12-36.

Rühl 2015
Rühl, G., 'Alternative and Online Dispute Resolution for (Cross-Border) Consumer Contracts: A Critical Evaluation of the European Legislature's Recent Efforts to promote Competitiveness and Growth in the Internal Market', *Journal of Consumer Policy*, 2015, Vol. 38, in print and <http://ssrn.com/abstract=2632117>.

Wagner 2014
Wagner, G., 'Private Law Enforcement through ADR: Wonder Drug or Snake Oil', *Common Market Law Review*, 2014, Vol. 51(1), p. 165–194.

Weber 2015
Weber, F., 'Is ADR the Superior Mechanism for Consumer Contractual Disputes?— An Assessment of the Incentivizing Effects of the ADR Directive', *Journal of Consumer Policy*, 2015, Vol. 38, p. 265–285.

N. Kornet

NORMATIVE FRAMEWORKS IN COMMERCIAL DISPUTE RESOLUTION: THE ROLE OF LEGAL AND NON-LEGAL NORMS IN MEDIATION AND ADJUDICATION

1. Introduction

When commercial actors enter into a transaction they aim to align their interests to achieve a mutually beneficial result. When a problem subsequently occurs in the performance of their transaction they will seek to resolve it with a view to maximising the value of the relationship. In the first place, they will seek resolution through cooperation in line with ordinary commercial practices and common-sense. If the parties are unable to resolve their conflicting interests together through negotiation, they may turn to other dispute resolution mechanisms that involve a neutral third party who will either assist the parties in creating a commercially-oriented solution, for instance through mediation, or who will decide on the dispute for the parties by enforcing legal rights, for instance through adjudication in the form of arbitration or litigation. These two forms of dispute resolution differ in nature and purpose. In mediation, a neutral third party - the mediator - intervenes to assist the parties in their attempt to reach a settlement agreement that preserves their transaction, salvages their on-going business relationship, and avoids escalation of their conflict into a legal dispute. In contrast, when parties pursue resolution of their dispute through adjudication, they seek strict enforcement of their legal rights laid down in their contract. The court or arbitral tribunal will assess the relative strength of the conflicting legal positions on the basis of an application of the legal norms applicable to the contractual relation. Although adjudication will lead to a resolution of the dispute, it will often have a destructive effect on the on-going business relationship between the parties.

From this brief introduction, it can be seen that these two approaches to dispute resolution have different objectives. Whereas mediation aims at a solution that meets the parties' commercial interests and expectations; adjudication leads to the settlement of a legal dispute. Due to their different nature and function, they therefore tend to give priority to different normative frameworks. Adjudication occurs entirely on the basis of the legal framework constituted by the law and the contract, while mediation, as a problem-solving process, allows a broader range of considerations to shape the outcome and thus incorporates norms and practices from other, non-legal frameworks. Nevertheless, despite this apparently clear-cut distinction, one of the controversial themes in contract law scholarship is whether contract law - and therefore the adjudicators who enforce it - should align itself more closely with commercial practice. In particular, socio-legal contract scholars call upon adjudicators to incorporate commercial norms in the law with a view to achieving results that align more closely with commercial practice and expectations. At the same time, the increasing participation of lawyers in the mediation process has an impact on the role of legal norms in mediation. The role that different normative frameworks play in these different dispute resolution mechanisms therefore may not be so straightforward.

This contribution aims to explore the different normative frames of reference that shape the commercial transaction and to examine the relative influence these normative frameworks should have in mediation and adjudication. To this end, the contribution is divided in three parts. In the first part, the different normative frames of reference that shape a commercial transaction are identified. The second part addresses the different nature and function of mediation and adjudication as dispute resolution mechanisms for commercial disputes. In the third part, the relative priority that different normative frames of reference should be given in mediation and adjudication is examined in light of the different nature and function of these dispute resolution mechanisms. In this contribution it is suggested that within each dispute resolution mechanism, the different normative frames of reference shaping the commercial transaction should be given greater or lesser weight depending on the nature and function of the dispute resolution mechanism. Thus, the nature and function of mediation, as a problem-solving process, may require the enforcement of legal norms to move to the background and allow the other normative frameworks that shape a commercial transaction to guide the resolution of a dispute. Indeed, it is posited that reliance on legal norms would actually jeopardize the nature and function of mediation. In contrast, an important function of adjudication in commercial transactions is to promote legal certainty and therefore adjudicatory proceedings should have their foundation in legal norms and adjudicators should remain wary of incorporating other normative frames of reference in the resolution of the legal dispute.

2. Normative Frameworks in Commercial Transactions

Commercial actors enter into a transaction with a view to exchanging goods and services for mutual gain in pursuit of a commercial objective. The commercial bargain they strike will be laid down in the contract concluded between them, which will contain the parties' legal rights and duties with respect to the performance of the transaction. Contracts can thus be seen to facilitate commercial transactions by providing a legal framework through which commercial actors can plan and coordinate their commercial activity.[1] In addition to the legal framework underlying the transaction, it is possible to identify two other frames of reference that inform the substance of the commercial relation.[2] Firstly, a commercial transaction is shaped by the commercial relationship within which it takes place. This commercial relationship is shaped by norms and values of a particular business or societal community concerning how individuals are expected to behave, but also by the norms and practices the parties develop between them over the course of time. The commercial relationship is established prior to a particular transaction and will continue to exist beyond its performance. The continued value of the commercial relationship, and thus the interest in adhering to norms and practices within this commercial context, will depend on the importance of maintaining a productive relation in the commercial actor's strategic business planning. Secondly, the commercial transaction aims at the exchange of goods or services on a market and therefore the economic framework, which is oriented on an economic, market-oriented rationale also impacts on commercial actors' expectations and behaviour. A commercial transaction is therefore shaped by the legal, commercial and economic frame of reference.

Each of these frames of reference shapes how commercial actors conduct their business, manage their commercial relationships, manage and allocate their commercial, economic and legal risks, as well as how the parties will behave when a problem arises in the transaction. Each frame of reference provides norms on how a particular problem or dispute should be resolved. For example, the legal framework is clearly oriented on the enforcement of the legal rights that stem from the contract and focuses on how the contract, as formulated by the parties, and the law view the dispute.[3] The commercial framework provides information on for instance the strategic commercial importance of a particular commercial relation. This normative framework focuses on the parties' past dealings and practice and the conventions of the market in which the transaction is embedded.[4] Within the commercial relation the parties will adhere to certain patterns of behaviour and social or commercial norms with respect to how they deal with a problem that arises.[5] The economic frame of reference focuses on the economic deal. It is important that the transaction works for the parties in the sense that they can maximize the value of the commercial relationship. The economic frame of reference consequently measures and assesses contractual behaviour the basis of economic rationality. Economic calculations may for instance indicate that short-term losses are worth accepting in light of long-term gains from the commercial relation.[6]

1 See e.g. Collins 1999, p. 149 *et seq.*
2 See Collins 1999, p. 128 *et seq.* and Collins 2003, p. 16, who identifies the business relation, the economic deal and the contract.
3 Collins 1999, p. 131; Collins 2003, p. 17.
4 Collins 1999, p. 180, 25 *et seq.*
5 See Collins, 1999.
6 Collins 1999, p. 130.

It is important to recognize that these various frames of reference impact on how commercial disputes are resolved. When a problem arises in a commercial transaction, the answer is not simply to be found in and determined by the legal framework created by the contract and the law, but will also engage the commercial and economic frames of reference within which the transaction is embedded. A decision not to rely on the strict enforcement of legal rights may reflect the influence of the commercial or economic context within which the transaction takes place. The contract and the law will be brought into play only if it is rational to do so, for instance when the parties anticipate that their commercial relationship is coming to an end or if economic considerations point to enforcement of the contract.[7]

One of the controversial themes in contract law scholarship is the relationship between contract law and commercial practice, expectations and norms, and the extent to which non-legal norms should be recognized and enforced in the adjudication of a commercial dispute. It is claimed by some that there is a misalignment between the legal rights stemming from the contract and contract law and the interests and expectations stemming from the commercial relation.[8] Socio-legal contract scholars have highlighted the divergence between the practice of commercial actors in the making and performance of their contracts and the law that is applied to their contracts. The results of empirical studies into contracting practice conducted by, for instance, Macaulay and Beale and Dugdale, provide evidence that commercial parties generally tend to focus on the performance aspects of their deal rather than the legal elements of the transaction.[9] When negotiating the deal and laying it down in a contract, they may refrain from addressing elements that could have a negative influence on the existing good business relationship. Although lawyers may insist on the details, commercial actors may view insistence on detailed contract terms as an indication of distrust and as 'blunt[ing] the demands of friendship, turning a cooperative venture into an antagonistic horse trade'.[10] These empirical studies also reveal that disputes are rarely resolved by contract litigation or the application of contract law.[11] Rather than threatening to sue if there is a defect in performance, for instance, commercial actors will tend to negotiate a solution and use other techniques, such as non-legal norms and sanctions, to induce performance of contractual obligations.[12] Often the commercial actors' primary interest will be to ensure the continuation of the commercial relationship through renegotiation.

In his seminal writings on contracts, Macneil emphasizes that all contracts are embedded, to a greater or lesser extent, in complex on-going relations shaped by

7 Collins 1999, p. 137; Collins 2003, p. 17.

8 See most recently Mitchell 2013. Also see the contributions in Worthington 2003.

9 Macaulay 1963; Beale & Dugdale 1975.

10 Macaulay 1963, p. 64; also Macaulay 2003, p. 46; Beale & Dugdale 1975, p. 47; Collins 1999, p. 151, 153 and 174.

11 Macaulay 1977, p. 509; Macaulay 1985, p. 467; Beale & Dugdale 1975, p. 48; also see Collins 1999, p. 137-140 on the 'non-use' of contracts.

12 Macaulay 1963, p. 61.

values such as trust, cooperation, solidarity and mutuality,[13] which renders it necessary to understand, recognize and consider all the relational elements that might affect the transaction. This highly contextual approach views the express terms of the contract as 'no more than an extremely important part of a dense web of relations'.[14] The relational patterns of behaviour and norms that arise from observation of contracting practices are considered to be equally important to understanding the commercial relation.

These sociologically-inspired insights suggest that contracts, contract law and contract enforcement through adjudication do not play the central role in resolving disputes envisaged by traditional perceptions of contract that attribute a central role to the contractual document and to the legal enforcement of contractual obligations. The underlying message of this scholarship is that contracts are not created in a vacuum, but within a particular social setting, contracting community or relationship. This broader, non-legal context can give rise to standards or norms that guide the parties' behaviour. The parties' relationship and the economic and commercial context within which the transaction takes place shape the parties' understandings and expectations of their transaction.

The question that arises is whether contract law should heed this commercial reality and incorporate the non-legal context into the legal framework. According to socio-legal scholars in particular, this commercial reality should have consequences for the law, and requires adjudicators to take a contextual approach when determining the rights and obligations of the parties.[15] From this perspective, the law best facilitates commerce when it identifies, aligns with and incorporates the non-legal, commercial norms that underlie the commercial transaction. This would mean that when interpreting and enforcing the express terms of the contract, the adjudicator should be open to 'the possibility that this wider context, and the norms generated by and within it, are relevant to how the contractual relationship should be understood, obligations derived and interpreted and disputes resolved'.[16] This requires a shift in contract law whereby norms of behaviour generated between the parties and those generated from industries or other commercial contexts are given effect within the legal framework.[17]

Other contract scholars disagree. Although they recognize that contracts are socially embedded, they question whether that should have implications for contract law and the rules that are applied by adjudicators.[18] They have argued that by incorporating the non-legal frames of reference into the legal, the effectiveness of such non-legal mechanisms would be undermined.[19] They highlight that the value of non-legal norms is precisely that they remain outside the legal framework and

13 See in particular Macneil 1978; Macneil 2000.

14 Macneil 2003, p. 208.

15 Collins 1999; also see Wightman 2003 and Mitchell 2013.

16 Mitchell 2013, p. 242.

17 Mitchell 2013, p. 423.

18 See Scott 2000a; Scott 2000b; Ben-Shahar 1999; Epstein 1999.

19 See Bernstein 1996; Bernstein 1999; Scott 2000a; Scott 2000b.

rely on non-legal and reputational sanctions. These scholars reject that contract law should be aligned with commercial norms and expectations. They explain that commercial actors make a variety of commitments during the course of their commercial relationship, but only some of these are intended to be legally binding. Others belong to the non-legal realm of their transaction.[20] For example, they will make concessions in order to demonstrate flexibility and cooperation. These practices develop while the parties trust one another and wish to preserve the relationship with a view to future dealings.[21] Although the parties are aware that these practices often vary from the express terms of the contract, they are willing to make such flexible adjustments (for instance accepting late payment, varying quantity terms, adjusting prices etc.) as long as the relationship is profitable and there is a prospect of future dealings.[22] These 'relationship preserving norms' are not always intended to reflect legally enforceable commitments. The contracting parties understand that these flexible adjustments are part of 'the give and take of ordinary mercantile life', and should not be made obligatory in the law.[23] Instead, once the contractual relationship breaks down, Bernstein explains, commercial parties want so-called 'end-game norms' to apply.[24] These end-game norms are contained in the express terms of the contract and in the law of contract. Patterns of behaviour that courts observe in search of commercial norms and practices often reflect these relationship-preserving norms, which do not necessarily reflect the norms the parties want to apply once trust and the likelihood of future dealings has dissipated. Therefore these commercial norms and practices, it is argued, do not provide useful information for a court confronted with a contract dispute.[25] By applying these norms in the end-game, the courts are misinterpreting their intended effect. Bernstein and Scott each explain that contracting parties allocate certain aspects of their contractual relationship between the legal and the non-legal realms in order to maximize the value of their commercial relationship.[26] They therefore argue that the division between the legal and the non-legal realm of the commercial relationship should be respected and the courts should not incorporate non-legal norms in the contract and the law. Following this line of reasoning, the contract should be subject to clear and simple rules, and the terms of the contract should be interpreted and enforced objectively without reliance on broader contextual information. These scholars furthermore have expressed a concern for judicial error because courts are unable to access reliable information on non-legal norms and, even if they could, they do not have the expertise needed to accurately assess the relevance of this broader contextual information for the particular legal dispute.[27]

20 See Bernstein 1996.
21 Bernstein 1999, p. 717.
22 Bernstein 1996, p. 1787-1788.
23 Bernstein 1999, p. 752; Bernstein 1996, p. 1801.
24 Bernstein 1996, p. 1797; Bernstein 1999, p. 754.
25 Bernstein 1999, p. 779-780.
26 Bernstein 1996, p. 1788; Scott 1990, p. 615; Charny 1999.
27 Scott 2000a; Bernstein 1996; Gava & Greene 2004.

To summarize, it can be seen that commercial relationships are highly complex. They are shaped and governed by norms that stem from different normative frameworks, reflecting different interests at different times in the commercial relationship. Although the legal framework as reflected in the contract and contract law is an important element of the commercial transaction, its function and significance fluctuates throughout the time span of the transaction, and often only becomes relevant once the commercial relationship comes to an end and there is no prospect for salvaging it. In the pre-contractual and performance stages of a commercial transaction, the commercial framework reflected in non-legal norms and practices play a significant role. When a dispute occurs, the question therefore arises, according to which norms the dispute should be resolved. It will be argued in section 4 that this will depend on the state of the commercial relationship at the time the dispute occurs and the nature of the dispute resolution mechanism that is used. Before returning to this question, however, different approaches to dispute resolution will first be reviewed with particular attention being given to mediation.

3. Mediation and Adjudication on the Continuum of Dispute Resolution Mechanisms

When a dispute arises in a commercial transaction, the parties have a range of approaches and procedures at their disposal to respond to and resolve the dispute. These different mechanisms for dispute resolution can be positioned along a continuum. The two ends of the continuum vary considerably in the way in which the dispute is addressed and settled. Dispute resolution mechanisms can be positioned along the continuum on the basis of who decides over the outcome of the dispute. At one end of the continuum, the parties decide the outcome; they must reach agreement on how the dispute is to be resolved. Such dispute resolution mechanisms are characterized by voluntary participation and cooperation between the parties. At the other end of the continuum, a neutral third party determines the outcome of the dispute and the parties must submit to the decision of the adjudicator. Dispute resolution mechanisms can also be positioned on the continuum depending on the way in which the outcome is achieved, ranging from informal proceedings to more formal proceedings. At one end, the parties retain control over the process and at the other end they cede control. This continuum is often depicted as in the figure below.

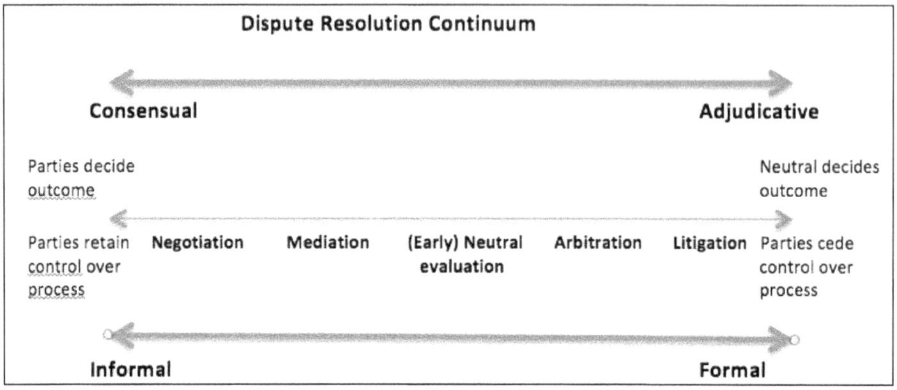

When a dispute arises in a commercial transaction, the preferred method of dispute resolution is negotiation. The commercial actors voluntarily entered into a transaction to collaborate in achieving an outcome that is mutually beneficial to them. When they encounter a problem in the performance of their transaction, they would ideally resolve it between them through negotiation, since it is the parties themselves who are in the best position to determine what solution best meets their interests. Through negotiation, the parties are able to achieve an outcome that offers mutual gain and achieves the outcome they initially set out to realize, thus preserving the transaction and the on-going commercial relationship. The aim of negotiation should be to identify the shared and compatible interests that reside behind the parties' opposed positions with a view to constructing a solution that leads to mutual gain.[28] When the parties are left to reach a solution on their own, however, their negotiations may dissolve into positional bargaining, with each party taking a position that best serves its own interests. This can lead to an escalation of the dispute since the parties are more concerned with convincing the other party of their own position than addressing the underlying interests that could offer a solution. The more the parties become locked into their positions, the more likely that negotiations will result in an impasse or a breakdown in the relationship since neither party will be willing to back down for fear of showing weakness. When this occurs, they will need to involve a third party. Depending on the dispute resolution method adopted, the role of the third party and the disputing parties will differ. The parties may decide to escalate their dispute and submit their dispute to adjudicatory proceedings to have a third party determine the outcome. An alternative approach is to involve a third party to move the parties beyond their impasse and refocus and assist in the negotiation process, for instance by engaging a mediator.

In mediation the parties use the assistance of a neutral third party with no authority to make binding decisions for the parties to solve the problem they have

28 See Fisher, Ury & Patton 1992.

encountered. Therefore mediation can be viewed as 'assisted and enhanced negotiation'.[29] The mediator intervenes in the dispute with the purpose of helping the parties to mend their fences and improve their relationship by facilitating effective communication and using constructive problem-solving and negotiation procedures to allow them to reach a voluntary and mutually acceptable resolution of their dispute.[30]

Voluntary participation constitutes the cornerstone of mediation.[31] Mediation revolves around the parties taking responsibility for the resolution of their dispute by collaborating with a view to constructing their own solution. A party who is coerced into mediation is less likely to participate actively in collaborative problem-solving than one who takes part voluntarily. The parties are responsible for creating a solution for the problem that has arisen, therefore in resolving their conflict, they must be able to accept or reject certain solutions based on a consideration of their needs and interests and the alternatives available to them. Nolan-Haley therefore characterizes mediation as 'a voluntary process of self-determination'.[32] The mediator does not possess decision-making power and does not function as an adjudicator determining how the dispute is to be resolved.[33] Rather than imposing an outcome upon the parties, the role of the mediator is to facilitate communication between the parties to assist them in identifying, understanding and articulating their needs and interests to each other. In this way, the parties are assisted in identifying mutually acceptable solutions that meet their underlying needs and interests. This lack of decision-making power on the part of the mediator is what makes mediation attractive to commercial parties, because it allows them to retain control over the process and outcome.[34] At the same time, the value of involving a mediator is that she is able to alter the dynamics of the existing negotiation procedure.[35] Whereas bilateral negotiations may dissolve in recriminations, posturing and entrenchment in positions, the involvement of a mediator can refocus the negotiations on the interests and needs of the parties that lie behind the positions they expounded.

Effective communication and exchange of information is crucial for successful mediation. For this reason, during the mediation process, the mediator will meet with the parties in joint sessions, but also in caucuses with each party separately. The mediator can use these caucuses to obtain background information, to ensure that the party is being heard and understood, to identify the underlying needs, interests and concerns the parties seek to have satisfied, and to explore the relative strengths and weaknesses of possible solutions without the other party being

29 Peters 2008, p. 1252.
30 Moore 2014, p. 20; Peters 2008, p. 1253.
31 Spencer & Brogan 2006, p. 87; Hopt & Steffek 2012, p. 11.
32 Nolan-Haley 2012, p. 68.
33 Spencer & Brogan 2006, p. 88; Hopt & Steffek 2013, p. 11; Moore 2014, p. 22.
34 Moore 2014, p. 22; Stipanowich & Lamare 2014, p. 36 and 51; Burton 1995, p. 638 and 641.
35 Moore 2014, p. 22-23.

present.[36] The mediator is thus able to gain a more complete picture of all the circumstances underlying the dispute, to view the issues from various angles, identify 'compatible, complementary and non-competitive interests' with a view to creating opportunities to collaborate towards a mutually beneficial resolution.[37] The mediator is to be seen as a 'broker of perspectives' between the parties, rather than a broker of information.[38] By meeting with parties separately, the mediator will acquire information that the parties may not immediately be willing to share with each other, especially when the information is commercially sensitive. Having a better understanding of each party's concerns, the mediator is able to refocus them on the joint endeavour they originally entered into, in particular the realization of the shared objective of the commercial transaction.

Although communication is essential for successful mediation, it is important that such communication takes place in a safe environment. Confidentiality is therefore another core feature of mediation, since it ensures that the parties are willing to participate and communicate effectively to discuss concerns, interests and issues with the mediator and each other without fears that such information will be disclosed.[39] The parties will wish to ensure that certain information, statements or admissions they make during mediation will not be used as evidence against them in other - adjudicatory - proceedings should mediation fail. If they fear that the information they share with each other or with the mediator will be made admissible as evidence in subsequent adjudicatory proceedings, or be made available to the public at large, this could reduce their willingness to engage in mediation. For this reason, in addition to confidentiality agreements, the law plays an important role in protecting confidentiality with a view to maintaining the effectiveness of the mediation process. Instruments dealing with mediation, such as the EU Mediation Directive and the UNCITRAL Model Law on International Commercial Conciliation, therefore contain provisions dealing with confidentiality and the disclosure of information and admissibility of evidence.

The objective of mediation is to solve the problem that lies at the root of the dispute between the parties. In constructing the solution, the parties are not confined to legal issues and solutions that stem from the enforcement of their legal rights as laid down in their contract and the law. In mediation, parties are free to develop a unique solution, even solutions that would not be possible within the legal system.[40] For example, in the case of an alleged breach of contract, the law would restrict the parties to remedies available under the law, such as a damages claim or the right to terminate the contract. In mediation, parties can brainstorm and develop creative solutions to remedy the effects of a breach that go beyond those provided in the law.[41] Indeed, mediation induces the parties to free themselves from

36 Moore 2014, p. 111, 122, 127.

37 Moore 2014, p. 127.

38 Dress 1988, p. 576

39 Spencer & Brogan 2006, p. 86.

40 Spencer & Brogan 2006, p. 99.

41 *Ibid*.

the encumbrances of rules and legal rights and instead allows them to work out their own rules.[42] In this way, the parties can address the interests and objectives that form the foundation of their transaction. Rather than focussing on legal rules, mediation allows the parties to address the interests and objectives that form the foundation of their transaction to achieve a win-win solution for the underlying problem. In reaching their solution, parties may be guided by commercial or social norms that are relevant to their relationship.[43] Indeed, this can be seen as one of the strengths of mediation, it allows for a solution to be constructed based on considerations that stem from the various frames of reference that impact on the commercial transaction. The outcome of successful mediation is a voluntary settlement in which the parties are able to 'craft individualized justice on their own terms based on their own interests and values'.[44] Since the parties are themselves responsible for creating the solution, it is likely that they will be more satisfied with it and therefore more likely to comply when compared to a solution imposed by a third party.[45]

Adjudicative procedures, such as arbitration and litigation, are positioned at the other end of the dispute resolution continuum. In contrast to mediation, where the mediator has no authority to impose an outcome on the parties, in arbitration and litigation, a neutral third party decides a dispute between the parties on the basis of legal rights and obligations. The adjudicator has the power to decide and the parties must abide by the decision. The difference between arbitration and litigation is primarily to be found in the nature of the proceedings. In litigation, the parties' dispute is submitted to the jurisdiction of a national court. The proceedings are conducted in public in accordance with the procedural law of the forum. Arbitration is positioned left of litigation on the continuum, not because the decision taken by the arbitral tribunal is any less binding than a court decision, but because the parties retain some control over the way in which the arbitral proceeding is conducted. The parties to arbitration can agree upon the place of arbitration and the procedural law and rules that are applicable to the conduct of the proceedings. They are also able to decide upon the persons who are to act as arbitrators; in this way they constitute their own private court. However, once arbitration is initiated, like litigation, the parties are bound by the formalities of the chosen procedure and the decision rendered by the tribunal. The court or arbitral tribunal render a decision based on an assessment of the relative strength of the legal positions of each of the parties and will decide which party 'wins' and which 'loses' in accordance with the law. Whereas court decisions are published and consequently have some precedential effect for future transactions, the decisions of arbitral tribunals, like the proceedings themselves, remain private.

42 Fuller 1971, p. 325-326.
43 Fuller 1971, p. 308.
44 Nolan-Haley 2012, p. 69.
45 Nolan-Haley 2012, p. 69; Stipanowich & Lamare 2014, p. 2; Stipanowich 2004.

At this stage it is possible to contrast mediation and adjudication in the way in which resolution of the dispute between the parties is sought. In adjudicative proceedings, the focus is on the legal issues and the basis for the dispute is the parties' conflicting legal positions. The court or arbitral tribunal examines the events and evaluates the contract and the parties' legal positions to render a decision that is based on legal norms. Where legal norms dictate the outcome, however, a barrier is set up to effective problem-solving and the search for a mutually beneficial solution. Indeed, the purpose of adjudication is to settle the dispute based on legal norms as opposed to solving the problem that forms the foundation of the dispute. In adjudication, the focus is on the conflicting legal positions, as opposed to conflicting needs and interests underlying the commercial transaction. In this way, adjudication is backward-looking, focusing on facts, evidence and arguments found in the contract that was originally concluded, rather than looking to develop solutions that are beneficial to the future of the commercial relationship.[46] Due to the polarization that occurs when parties focus on competing legal positions, the consequence of this approach is that adjudicatory proceedings more often end rather than repair commercial relationships and they do not resolve the problem that led to the dispute.[47] Not only do adjudicatory proceedings have destructive effects on the commercial relationship, it can also have a negative impact on the company's reputation, which in turn makes it difficult to establish new relationships.[48]

In contrast, the objective of mediation is to focus on mending fences, restoring relationships, and solving the problem that underlies the dispute. In his seminal piece on mediation, Lon Fuller highlights mediation's capacity to 'reorient the parties toward each other not by imposing rules on them, but by helping them to achieve a new and shared perception of their relationship, a perception that will direct their attitude and dispositions toward one another'.[49] Consequently, mediation is not concerned with enforcing legal rights, but with creating mutually beneficial solutions for the problems that have led to the dispute. This focus on interests means that the parties' legal rights and claims will move to the background, and commercial norms can be given greater weight. When contrasting adjudication and mediation, it can be seen therefore that adjudicatory procedures, with their focus on legal positions and legal norms, lead to competition between the parties to win the case. Adjudication thus ends a dispute by determining which party wins. In contrast, mediation is not simply aimed at ending the dispute, but at promoting collaboration between the parties with a view to creating additional value, for instance by restructuring the relationship to make it as commercially advantageous as possible for both parties.[50]

46 Peters 2008, p. 1261; Moore 2014, p. 22.
47 Reiff 2007, p. 24.
48 Wälde 2006, p. 207; Dress 1988, p. 572.
49 Fuller 1971, p. 325.
50 Wälde 2006, p. 206.

4. Normative Frameworks in Commercial Dispute Resolution

When a dispute arises in a transaction, commercial actors can rely on a range of norms and different dispute resolution mechanisms to reach a resolution. The question is which norms should be given precedence for resolving the dispute and does this depend on the dispute resolution mechanism the parties opt for. The answer to this question depends on the state of the commercial relationship at the time of dispute resolution and the nature of the dispute resolution mechanism that is used. It is suggested that while the parties seek to collaborate on constructing a solution that preserves the transaction and the on-going business relationship but are unable to reach an acceptable solution without third party intervention, they should opt for mediation. Conversely, where the dispute has escalated so that the parties no longer perceive a future for their on-going relationship and/or they require a determination on legal rights, adjudication is the appropriate method of dispute resolution. This clearly aligns with the nature and function of these two distinct dispute resolution mechanisms. Whereas mediation is aimed at solving the problem that has arisen in the commercial relationship and placing the responsibility to construct a solution that is mutually beneficial on the parties; adjudication involves a third party to settle the dispute for the parties once it has escalated to a stage that they are no longer able or willing to reach a solution on their own and seek enforcement of their legal rights. Whereas mediation is oriented on the commercial interests and relationship underlying the transaction; adjudication is oriented on legal rights that stem from the contract. Due to their different nature and function, the choice for the appropriate dispute resolution mechanism consequently should influence the relative weight to be given to the different normative frameworks that shape the commercial transaction.

The core feature of mediation is that the parties voluntarily participate in the resolution of their dispute and that they are flexible in constructing a solution that reflects their shared interest in preserving the transaction and the on-going relationship. The focus is on the parties' commercial and economic needs and interests, rather than on the legal rights and obligations laid down in the contract. Belhorn identifies the following cognitive tools the parties use to evaluate their interests: '(i) legal norms, which are related to the parties' expectations of a disputes' outcome at trial; (ii) social norms, which are related to the parties' expectations of the social sanctions they may incur or avoid depending on whether mediation is successful or abortive; and (iii) personal interests, which are related to the parties' own perceptions of their autonomous preferences and needs'.[51] In creating their solution, therefore, the parties can rely on a multitude of norms and practices. The legal framework, as laid down in the contract and the law, is consequently relevant, but it is not determinative of the outcome. After all, commercial transactions are founded on party autonomy, and the parties remain free to modify their legal rights and obligations if they consider that to be in their

51 Belhorn 2005, p. 1006.

mutual interest. Mediation allows the parties to move away from a legal understanding of their dispute and seeking a solution that conforms to pre-existing legal norms.[52] Instead they can acquire a greater appreciation of non-legal norms and the non-legal incentives that can influence their settlement choices.[53] Because these non-legal norms form a valid part of the dispute resolution process, mediation can add more value to solving the underlying problem than adjudication which is aimed at settling the dispute on the basis of legal norms.[54] Nevertheless, the legal framework can provide the yardstick against which the failure to reach a settlement can be measured.[55] Thus legal norms do play a role, and they can constitute bargaining chips.[56] At the same time, it should be observed that giving too much weight to the legal framework in mediation could jeopardize the very nature and usefulness of this dispute resolution mechanism. When parties invest significantly in obtaining a legal analysis of their dispute, they will seek to capitalize on their investment in acquiring the legal opinion and be less likely to take advantage of the unique, non-legal benefits of mediation, which allows them to seek solutions outside the legal framework.[57] Where legal norms are allowed to dominate, mediation moves away from its focus on the identification of interests and constructing a solution that creates additional value for the parties by resolving the actual problem that lies beneath the dispute.[58] The increasing involvement of lawyers in mediation consequently threatens to turn commercially-oriented mediation into legal mediation. In the end, the key to mediation is that it is the parties who are responsible for the outcome and therefore they are responsible for deciding the relative weight to be given to the different normative frameworks in resolving the dispute.

Mediation is thus not to be viewed as an alternative forum for the private enforcement of legal rights, but as a forum for collaborative problem-solving and dispute resolution based on a broader set of norms. Mediation provides the parties a forum in which they can develop different incentives to bring about performance in conformity with their expectations. By incorporating broader dimensions of the transaction, including the commercial and economic framework, mediation thus provides a forum for the evolution, recognition and enforcement of non-legal norms, although these will remain private and hidden, due to the privacy of the proceedings. Furthermore, the settlement agreement reached by the parties is private and confidential, and consequently the outcome, and the norms and practices on which it is based, remains unknown. As a result, the parties may be able to develop unique, innovative and flexible solutions, knowing they will not create legal norms for other transactions. Mediation can therefore lead to norm-

52 Fuller, 1971, p. 308; Waldman 1997, p. 705.
53 See Belhorn 2005.
54 Belhorn 2005, p. 988.
55 Bühring-Uhle, Kirchhoff & Scherer 2006, p. 148.
56 *Ibid.*
57 Belhorn 2005, p. 1000.
58 Wälde 2006, p. 213.

generation by private actors, however, such norms will not have precedential or law-making value since they remain in the private realm.

If parties seek to resolve their dispute through adjudication, they usually do so because they have been unable to reach a solution by negotiation or mediation and have reached the end of the commercial relationship. Parties may also proceed to adjudication if there is a legal issue that needs to be settled, for instance in light of other transactions they have entered into or will enter into in the future. In adjudication, whether through arbitration or litigation, the parties' dispute is framed in strictly legal terms, and the adjudicator is charged with determining the proper interpretation and application of legal norms stemming from the contract concluded between the parties or the law that applies to it. The question that has arisen in contract law scholarship is what role should non-legal, commercial norms and expectations play in determining the parties' legal rights. The position forwarded in this contribution is that adjudicators should be extremely wary of incorporating non-legal norms in the legal framework of adjudication for three main reasons.

Firstly, the incorporation of non-legal norms into the legal framework would jeopardize legal certainty. Scott highlights that certainty, predictability and stability are the 'bedrock desiderata of commercial law'.[59] Commercial actors use contracts to create a legal framework for planning and coordinating their commercial activities and managing the risks associated with the transaction and the possible problems that could arise. To do so effectively, they must know with some clarity and predictability to which legal norms they are bound. The contract and contract law determine how the parties will deal with contingencies, defective performance or opportunistic behaviour if the parties cannot resolve the problem themselves in accordance with commercial norms and practices. Where the law is uncertain, commercial actors will need to provide greater detail in their contract in order to restore clarity and predictability concerning the legal norms that will apply in case adjudicatory proceedings are initiated, which increases the transaction costs associated with the contract. Clarity and predictability of the norms in the legal framework are also important for the proper functioning of other, non-adjudicatory dispute resolution mechanisms. Commercial parties engage in negotiation and mediation in the shadow of the law. The legal framework therefore provides the yardstick for the alternative to not reaching an agreement.[60] If the parties are unable to reach settlement through negotiation or mediation, they know that the dispute will need to be resolved by an adjudicator. Uncertainty in the law is created when the contracting parties are not able to predict how the adjudicator will apply a certain rule. It is increased when the adjudicator steps outside the existing legal framework on which the parties have based their contractual framework to incorporate non-legal norms.

59 Scott 2000b, p. 149.
60 Bühring-Uhle, Kirchhoff & Scherer 2006, p. 148.

It could be argued that the incorporation of non-legal norms that guide commercial conduct is not necessarily a great threat to certainty and predictability since the parties would abide by the norms that stem from their own commercial framework in any event, but this leads to a second objection to the incorporation of non-legal norms in adjudicatory proceedings. The incorporation of non-legal norms supposes that it is possible to identify these norms with some certainty and predictability. It has to be recognized, however, that non-legal, commercial norms do not constitute bright-line rules.[61] It can be questioned whether there is reliable evidence of the existence of certain commercial norms and practices and even if there is, whether it can be used by adjudicators in a reliable way.[62] To find such information would require empirical studies and would require adjudicators who possess the skills that are necessary to analyze economic and sociological information.[63] Adjudicators are experts in law, they do not have the expertise and knowledge needed to put such information into the proper commercial perspective.[64] Such information would likely also go through a 'legal filter' in order to attribute it a 'reasonable' meaning in the eyes of the law. Bernstein even challenges the existence of commercial customs that can be useful to courts. She explains that the customs that can be identified provide commercial parties 'with a set of vaguely defined yet workable relationship-preserving norms', rather than clear rules that an adjudicator could use to settle a dispute.[65] Even where these social norms can be identified, they will need to be evaluated against other, competing norms, as well as the objective of the transaction to realize an immediate profit or to build a long-term commercial relationship.[66] Gava and Greene doubt whether the courts are in the best position to make such an evaluation and suggest that this is better left to the market players themselves.[67] Due to the lack of reliable information and clear-cut norms, the risk of judicial error is greater when the courts enforce non-legal norms than when they simply restrict themselves to enforcing the terms of the contract.[68]

A third reason why adjudicators should be reluctant to incorporate non-legal norms in legal proceedings is that it misconceives the nature of non-legal norms and the intentions of the parties when they rely on them during performance of the transaction. If the parties had wanted to be legally bound by these non-legal norms and practices, they could have expressly included them in the contract, however they opted not do so. Bernstein identifies a number of reasons why parties may decide against incorporating non-legal norms and highlights the distinction to be

61 See for instance Bernstein 1999.
62 See Gava & Greene 2004, p. 621 *et seq.*
63 Gava & Greeene 2004, p. 618, 623.
64 Also see Posner 2000, who refers to the 'radical incompetence' of judges to be able to deal with this type of information.
65 Bernstein 1999, p. 717; Gava & Greene 2004, p. 621.
66 Gava & Greene 2004, p. 622.
67 Gava & Greene 2004, p. 624.
68 Bernstein 1996, p. 1795.

made between relationship-preserving and end-game norms.[69] Relationship-preserving norms are the 'performance norms' that govern the relationship whilst the parties continue to trust each other and are focussed on the value of preserving the commercial relationship.[70] These norms may be quite different from the end-game norms that are contained in the parties' contract and which the parties intend to have applied by the adjudicator when they are unable to collaborate to resolve a dispute.[71] While the parties continue to trust each other and value potential future dealings, they will tend to refrain from relying on strict enforcement of their legal rights, and instead demonstrate flexibility and cooperation; behaviour that is essentially contrary to the express terms they have laid down in their contract. A classic example is where a buyer waives his contractual rights in case of a breach of a strict delivery date. With a view to preserving the on-going commercial relationship with the seller, the buyer may be willing to forego his claim to damages or termination. However, where this occurs on a regular basis, the buyer may no longer trust his counterpart and at a certain point seek enforcement of his contractual rights. An adjudicator who observes this pattern of behaviour may be inclined to attribute legal consequences to the buyer's behaviour and deny the buyer's claim in relation to the breach of the strict delivery date. In doing so, the adjudicator could be misinterpreting the buyer's behaviour, however, and may fail to realize that the buyer had opted to be flexible while there was still a future for the commercial relationship. When the adjudicator incorporates these relationship-preserving norms in the legal framework, he consequently undermines the parties' choice to have different stages of their relationship be governed by different normative frameworks in order to maximize the value of their transaction.[72] Only the parties are able to determine which normative framework meets their interests at a particular stage in their relationship; the adjudicator does not have the necessary information or expertise to make this decision for the parties, and therefore should not impose a non-legal normative framework upon them when the parties have clearly chosen to shift their dispute from the non-legal to the legal realm. Furthermore, by incorporating non-legal norms into the legal framework, the adjudicator makes it difficult for commercial parties to enter into purely non-legal arrangements since they will be fearful of the consequences that demonstrating flexibility for instance will have once the commercial relationship comes to an end and they seek enforcement of their legal rights.[73] Thus, Bernstein emphasizes that when trust has dissipated and the parties no longer see a future for their commercial relationship they prefer to have the end-game norms laid down in the contract govern their commercial relationship.

In the end, party choice determines which normative framework should take precedence in different dispute resolution mechanisms. When commercial actors

69 Bernstein 1996, p. 1797-1798.
70 Bernstein 1996, p. 1796.
71 *Ibid.*
72 Bernstein 1996, p. 1778.
73 Bernstein 1996, p. 1771, 1794.

opt for mediation, they retain control over the outcome. Commercial actors perceive the retention of control as one of the main advantages of mediation.[74] The mediator has no decision-making power and cannot impose a solution upon the parties; the parties must construct the solution themselves. In developing their solution, the parties can choose to give preference to a wide range of considerations and norms, and ultimately they can generate the relevant norms for their own relationship, whether based on commercial, economic or legal considerations, with a view to maximizing the value of their commercial relationship. If the parties do not engage in mediation, or if mediation is unsuccessful, and their dispute escalates to the end-game stage, the parties can choose to have their dispute settled through adjudication. Once adjudicatory proceedings are initiated, it has to be recognized that the parties lose control over the outcome and they must abide by the decision rendered by the adjudicator. They consequently also lose control over the norms that will be determinative of the outcome. It should be recognized that commercial parties only decide to initiate legal proceedings once they have attempted and failed to reach a solution outside the law or where resolution of the legal issue is important for the conduct of future transactions. The initiation of adjudicatory proceedings should therefore be seen as a deliberate choice to move the dispute from the non-legal to the legal realm, and with that as a conscious choice to have the outcome determined by the legal framework created by the contract and the law. In light of the objections made previously to the incorporation of non-legal norms in the legal framework, the adjudicator must recognize that certainty and predictability is best ensured when the dispute is settled on the basis of legal norms, that it does not have the expertise and knowledge to interpret the relevance of non-legal norms for the particular contractual relationship even if it would be possible to obtain reliable evidence of such norms, and that by initiating adjudicatory proceedings, the parties have chosen to move the dispute from the non-legal to the legal realm. Consequently, the normative framework created by the contract and the law should govern the resolution of the dispute. Incorporation of other normative frameworks should only be pursued in adjudicatory proceedings if there is reliable evidence of such norms and the way in which they impact on the particular commercial transaction and the parties have clearly chosen to have such norms incorporated in the legal framework.

5. Conclusion

Commercial transactions are highly complex and multifaceted. They are shaped by interests, norms and practices stemming from the commercial, economic and legal context within which they are embedded. When a dispute arises between the parties, the solution is not simply to be found in the terms of the contract and the law. It will also be necessary to engage the commercial and economic frames of reference, and usually this is what the parties will do first. The purpose of this

[74] Stipanowich & Lamare 2014.

contribution was to explore the different normative frames of reference that shape the commercial transaction and to examine the relative influence these normative frameworks should have in mediation and adjudication. It was suggested that within each dispute resolution mechanism, the different normative frames of reference shaping the commercial transaction should be given greater or lesser weight depending on the nature and function of the dispute resolution mechanism. It can be concluded that the importance of legal norms increases along the continuum. Thus, the nature and function of mediation, as a problem-solving process, may require the enforcement of legal norms to move to the background and allow the other normative frameworks that shape a commercial transaction to guide the resolution of a dispute. Indeed, it is posited that reliance on legal norms could actually jeopardize the nature and function of mediation. At the same time, it has to be recognized that the core feature of mediation is that the parties take responsibility for the outcome, and therefore they also control which norms prevail in the creation of a solution. Consequently, if they choose to rely on legal norms to resolve their dispute, they are free to do so. In contrast, an important function of adjudication in commercial transactions is to promote legal certainty and therefore adjudicatory proceedings should have their foundation in legal norms. Adjudicatory proceedings frame the dispute in strictly legal terms, and consequently, where legal issues are at stake, legal norms should prevail. Where commercial actors have exhausted other avenues for resolving their dispute and turn to an adjudicator to decide the outcome of their dispute, it would seem that non-legal norms have not been capable of providing a solution, therefore adjudicators should remain wary of incorporating other normative frames of reference in the resolution of the legal dispute.

Bibliography

Beale & Dugdale 1975
Beale, H. & Dugdale, T., 'Contracts Between Businessmen: Planning and the Use of Contractual Remedies', *British Journal of Law and Society*, 1975, Vol. 2, p. 45-60.

Belhorn 2005
Belhorn, S.R., 'Settling Beyond the Shadow or the Law: How Mediation Can Make the Most of Social Norms', *Ohio State Journal on Dispute Resolution*, 2005, Vol. 20, p. 981-1026.

Ben-Shahar 1999
Ben-Shahar, O., 'The Tentative Case Against Flexibility in Commercial Law', *University of Chicago Law Review*, 1999, Vol. 66, p. 781-820.

Bernstein 1996
Bernstein, L., 'Merchant Law in a Merchant Court: Rethinking the Code's Search for Immanent Business Norms', *University of Pennsylvania Law Review*, 1996, Vol. 144, p. 1765-1821.

Bernstein 1999
Bernstein, L., 'The Questionable Empirical Basis of Article 2's Incorporation Strategy: A Preliminary Study', *University of Chicago Law Review*, 1999, Vol. 66, p. 710-780.

Bühring-Uhle, Kirchhoff & Scherer 2006
Bühring-Uhle, C., Kirchhoff, L. & Scherer, G., *Arbitration and Mediation in International Business*, Alphen aan den Rijn: Kluwer Law International, 2006.

Burton 1995
Burton, S.J., 'Combining Conciliation with Arbitration of International Commercial Disputes', *Hastings International and Comparative Law Review*, 1995, Vol. 18, p. 637-658.

Charny 1999
Charny, D., 'The New Formalism in Contract', *University of Chicago Law Review*, 1999, Vol. 66, p. 842-857.

Collins 1999
Collins, H., *Regulating Contracts*, Oxford: Oxford University Press, 1999.

Collins 2003
Collins, H., *The Law of Contract*, 4th edn., London/Edinburgh: Lexis Nexis, 2003.

Dress 1988
Dress, T.P., 'International Commercial Mediation and Conciliation', *Loloya L.A. International and Comparative Law Journal,* 1988, Vol. 10, p. 569-581.

Epstein 1999
Epstein, R.A., 'Confusion about Custom: Disentangling Informal Customs from Standard Contractual Provisions', *University of Chicago Law Review,* 1999, Vol. 66, p. 821-835.

Fisher, Ury & Patton 1999
Fisher, R., Ury, W. & Patton, B., *Getting to Yes: Negotiating Agreement without Giving In,* London: Random House Business Books, 1999.

Fuller 1971
Fuller, L., 'Mediation - Its Form and Functions', *Southern California Law Review,* 1971, Vol. 44, p. 305-339.

Gava & Greene 2004
Gava, J. & Greene, J., 'Do we Need a Hybrid Law of Contract? Why Hugh Collins is Wrong and Why it Matters', *Cambridge Law Journal,* 2004, Vol. 63, p. 605-631.

Hopt & Steffek 2012
Hopt, K.J. & Steffek, F., 'Mediation: Comparison of Laws, Regulatory Models, Fundamental Issues', in: Hopt, K.J. & Steffek, F. (eds.), *Mediation: Principles and Regulation in Comparative Perspective,* Oxford: Oxford University Press, 2012, [accessed via Oxford Scholarship Online]

Macaulay 1963
Macaulay, S., 'Non-contractual Relations in Business: A Preliminary Study', *American Sociological Review,* 1963, Vol. 28, p. 55-69.

Macaulay 1977
Macaulay, S., 'Elegant Models, Empirical Pictures and the Complexities of Contract', *Law & Society Review,* 1977, Vol. 11, p. 507-528.

Macaulay 1985
Macaulay, S., 'An Empirical View of Contract', *Wisconsin Law Review,* 1985, p. 465-482.

Macaulay 2003
Macaulay, S., 'The Real Deal and the Paper Deal: Empirical Pictures of Relationships, Complexity and the Urge for Transparent Simple Rules', *Modern Law Review,* 2003, Vol. 66, p. 44-79.

Macneil 1978
Macneil, I.R., 'Contracts: Adjustment of Long-term Economic Relations under Classical, Neoclassical, and Relational Contract Law', *Northwester University Law Review*, 1978, Vol. 72, p. 854-905.

Macneil 2000
Macneil, I.R., 'Relational Contract Theory: Challenges and Queries', *Northwestern University Law Review*, 2000, Vol. 94, p. 877-907.

Macneil 2003
Macneil, I.R., 'Reflections on Relational Contract Theory after a Neo-classical Seminar', in: Campbell, D. & Collins, H. (eds.), *Implicit Dimensions of Contract. Discrete, Relational and Network Contracts*, Oxford: Hart Publishing, 2003, p. 207-217.

Mitchell 2013
Mitchell, C., *Contract Law And Contract Practice: Bridging The Gap Between Legal Reasoning And Commercial Expectation*, Oxford: Hart Publishing, 2013.

Moore 2014
Moore, C.W., *The Mediation Process. Practical Strategies for Resolving Conflict*, 4th edn. San Francisco: Jossey-Bass, 2014.

Nolan-Haley 2012
Nolan-Haley, J., 'Mediation: The "New Arbitration"', *Harvard Negotiation Law Review*, 2012, Vol. 17, p. 61-95.

Peters 2008
Peters, D., 'Can We Talk? Overcoming Barriers to Mediating Private Transborder Commercial Disputes in the Americas', *Vanderbilt Journal of Transnational Law*, 2008, Vol. 41, p. 1251-1305.

Posner 2000
Posner, E.A., 'A Theory of Contract Law under Conditions of Radical Judicial Error', *Northwestern University Law Review*, 2000, Vol. 94, p. 749-774.

Reiff 2007
Reiff, L.C., 'The Use of Conciliation or Mediation for the Resolution of Commercial Disputes', *Canadian Business Law Journal*, 2007, Vol. 45, p. 20-47.

Scott 1990
Scott, R.E., 'A Rational Theory of Default Rules for Commercial Contracts', *Journal of Legal Studies*, 1990, Vol. 19, p. 597-616.

Scott 2000a
Scott, R.E., 'The Case for Formalism in Relational Contracts', *Northwestern University Law Review*, 2000, Vol. 94, p. 847-876.

Scott 2000b
Scott, R.E., 'The Uniformity Norm in Commercial Law: A Comparative Analysis of Common Law and Code Methodologies', in: Kraus, J.S. & Walt, S.D. (eds.), *The Jurisprudential Foundations of Corporate and Commercial Law,* Cambridge: Cambridge University Press, 2000, p. 149-192.

Spencer & Brogan 2006
Spencer, D. & Brogan, M., *Mediation Law and Practice,* Cambridge: Cambridge University Press, 2006.

Stipanowich 2004
Stipanowich, T.J., 'ADR and the "Vanishing Trial": The Growth and Impact of Alternative Dispute Resolution', *Journal of Empirical Legal Studies,* 2004, Vol. 1, p. 843-912.

Stipanowich & Lamare 2014
Stipanowich, T.J. & Lamare, J.R., ; Living with ADR: Evolving Perceptions and Use of Mediation, Arbitration and Conflict Management in Fortune 1000 Corporations', *Harvard Negotiation Law Review,* 2014, Vol. 19, p. 1-68.

Wälde 2006
Wälde, T.W., 'Efficient Management of Transnational Disputes: Mutual Gain by Mediation or Joint Loss in Litigation', *Arbitration International,* 2006, Vol. 22, p. 205-232.

Waldman 1997
Waldman, E.A., 'Identifying the Role of Social Norms in Mediation: A Multiple Model Approach', *Hastings Law Journal,* 1997, Vol. 48, p. 703-769.

Wightman 2003
Wightman, J., 'Beyond Custom: Contracts, Contexts, and the Recognition of Implicit Understandings', in: Campbell, D., Collins, H. & Wightman, J. (eds.), *Implicit Dimensions of Contract. Discrete, Relational and Network Contracts,* Oxford: Hart Publishing, 2003, p. 143-186.

Worthington 2003
Worthington, S. (ed.), *Commercial Law and Commercial Practice,* Oxford: Hart Publishing, 2003.

A. Beckers

LAW OR SOCIAL ORDERING: A CHOICE FOR COMMERCIAL PARTIES IN DISPUTE RESOLUTION? A COMMENT ON KORNET

1. Introduction

In her contribution, *Nicole Kornet* focuses on what she defines as normative frameworks that shape the business relation and their influence on dispute resolution. It is the normative frameworks, she proceeds, that should be guiding in dispute resolution and, depending on whether the nature of the dispute-solving body is mediation or adjudication, the framework should be given different weight. The normative frameworks that *Kornet* is interested in are the legal contract that binds the contracting parties and creates the legal rights and obligations that govern their relation, the social relation between two businessmen that is strongly influenced by social expectations within the business community and, finally, the economic rules of market exchange that shape the expectations related to the exchange of a good or service. In that respect, *Kornet* firmly embeds her contribution within the tradition in contract theory that focuses on contracts as consisting of different 'points of reference', 'normative systems'[1] or 'contracting worlds'.[2] One can also view her contribution as being related to the recent research on 'contract governance' in which one aspect is described as being about 'the analysis and structure of legal and extra-legal institutions and factors which constitute the framework for private transactions'.[3] While the analysis of the normative frameworks seems thus to be firmly embedded in what has been already revealed by (sociological and economic strands in) contract research, a thought-provoking novelty of her contribution relates to the endeavour of instrumentalising the insights of this strand of research to an explicit normative undertaking in relation to the appropriate dispute resolution forum and the way it is organised. She argues that these frameworks should influence the way disputes on contracts are solved and, furthermore, that their relevance should be different depending on the

1 Collins 1999, p. 128.
2 Teubner 2000.
3 Möslein & Riesenhuber 2009, p. 268.

character of the dispute solving institution. To her, in mediation the legal framework should move to the background with a focus on social and economic norms whereas adjudication should - due to the need for certainty - be more strongly guided by legal considerations with a significantly lower weight given to the more ambiguous economic and social norms.[4] By emphasising the importance of party choice as to the appropriate forum for solving their disputes, *Kornet* also inherently promotes the idea that the preference for a specific normative framework to govern a dispute is a matter of what the contracting parties choose. As a result, the two core arguments in the contribution is that the normative framework to govern a dispute between two commercial parties is to be oriented on, firstly, party choice, which is, secondly, dependent on the availability of two firmly separated dispute resolution mechanisms in which different frameworks are guiding.

While I generally share much sympathy for both of these assumptions, I seek to emphasise in this comment the need for some refinement of both of them with a view to the complex organisation of business relations and their embedding in a globalised society.

Firstly, I will focus on the suggestion that the weight given to law, social norms and market exchange is ultimately a decision of the contracting parties that they take when opting for a specific dispute resolution mechanism. Or, as *Kornet* puts it: 'In the end, party choice determines which normative framework should take precedence in different dispute resolution mechanisms'.[5] I will argue that the suggested atomistic view on only the choices and interests of the commercial relation is too narrow, in particular when commercial relations are organised as a complex network of different bilateral contracts or when the contract dispute concerns an adverse impact on the interests of outsiders or the public interest. Therefore, a broader perspective that focuses on the interests of the contracting parties, third parties and the public seems to my understanding necessary.

Secondly, I focus on the argument that a clear distinction between mediation and adjudication can and should be made in terms of the frameworks that govern the dispute. Or, in *Kornet*'s terms: '(...) the nature and function of mediation (...) may require the enforcement of legal norms to move to the background (...)' and 'adjudicatory proceedings should have their foundation in legal norms and adjudicators should remain wary of incorporating other normative frames of reference in the resolution of the legal dispute'.[6] This distinction is certainly persuasive against the background of the origin that each of these dispute solving mechanisms comes from. Yet it seems, to me, not to capture entirely the reality of dispute resolution, in particular insofar as the available and preferred spectrum of dispute resolution under the premises of globalization is concerned. As can be observed, mediation and adjudication have already become much more interwoven and dispute resolution mechanisms with mediation and adjudication elements

4 Kornet, section 4.
5 See Kornet, section 4.
6 See Kornet, section 1.

prove to be increasingly attractive. This arguably suggests that the clear distinction between non-legal mediation and legal adjudication, as proposed by *Kornet*, might need some further consideration as to the constellations in which it is valid.

2. The Commercial Relation as Determining the Dispute Solving Mechanism

Kornet departs from the understanding that the normative framework to governs the dispute could also depend 'on the dispute resolution mechanism that the parties opt for'.[7] This argument seems very much in line with her earlier writings on contract interpretation in which she argued to treat the parties as being at the heart of the contractual relation.[8] If the interpretation of contracts should be left primarily to the parties, it seems only logical that this should also remain valid in deciding the appropriate dispute solving mechanism and the normative frameworks that govern it.

Nonetheless, as persuasive as the preference for party choice may be, I see some difficulties in granting the commercial parties to a contract full discretion in deciding how their dispute is resolved. My discomfort stems firstly from the fact that research focusing on the practice of commercial contracting has revealed that contracts do not always occur in (a) bilateral form, although contract lawyers still treat this as the ideal. To the contrary, complex multilateral contracts and linked bilateral contracts seem to have become a dominant feature in organising commercial relations.[9] The often-mentioned examples are complex interdependent supply chains and multilateral contract arrangements,[10] yet there is even more variety. *Grundmann*, for instance, has classified the different forms of contract networks into chain, star, triangle, and circle.[11] For at least these constellations, the choice of the commercial parties to let their dispute be solved in a particular dispute resolution forum is not a clear-cut criterion handily available. First of all, the choice of the parties seems difficult to determine. When a dispute on a contract within a network arises, several, potentially even conflicting, party choices come into play: The interests of the parties of the bilateral contract within the network that is under dispute, the interest of parties within the network that remain outside the contractual relation under scrutiny whose contract is nonetheless linked to this contract, and the interest of the all parties in having the network objective realised. The parties to a bilateral contract might already be at a stage where the dispute has escalated, which according to *Kornet* would lead most likely to adjudication and a focus on the legal rights and obligations rather than social and economic norms. Notwithstanding this preference, other parties within the network might have an

7 See Kornet, section 4.

8 In particular Kornet 2006, p. 382-384, 388-400.

9 See extensively on these contract networks from the legal perspective Grundmann 2007; Cafaggi 2008; Amstutz & Teubner 2009; Teubner & Collins 2011.

10 See for a good overview Cafaggi 2008, p. 11-16.

11 Grundmann 2007, p. 721-723.

interest in preserving the relation and remaining co-operative in order not to jeopardise the functioning of their own bilateral contracts and the network as a whole. Who should then be in the position to choose the dispute resolution and herewith the normative frame of reference? I would, for these constellations, argue that a refinement of the criterion of party choice would be necessary to capture the reality of not only bilateral, but also multilateral and interlinked contractual relations. A conceivable option could in this case be to suggest court-mandated mediation for the contract within the network, which the contracting parties seek to take to court rather than uncritically accepting the choice of the parties.[12] This could at least be one option to pay due respect not only to the interest of the parties to a contract, but also the interests of the broader contractual setting, the 'network interest', in which they are embedded.

There is a second additional discomfort that I have with the wide acceptance of party choice, which is related to the embedding of the business relation within a broader social context. Should the interests of the social context be excluded from the choice for the appropriate dispute resolution mechanism? *Kornet* remains silent on this question, though her argument that the parties should be at the core of the dispute resolution seems to suggest that this should be the case. However, I am advocating the need to at least consider these external interests when determining the appropriate forum for dispute resolution. A specific example for a constellation of a contract having adverse impact on social interests is one containing obligations of one contracting party to respect the interest of a third party, such as the employees in factories, or consumers, or to safeguard public interests, such as not to pollute the environment, to prevent corruption, or to respect human rights. Such contracts have recently received attention in the contracting literature as so-called 'regulatory contracts'.[13] I will take the example of contracts on the supply of goods that have incorporated provisions to comply with fundamental workplace standards when producing goods. Empirical research on these types of contracts suggests that the commercial parties contracting on such obligations are prone to preferring relational non-judicial and informal collaborative solving of a dispute whenever it arises.[14] The interest in confidential and informal dispute resolution seems also quite natural, given the parties' interest to uphold the exchange relation that remains mutually beneficial for them or, if that is not possible, to terminate the contract without adjudicating on it. It is eventually only a third party that is adversely affected by an otherwise mutually beneficial exchange of goods. Conversely, it is probably in the least interest of the third party benefitting from such contractual obligation that an informal confidential settlement is reached without its interests being heard. The third party, i.e. the worker being centrally affected by the contract breach, is likely to be interested in having the dispute

12 Court-mandated (and thus prescribed) mediation is already a recognised form of mediation practice. See, e.g., for a good analysis of the spectrum between prescribed and voluntary mediation Alexander 2004.

13 See, e.g., Backer 2008; Cafaggi 2013; Verbruggen 2014.

14 McBarnet & Kurkchiyan 2007, p. 79; Peterkova Mitkidis 2014, p. 20-22.

solved in a forum on which he has a choice. This can still be a specific form of mediation, yet most likely not under the condition that the commercial parties retain the choice over the setting. In these cases, the necessity for the contracting parties to respect a neutral mediation as preferred by the affected third party seems, to my understanding, a need worth considering.[15]

A third constellation in which the choice of the parties for a specific dispute resolution mechanism becomes arguably problematic are contracts in which the breach of public interests is at stake. For such contracts, it seems to equally a matter of controversy whether the nature of the dispute resolution should be entirely at the choice of the contracting parties. In the cases where fundamental social interests are affected, mediation solving the dispute in the interests of the contracting parties neglects the interest of the public in having public interests respected even against the will of the contracting parties. A short example to illustrate is the disrespect of mandatory rules by the contracting parties. Should a dispute on the proper performance of a contract on the supply of goods violating embargo provisions[16] be indeed subject to collaborative mediation with a focus on social and economic norms and a less stronger role of the legal norms? It is likely that in these constellations it is in the interest of the parties to have their dispute on the delivery of the goods be solved by mediation, possibly uphold their business relation, without receiving a decision on the legal rights and obligations that their contract is void for breach of mandatory laws. Yet, if so, some discomfort remains with providing parties with free discretion to 'opt out' of laws in choosing their dispute resolution mechanism that are generally considered mandatory.

3. The Distinction between Mediation and Adjudication

A necessary prerequisite for the focus on party choice is the availability of different forms of dispute resolution. *Kornet* advocates in this regard separating mediation from adjudication and viewing them as two different forms of dispute resolution. Her argument is certainly persuasive if one considers the origin of each of these dispute-solving mechanisms. Adjudication is based on the idea that a conflict (that is) impossible to solve is brought to a third party who is asked to decide on it on the basis of a 'neutral' frame of reference, i.e. law. From this perspective, the law with its system of adjudication acts as (a) last resort for solving disputes when social conflicts escalate. Mediation, in contrast, remains part of the informal ordering mechanisms within the private sphere that operate outside the law. It relies heavily on the willingness of the actors themselves, their capability to solve their disputes

15 On this point, one should consider linking commercial mediation to the developments in the business and human field, in particular the work being done on developing appropriate dispute resolution mechanisms to remedy human rights violations by companies as prescribed in the UN Guiding Principles on Business and Human Rights, see generally, Rees 2010.

16 See for just one example for such a constellation *Ameropa AG v Havi Ocean*, United States District Court 10 Civ. 3240.

with only an indirect and more guiding role of a third party, and their interest in not spoiling their social relations by a court dispute. The law is not required for this undertaking, at least not in its capacity as a system based on decision-making. It may even be counterproductive as the law may be able to destroy social trust between the parties.[17]

As clear as this distinction between adjudication as part of the legal system and mediation as part of the social sphere might be, I would see the reality to be more strongly characterised by shades of grey. The influence of the law on mediation is already apparent in the institution of mediation itself. In the mediation literature, a classification of different forms of mediation is made, in particular the distinction between facilitative and evaluative mediation. Evaluative mediation is in this regard already seen as a 'hybrid of mediation and arbitration' in which 'the mediator may provide evaluative information on possible legal or legislative outcomes (...)'.[18] In fact, the mediator in evaluative mediation adopts strategies that are akin to those of a judge, such as to assess the strength and weaknesses of the position of each party and predict and present to the parties the likely outcome of a court case.[19] While the influence of the law is in this form of mediation still quite subtle as the mediator is ultimately not taking a decision on the basis of the law, it is in particular dispute resolution a global level that has rendered this clear-cut distinction increasingly blurred. To be sure, *Kornet* also observes this development when she presents the arguments of socio-legal and economic contract law scholars that are in favour of orientating adjudication on commercial practice and efficiency and when mentioning the increasing participation of lawyers in the mediation process. Yet, while she views this development with inherent scepticism, I also see two advantages of this development, namely the contribution of these hybrid forms of dispute resolution to the evolution of global governance and their attractiveness to commercial parties.

3.1. *Law-oriented Mediation as a Contribution to Global Governance*

On a global level, the changing character of mediation into a more adjudicative form of dispute resolution has in some areas already contributed to the gradual evolution of a nascent system of global law making. The fact that litigation, as the most formalised and adjudicative form of dispute resolution, is mainly organised on a national level has made it highly unattractive for commercial parties even when they seek to solve their disputes with a view to their legal rights.[20] In the absence of genuine global courts, the need of commercial parties to solve disputes with a view to legal norms is increasingly fulfilled by forums that were initially set up to provide mediation rather than adjudication. This has resulted in a change of their

17 See, e.g., fundamentally Macaulay 1963.

18 Spencer & Brogan 2006, p. 103.

19 Fundamentally on the strategies of mediators in evaluative mediation Riskin 1996, p. 26-28.

20 See for empirical evidence for the declining attractiveness of courts for cross-border commercial disputes, e.g., Hoffmann & Maurer 2010.

character towards being less oriented toward the goal of mediation. Mediation has partly *compensated* for the lack of adjudication and hereby contributed to the creation of what in legal theory is currently discussed as the evolving body of non-state law that provides for the ordering of globalised society.[21] To illustrate this shift and its potentials in ordering the globalised society, I would like to focus on one specific forum for mediation, which has gradually shifted towards becoming more legalised in terms of substance (i.e. the normative framework used to solve the dispute is the law) and procedure (the way in which the mediation is organised becoming more legalised).

Rules on socially responsible conduct for companies including supply chains are laid down in the OECD Guidelines for Multinational Enterprises, which is a non-binding 'soft law' framework adopted by the OECD. In the OECD Guidelines for Multinational Enterprises, it is laid down as an obligation for governments to have in place a so-called National Contact Point (NCP). These NCP are intended to provide a forum that aims at 'contributing to the resolution of issues that arise relating to the implementation of the Guidelines in specific instances'.[22] This specific instance procedure was initially envisaged as a form that largely relies on mediation,[23] but it has in some countries started to function as a quasi-legal body making use of procedures akin to legal procedures and dispute resolution with reference to the law.[24] In fact, affected third parties and Non-governmental organisations opt for this forum also in order to obtain a decision on whether particular corporate behaviour is in compliance with the OECD Guidelines. Taking the perspective of *Kornet*, this gradually evolving juridification of the National Contact Point procedure would have to be viewed with dread. The combination of a confidential mediation procedure and a subsequently neutral assessment and published decision of the NCP if the parties do not reach an agreement,[25] can be criticised for making the procedure unpredictable for the parties. On the other hand, it is, arguably for good reasons, emphasised that the increasing legalisation of the procedure the NCP adopts and the substantive reference to legal rights in its assessments has contributed to the evolution of an ordering mechanism that fills a gap on a global level.[26] By means of issuing final statements on corporate compliance with the OECD Guidelines, the NCP begins to develop and publish rules on socially responsible corporate conduct, which contributes in a productive way to developing a governance framework for the behaviour of companies. And, as Backer pointedly observes: 'Critically in that development, of course, is the work

21 On the debate, see generally, e.g., Teubner 1997; Calliess 2002, Backer 2007; Berman 2007; Michaels 2007; Calliess & Renner 2009; Calliess & Zumbansen 2010.

22 OECD Guidelines for Multinational Enterprises 2011, Part II, No. 1, para. (1).

23 OECD Guidelines for Multinational Enterprises 2011, 'Procedural Guidance', C., No. 2, para. (d).

24 See extensively Backer 2009 with a view to the UK National Contact Point.

25 OECD Guidelines for Multinational Enterprises 2011, 'Procedural Guidance', C., No. 3, para (c).

26 Backer 2009, p. 283-287; Calliess & Renner 2009, p. 274 *et seq.*

of the NCPs, the royal *courts* of this developing common law',[27] that were initially understood as a forum to provide mediation.

3.2. *Legalized Mediation as an Attractive Form for Commercial Parties*

Kornet could of course counter this argument by insisting on the fact that her contribution views dispute resolution not as a mechanism that should serve society and its interest in establishing an ordering mechanism on a global level. Instead, she would argue, dispute resolution on commercial matters should primarily be in place to serve the needs of commercial parties. Parties should be in the position to opt (and according to *Kornet* they also should opt) for mediation when they 'seek to collaborate on constructing a solution that preserves the transaction and the on-going business relationship' and for adjudication 'where the dispute has escalated so that the parties no longer perceive a future for their on-going relationship'.[28] But is that really the case? I would argue that not only for society, but also for the commercial parties, a dispute resolution mechanism containing elements of mediation and adjudication and being oriented on social, economic and legal norms could be attractive for the parties when resolving their disputes. The constellation that I have in mind is commercial arbitration, which seems interestingly a dispute resolution mechanism that is not easy to classify. While *Kornet* seems to situate arbitration in the realm of adjudication with only marginal elements of mediation,[29] this form of dispute resolution is defined by others as part of alternative dispute resolution (ADR), to which also mediation belongs.[30] In fact, commercial arbitration shares some features with litigation as well as with mediation. With litigation, it has in common its organisation as a dispute resolution mechanism that involves the decision of a third party and its orientation on legal rights and obligation. Yet, with mediation it has in common that the parties retain control over the situation. Decisions are not taken without their influence. Parties can influence the arrangement of the dispute resolution, such as the choice for the institution where to arbitrate and the procedure. An important characteristic making it akin to mediation is also the confidentiality of the proceedings, the quicker and less formalised procedure in comparison to litigation and the fact that parties need to opt in for it to be applicable. Given the attractiveness of arbitration on a global level, one might consider that it actually makes sense for commercial parties to opt for such an integrated form of dispute resolution that provides for the opportunity to solve conflicts in a quick, efficient and informal way with the advantage of having clarity on their legal rights rather than having to choose between either lengthy, formalised and public litigation or informal, confidential, but in its outcome rather uncertain, mediation as a solution.

27 Backer 2009, p. 289 (Emphasis added).

28 Kornet, section 4.

29 Kornet, section 3.

30 See in particular Martin Brink's presentation on the conference, described by Cavusoglu & Meurkens 2014, p. 475.

This is certainly not to say that adjudication in courts, arbitration and mediation should not be distinguished at all; yet to combine different elements used in mediation, arbitration and court adjudication could also have advantages. It could result in having in place a form of dispute resolution that is in fact attractive for commercial parties when they determine an appropriate forum to have their dispute resolved with a view to social, economic and legal concerns. This could strengthen *Kornet*'s first argument that the organisation of the dispute resolution is ultimately to be oriented on the choice and interests of commercial parties.

Bibliography

Alexander 2004
Alexander, N., 'Visualising the ADR Landscape', *ADR Bulletin*, 2004, Vol. 7, p. 46-48.

Amstutz & Teubner 2009
Amstutz, M. & Teubner, G. (eds.), *Networks. Legal Issues of Multilateral Co-operation*, Oxford: Hart Publishing, 2009.

Backer 2007
Backer, L.C., 'Economic Globalization and the Rise of Efficient Systems of Global Private Law Making: Wal-Mart as Global Legislator', *Connecticut Law Review*, 2007, Vol. 39, p. 1739-1784.

Backer 2008
Backer, L.C., 'Multinational Corporations as Objects and Sources of Transnational Regulation', *ILSA Journal for International & Comparative Law*, 2008, Vol. 14, p. 499-523.

Backer 2009
Backer, L.C., 'Rights and Accountability in Development. ('Raid') v. Das Air and Global Witness v. Afrimex', *Melbourne Journal of International Law*, 2009, Vol. 10, p. 258-307.

Berman 2007
Berman, P.S., 'Global Legal Pluralism', *Southern California Law Review*, 2007, Vol. 80, p. 1155-1237.

Cafaggi 2008
Cafaggi, F., 'Contractual Networks and the Small Business Act: Towards European Principles?', *EUI Working Papers, Department of Law*, 2008.

Cafaggi 2013
Cafaggi, F., 'The Regulatory Functions of Transnational Commercial Contracts: New Architectures', *Fordham International Law Journal*, 2013, Vol. 36, p. 1557-1618.

Calliess 2002
Calliess, G.-P., 'Reflexive Transnational Law. The Privatisation of Civil Law and the Civilisation of Private Law', *Zeitschrift für Rechtssoziologie*, 2002, Vol. 23, p. 185-216.

Calliess & Renner 2009
Calliess, G.-P. & Renner, M., 'Between Law and Social Norms: The Evolution of Global Governance', *Ratio Juris*, 2009, Vol. 22, p. 260-280.

Calliess & Zumbansen 2010
Calliess, G.-P. & Zumbansen, P., *Rough Consensus and Running Code. A Theory of Transnational Law*, Oxford: Hart Publishing, 2010.

Cavusoglu & Meurkens 2014
Cavusoglu, D. & Meurkens, L., 'Conference Report: "The Citizen in European Private Law: Norm-Setting, Enforcement and Choice", Conference Held in Maastricht, The Netherlands, 18 October 2013', *European Review of Private Law,* 2014, p. 469-480.

Collins 1999
Collins, H., *Regulating Contracts,* Oxford: Oxford University Press, 1999.

Grundmann 2007
Grundmann, S., 'Die Dogmatik der Vertragsnetze', *Archiv für die civilstische Praxis,* 2007, Vol. 207, p. 718-767.

Hoffmann & Maurer 2010
Hoffmann, H. & Maurer, A., 'Entstaatlichung der Justiz: Empirische Belege zum Bedeutungsverlust staatlicher Gerichte für internationale Wirtschaftsstreitigkeiten (The vanishing trial in German commercial courts. Empirical evidence for the decrease in importance of national courts in international trade cases)', *Zeitschrift für Rechtssoziologie,* 2010, Vol. 31, p. 279-302.

Kornet 2006
Kornet, N., *Contract Interpretation and Gap Filling: Comparative and Theoretical Perspectives*, Antwerp: Intersentia, 2006.

Macaulay 1963
Macaulay, S., 'Non-Contractual Relations in Business: A Preliminary Study', *American Sociological Review,* 1963, Vol. 28, p. 55-67.

McBarnet & Kurkchiyan 2007
McBarnet, D. & Kurkchiyan, M., 'Corporate social responsibility through contractual control? Global supply chains and 'other regulation'', in: McBarnet, D., Vioiculescu, A. & Campbell, T. (eds.), *The New Corporate Accountability. Corporate Social Responsibility and the Law,* Cambridge/Mass.: Cambridge University Press, 2007, p. 59-92.

Michaels 2007
Michaels, R., 'The True Lex Mercatoria: Law Beyond the State', *Indiana Journal of Global Legal Studies,* 2007, Vol. 14, p. 447-468.

Möslein & Riesenhuber 2009
Möslein, F. & Riesenhuber, K., 'Contract Governance - A Draft Research Agenda', *European Review of Contract Law,* 2009, Vol. 5, p. 248-289.

Peterkova Mitkidis 2014
Peterkova Mitkidis, K., 'Sustainability Clauses in International Supply Chain Contracts: Regulation, Enforceability and Effects of Ethical Requirements', *Nordic Journal of Commercial Law,* 2014, p. 1-30.

Rees 2010
Rees, C., 'Mediation in Business-Related Human Rights Disputes: Objections, Opportunities and Challenges', *Harvard Kennedy School, Working Paper,* 2010, Vol. 56, p. 1-22.

Riskin 1996
Riskin, L., 'Understanding Mediators' Orientations, Strategies, and Techniques: A Grid for the Perplexed', *Harvard Negotiation Law Review,* 1996, Vol. 1, p. 7-51.

Spencer & Brogan 2006
Spencer, D. & Brogan, M., *Mediation Law and Practice,* Cambridge: Cambridge University Press, 2006.

Teubner 1997
Teubner, G., 'Global Bukowina: Legal Pluralism in the World Society', in: Teubner, G. (ed.), *Global Law Without A State,* Aldershot: Dartmouth Gower, 1997, p. 3-28.

Teubner 2000
Teubner, G., 'Contracting Worlds: The many autonomies of private law', *Social and Legal Studies,* 2000, Vol. 9, p. 399-417.

Teubner & Collins 2011
Teubner, G. & Collins, H., *Networks as connected contracts. With an Introduction by Hugh Collins,* Oxford: Hart Publishing, 2011.

Verbruggen 2014
Verbruggen, P., 'Regulatory Governance by Contract: The Rise of Regulatory Standards in Commercial Contracts', *Recht der Werkelijkheid,* 2014, Vol. 35, p. 79-100.

IUS COMMUNE EUROPAEUM

A peer-reviewed book series in which the common foundations of the legal systems of the Member States of the European Union are the central focus.

The *Ius Commune Europaeum* series includes horizontal comparative legal studies as well as studies on the effect of treaties within the national legal systems. All the classic fields of law are covered. The books are published in various European languages under the auspices of METRO, the Institute for Transnational Legal Research at the Maastricht University.

Recently published:

Volume 132: *Property Law Perspectives III*, A. APERS, S. BOULY, E.L.C. DEWITTE and D. GRUYAERT (eds.)
Volume 133: *Multi-Party Redress Mechanisms in Europe: Squeaking Mice?*, V. HARSÁGI and C.H. VAN RHEE (eds.)
Volume 134: *Europe at the Edge of Pluralism*, D. GOZDECKA and M. KMAK
Volume 135: *Cooperative Agreements between Public Authorities. The Influence of CJEU Case Law on National Legal Systems*, K. WAUTERS
Volume 136: *Common Core, PECL and DCFR: Could They Change Shipping and Transport Law?*, W. VERHEYEN, F.G.M. SMEELE and M.A.I.H. HOEKS
Volume 137: *Who Does What? On the Allocation of Competences in European Private Law*, B. AKKERMANS, J. HAGE, N. KORNET and J.M. SMITS
Volume 138: *The Nature of Mutual Recognition in European Law. Re-examining the Notion from an Individual Rights Perspective with a View to Its Further Development in the Criminal Justice Area*, W. VAN BALLEGOOIJ
Volume 139: *Evidence in Contemporary Civil Procedure. Fundamental Issues in a Comparative Perspective*, C.H. VAN RHEE and A. UZELAC (eds.)
Volume 140: *The Effect of D&O Insurance on Managerial Risk Taking*, M. GABER
Volume 141: *Information and Notification Duties*, I. SAMOY and M.B. LOOS
Volume 142: *The Application of the Theory of Efficient Breach in Contract Law. A Comparative Law and Economics Perspective*, W. LIAO
Volume 143: *A European Legal Framework for Nuclear Liability. Rethinking Current Approaches*, T. HELDT
Volume 144: *The Development of European Private Law in a Multilevel Legal Order*, E.A.G. VAN SCHAGEN
Volume 145: *Property Law Perspectives IV*, D. GRUYAERT, E. RAMAEKERS and L. ROSTILL (eds.)

www.ingramcontent.com/pod-product-compliance
Ingram Content Group UK Ltd.
Pitfield, Milton Keynes, MK11 3LW, UK
UKHW051927100926
8556IPUK00022B/1419

9 781780 683737